AN INTRODUCTION TO
THE PHILOSOPHY OF INDUCTION AND
PROBABILITY

D1594267

AN INTRODUCTION TO
The Philosophy of Induction
and Probability

L. JONATHAN COHEN

CLARENDON PRESS · OXFORD
1989

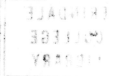

Oxford University Press, Walton Street, Oxford OX2 6DP

Oxford New York Toronto
Delhi Bombay Calcutta Madras Karachi
Petaling Jaya Singapore Hong Kong Tokyo
Nairobi Dar es Salaam Cape Town
Melbourne Auckland

and associated companies in
Berlin Ibadan

Oxford is a trade mark of Oxford University Press

Published in the United States
by Oxford University Press, New York

British Library Cataloguing in Publication Data
Cohen, L. Jonathan (Laurence Jonathan)
An introduction to the philosophy of induction and probability.
1. Probabilities – Philosophical perspectives
2. Inductive inference – Philosophical perspectives
I. Title
121'.63
ISBN 0-19-875079-X
ISBN 0-19-875078-1 Pbk

Library of Congress Cataloging in Publication Data
Cohen, L. Jonathan (Laurence Jonathan)
An introduction to the philosophy of induction and probability/L. Jonathan Cohen.
1. Induction (Logic) 2. Probabilities. I. Title
BC91.C6 1988 161—dc19 88-21674
ISBN 0-19-875079-X
ISBN 0-19-875078-1 (pbk.)

Set by Colset Private Limited, Singapore
Printed in Great Britain
at the University Printing House, Oxford
by David Stanford
Printer to the University

'Nostra autem ratio . . . ea . . . est ut certitudinis gradus constituamus.'

(Francis Bacon, *Novum Organum*, preface)

But our method is such that we establish degrees of certainty.

'Probabilitas enim est gradus certitudinis'.

(James Bernoulli, *Ars Conjectandi*, pt. 4, ch. 1)

For probability is degree of certainty.

PREFACE

The purpose of this book is to introduce the reader to philosophical issues and arguments about probability and induction, not to survey the past and present range of those issues and arguments. The text is therefore highly selective both in the topics and authors that it discusses and also in the points that it makes about them. It seeks to engage the reader's interest by presenting a coherent and readily intelligible picture of the field, with due regard to the depth and difficulty of the fundamental philosophical issues, rather than to aim at a more comprehensive and encyclopaedic type of treatment (which might also be more superficial). And it economizes as much as possible in the use of mathematical symbolism, the statement of mathematical results and the derivation of statistical algorithms, because its concern is with the philosophical issues rather than with the mathematical ones.

In trying to show how strong or how weak a particular philosophical theory really is I have not hesitated to include new arguments where they seem to be needed, and to exclude familiar ones where they seem to be of little value. No doubt others might wish to distribute their emphases differently. But that is inevitable in philosophy. In any case my overall purpose is not to make converts, but to excite interest by the exploration and comparison of alternative options. For those who then wish to go further the footnotes include relevant bibliographical suggestions.

I have adopted a broadly historical approach in the first chapter, in order to show how the central problems developed. The other five chapters seek to impose a clarificatory structure on the consideration of those problems. In order to assist understanding, each section is preceded by a summary of its contents. But, as newcomers to philosophy may need to be reminded, the nature of philosophical argument makes it impossible for reading such summaries to be a worthwhile substitute for reading the text. Also, for the benefit of those new to the subject, I have included in the footnotes some brief biographical notes in order to help locate historically important writers on probability within their cultural contexts.

In order to avoid unnecessary quotation-marks I have normally left it to the context to determine whether symbolic expressions are being used or mentioned. Also, unless there are contextual reasons to suppose otherwise, the pronoun 'he' is to be understood in the text as meaning 'he or she', the pronoun 'him' as meaning 'him or her' and the pronoun 'his' as meaning 'his or her'.

The origins of this book are in a course of lectures that I have given for some years within the Sub-Faculty of Philosophy at Oxford. I owe much to the questions and criticisms that have been voiced at those lectures. But I am most indebted to Jonathan Adler, Menachem Fisch, Greg Hunt, Jim Logue, and Dave Schum, who read an earlier draft of the text and raised many important points about it. None of them will be satisfied with everything that is in the final version, and any mistakes in it are mine, not theirs. But I have profited enormously from the time and care which each of them devoted to reading the earlier draft, and am deeply grateful to them all.

I am also very grateful to the Press's copy-editor, who has saved me from many infelicities of style, and to Pat Lloyd, who has contributed much by the care and attention with which she has typed and processed so many pages so many times.

A portion of Section 12 was published previously in Evandro Agazzi (ed.), *Probability in the Sciences* (Kluwer: 1988), 69–77.

L.J.C.

The Queen's College, Oxford
21 March 1988

CONTENTS

I

The Origins of the Problem

§ 1. AN OUTLINE OF THE ISSUES

Induction is termed 'ampliative' when it extrapolates beyond the
existing data. Ampliative induction may concern hypotheses
about what ought to happen as well as hypotheses about what
does happen. One main question about it concerns whether the
variety or the multiplicity of evidential instances is crucial in the
evaluation of inductive support. Another concerns whether
inductive support is a kind of probability that conforms to the
laws of the calculus of chance.

In contemporary philosophical dialogue about induction one
question is central.[1] What kind of support can the results of
scientific experiments give to hypotheses about laws of nature or
about uniformities of causal connection? What kind of
knowledge can we have that energy and mass are related by the
equation $e = mc^2$ or that appropriate doses of penicillin normally
cure septicaemia?

Such hypotheses always generate predictions that extrapolate
beyond the existing data. That is why they may be useful as a
basis for building another rocket, curing new cases of septicaemia, producing more food, etc. So induction about them is
conveniently labelled 'ampliative'. It involves reasoning to
conclusions that cover not only the evidential instances but
others also. It amplifies our knowledge. And it contrasts with the

[1] Modern conceptions of the problem-area may be traced through H.W.B. Joseph,
An Introduction to Logic, 2nd edn. (Oxford: Clarendon Press, 1916), 378–565; W.E.
Johnson, *Logic* (Cambridge: Cambridge University Press), Pt. II (1922), 189–253, and
Pt. III (1924); M.R. Cohen and E. Nagel, *An Introduction to Logic and Scientific Method*,
(London: Routledge and Kegan Paul, 1934), 151–72, 197–288, 302–51; W. Kneale,
Probability and Induction (Oxford: Clarendon Press, 1949); H.E. Kyburg, Jun., *Probability
and Inductive Logic* (London: Macmillan, 1970—contains a good bibliography); and R.
Swinburne, *An Introduction to Confirmation Theory* (London: Methuen, 1973).

'summative' induction that, rather unproblematically, establishes a generalization on the basis of what are known to be all its instances, as when a railway inspector, passing down the whole train, establishes that every passenger on the train has a ticket.

Nor is all ampliative induction concerned with laws or causes. Sometimes purely descriptive generalizations are at issue, such as 'All crows are black' or 'All emeralds are green'. And sometimes inductive reasoning operates in relation to generalizations that are not about what in fact always happens in nature but rather about what ought properly to happen in human society (though it may not always do so), as when in Anglo-American jurisprudence a general statement of the law about a particular kind of issue is supported by argument from certain past judicial decisions within the pertinent jurisdiction. Perhaps it will be stated that a breathalyser result ought to be accepted as legitimate evidence of what a motorist's blood-alcohol content was two hours previously because in one such case it was treated as legitimate by an appropriate court.

It follows that the question about inductive support needs to be posed more abstractly, so as to transcend such differences of subject-matter. The fundamental problem is: how does ampliative induction operate? And this problem raises two main issues which combine with one another to form the framework of discussion.

First, do generalizations derive more support from the variety of instances that are cited as evidence for them or from the multiplicity of those instances? We shall see, for example, that Francis Bacon, who founded the modern study of induction, preferred instantial variety, while Rudolf Carnap, who has been the most influential writer on the subject in the twentieth century, attached primary importance to instantial multiplicity. The former mode of reasoning is known as 'variative' or, for reasons which will soon emerge, 'eliminative' induction, the latter as 'enumerative' induction.

Secondly, what is the relation between inductive support and the kind of probability that conforms to the theorems of the calculus of chance as developed originally by the seventeenth-century mathematicians Blaise Pascal and Pierre Fermat? Because Pascalian probabilities are measured by numbers (on a scale that runs from 0 to 1) they hold out the prospect of supplying a mode of gradation for inductive support. Such support can apparently be conceived in Pascalian terms as existing at various levels on an ascending scale of rationality rather than as existing only at zero level or at the level of conclusive proof. But there have been many disputes about how this Pascalian analysis of induction is to be carried out and not everyone even agrees that Pascalian probability is the right basis for inductive gradation.

An introductory account of the subject can usefully begin with a historical sketch of how it has arrived at its present state. We shall see (§§ 2–3) how the Baconian and Pascalian traditions developed largely in independence of one another for about two centuries, until (§ 4) J.S. Mill began to apply Pascalian modes of gradation to Baconian induction. It was then possible for other philosophers, like J.M. Keynes, to develop variations on this theme, because more than one proposal had emerged for measuring probability in a way that conformed to Pascalian principles. But, whereas Keynes still stressed the importance of instantial variety in inductive evidence, as Bacon and Mill had done, more recently Carnap and others have proposed Pascalian analyses that would primarily display the value of instantial multiplicity. And yet a third Pascalian position is possible. The most recently popular mode of Pascalian analysis (called 'Bayesianism'), by concerning itself with the subjective gradation of an inductive reasoner's belief, however derived, rather than with the objective gradation of evidential strength, is able to avoid taking sides on the issue of instantial variety versus instantial multiplicity.

Faced with this rich diversity of philosophical positions we need first to examine how philosophical controversy about the nature of Pascalian probability may best be resolved (§§ 5–15). Only when that has been done shall we be able to explore the extent to which ampliative induction submits to a Pascalian analysis (§§ 16–19) and the extent to which non-Pascalian principles apply (§§ 20–22). And we shall then also have to allow (§§ 23–26) for the impact of several important puzzles and paradoxes that have been propounded as problems about the rationality of induction. For example, David Hume pointed out that, if a generalization goes beyond the observed evidence, then even though this evidence is uniformly favourable and enormously extensive, the logical possibility remains that the generalization may be false. So for Hume in the eighteenth century, as for Karl Popper in the twentieth, ampliative induction can never be a rational procedure. Perhaps you may think instead that ampliative induction can be rational just so long as it conforms to appropriate principles of its own, whether Baconian or Pascalian: all that is needed is to uncover the laws of this 'inductive logic'. But in certain important respects any such principles are difficult to state plausibly and coherently. For example, as Carl Hempel pointed out, if any favourable instance gives a generalization some confirmation, however small, and if anything that confirms a proposition must also confirm any logically equivalent proposition, then—paradoxically—even a white handkerchief gives some confirmation to the generalization 'All ravens are black', because it is a favourable instance for the equivalent generalization 'All non-black things are non-ravens'. These problems are very serious ones. But a satisfactory philosophy of induction ought to resolve them all. So the puzzles and paradoxes discussed in §§ 23–26 may be seen as a test for the adequacy of the analyses and evaluations propounded in §§ 16–22.

§ 2. THE BACONIAN TRADITION IN THE PHILOSOPHY OF INDUCTION

Bacon had a gradualist conception of inductive enquiry, both in science and in jurisprudence. This gradualism was echoed by Herschel and Whewell. Bacon and Whewell also emphasized the role of conceptual innovation in the progress of inductive enquiry, though Mill disagreed. Bacon did not however distinguish, as Mill did, between induction as a method of discovery and induction as a pattern of proof or graded justification.

The idea that ampliative induction may issue in judgements of comparison or gradation is one that may be traced back at least as far as Francis Bacon's *Novum Organum* (published in 1620), though it is hard to find a clear and systematic development of it in the work of any ancient or medieval philosopher. Indeed Bacon's gradualist epistemology was very highly regarded by many leading experimental scientists in the seventeenth century, like Robert Hooke and Robert Boyle.[2] But he has not been well served by his modern interpreters. All too often they have echoed the misrepresentation that was promoted by R.L. Ellis in the latter half of the nineteenth century. They have held that 'absolute certainty is . . . one of the distinguishing characters of the Baconian induction'.[3] Yet what Bacon wrote in the preface of his *Novum Organum* was that his principle of method, 'though hard to practise, is easy to state: it is such that we set up degrees of certainty . . .'. Where degrees of certainty are said to be admissible, it is clearly wrong to impute insistence at every stage on absolute certainty, even if that were ultimately what we seek.

Bacon advocated that scientists interrogate Nature in order to be able to tabulate both the various circumstances in which instances of the phenomenon (the 'nature') under investigation have been found to be present and also the circumstances under which they have been found to be absent. Thus he found heat present in the sun's rays, in flame, and in boiling liquids, but absent in the moon's and stars' rays, in phosphorescence, and in natural liquids.[4] To the extent that scientists discover a circumstance which correlates uniquely with the phenomenon—i.e. is *always* present when it is present and absent when it is absent—they have discovered its proximate explanation (or 'form') and have acquired power to reproduce it at will. Thus he says that what constitutes finding the form for a particular nature is that 'another nature should be discovered which is convertible with the given nature and yet is a limitation of a

---

[2] e.g. *The Posthumous Works of Robert Hooke*, (London: R. Waller, 1705), 6, and R. Boyle, *Works* (London: A Millar, 1744), i. 199. Francis Bacon (1561-1626) was by training a lawyer and was Lord Chancellor for a few years under James I. His philosophy of science was concerned with the social as well as the intellectual conditions for the advancement of knowledge and with the social as well as the intellectual benefits of properly directed research. In jurisprudence he sought a systematic statement of the principles of Common Law from the study of reported cases.

[3] R.L. Ellis, 'General Preface to Bacon's Philosophical Works', in *The Works of Francis Bacon*, ed. J. Spedding, R. Ellis, and D.N. Heath (London: Longmans, 1859), i. 23.

[4] For detailed references to Bacon's writings on this subject see L. Jonathan Cohen, 'Some Historical Remarks on the Baconian Conception of Probability', *Journal of the History of Ideas*, 61 (1980), 219-31.

more intelligible nature, like a true natural kind', and this more fundamental nature may itself have a form that investigators can seek to discover. For example, on Bacon's view the nature of which heat is a limitation is motion: 'heat is a motion expansive, restrained, and acting in its strife upon the smaller particles of bodies'. And motion itself must be supposed to be a limitation of a more fundamental property. So there is a hierarchy of explanatory laws to be discovered. The investigator should expect to make a gradual ascent to more and more comprehensive laws, acquiring greater and greater certainty as he moves up the pyramid, and each law that is reached should lead him to new experiments, that is, to experiments over and above those that led to the discovery of the law. But in regard to the apex of the pyramid, at which discovery of the 'summary law of Nature' would generate absolute certainty, Bacon says that we do not know whether this is within human reach.[5] (Contrast Ellis's misinterpretation.)

Bacon held that at each stage of the investigation greater significance should be attached to some kinds of observable instances than to others. Thus there are twenty-seven types of 'prerogative' instances that deserve preferential consideration, and some of these are more valuable than others in terms of their ability to exclude alternative explanations and thus contribute to greater certainty. But Bacon repudiated as 'childish' the method of induction by simple enumeration, whereby a generalization that is as yet unfalsified is supposed to acquire support that varies in strength with the number of known instances that verify it. On his view it is not the mere number of known instances that counts but the variety of circumstances that have been canvassed in the attempt to exclude alternative explanations. And this is because there is only a limited number of ultimate forms and so falsificatory evidence, by conclusively excluding incorrect hypotheses, permits firmer progress than verificatory[6] evidence does towards identifying the correct hypothesis. Even a well-verified hypothesis may still turn out to be false, but the truth-value of a falsified hypothesis is known

---

[5] *Of the Advancement of Learning* (*Works*, iii. 356). Contrast, however, Bacon's more optimistic claim in his *Parasceve* (*Works*, iv. 252).

[6] *Novum Organum*, bk. I, aphorism xlvi (*Works*, i. 166).

once and for all. Moreover, on Bacon's view,[7] at each level of investigation the kinds of circumstances that vary independently of one another are few enough to be examined, and thereby we may eventually come to hope that every false hypothesis has been eliminated, with an appropriate degree of certainty established for the remaining hypothesis. Eliminative induction is promoted by successive variations of experimental circumstances because, for example, if you test a hypothesis 'All A are B' unsuccessfully in circumstances C, you have thereby eliminated not only the hypothesis 'All A are B' but also the hypothesis 'All AC are B', while perhaps leaving open as yet the hypothesis 'All AD are B'.

Bacon's gradualist methodology reflects a theme that came to dominate seventeenth-century English attitudes towards knowledge of Nature. This theme was that scientific achievement—of the kind that brings power over Nature—is a matter for gradual progress in the future through open-minded, systematic, first-hand investigation. It is not—as implicitly categorized in much medieval and Renaissance writing—something that has already been perfected from observation in the past and can largely be recaptured second-hand from the texts of appropriately empiricist authorities (Aristotle, Galen, etc.). Nor is it something to be deduced from self-evident first principles in one glorious exercise of logical or mathematical skill, as Descartes suggested.[8] Moreover, one could not adopt Bacon's gradualism without rejecting the view that the truth of a scientific theory had to be absolutely certain if it were to be of any importance at all. On Bacon's view worthwhile results could be achieved at many stages on the way to certainty. So Bacon's inductivist epistemology cohered with the increasingly prevalent assumption that different levels of credibility were possible not only in regard to scientific contentions but also in regard to testimony about facts of religious or forensic importance. His philosophy was thus part of a general movement of thought that was coming to provide an intellectual

---

[7] *Valerius Terminus*, ch. 13 (*Works*, iii. 243).

[8] *Discourse on Method*, pt. V, in *The Philosophical Works of Descartes*, trans. E.S. Haldane and G.R.T. Ross (Cambridge: Cambridge University Press, 1931) i. 106–18.

basis for religious tolerance and for more practicable standards of proof in the courts, as well as for scientific gradualism.[9] But it should be noted that within this movement the scale of proof on a particular issue ran downwards from the justification of certainty that the proposition in question was true to the absence of any justification for belief in its truth: the lower limit of proof was not, as a Pascalian conception of probability requires, the presence of justification for belief in the proposition's falsity.[10]

Bacon insisted that his methodology is just as applicable to normative as to factual issues. It has a role in jurisprudence, for example, as well as in natural science because in Common Law, as Bacon pointed out, legal maxims, just like the axioms of Nature in science, are reached by induction from individual cases and then, once formulated, are applied back to determine new particulars. Bacon was therefore as emphatic on the value of good legal reports for jurisprudential induction as on that of good natural history for scientific induction. By the former we reduce uncertainty about our legal rights and duties; by the latter we reduce uncertainty about what is the case in Nature. And negative instances, he held, are of primary importance in both enquiries, in order to eliminate false propositions.[11] So too in the establishment of ethical principles from moral judgements in particular cases. Bacon was thus able to claim that the generality of his inductive logic paralleled that of syllogistic logic.[12] Both of them embraced not only propositions about actual facts but also propositions about what ought to happen.

Bacon's philosophy of science retained much of its reputation into the earlier half of the nineteenth century. J. F. W. Herschel, for example, proclaimed his Baconian allegiance by placing a picture of Bacon's bust on the very title page of his *Preliminary*

---

[9] See B. J. Shapiro, *Probability and Certainty in Seventeenth-Century England: A Study of the Relationships between Natural Science, Religion, History, Law and Literature* (Princeton: Princeton University Press, 1983). Cf. S. Shaffer's review of this book, 'Making Certain', *Social Studies of Science*, 14 (1984), 137–52, which is more critical in tone than in substance. Bacon even allowed the possibility that his own methodology was capable of improvement: *Novum Organum*, bk. I, aphorism cxxx (*Works*, i. 223).

[10] Shapiro, *Probability and Certainty*, p. 33. On this question of the lower limit of proof see further pp. 112–13 below.

[11] See P. H. Kocher, 'Francis Bacon on the Science of Jurisprudence', *Journal of the History of Ideas*, 18 (1957), 3–26.

[12] *Novum Organum*, bk. I, aphorism cxxvii (*Works*, i. 220).

Discourse on the Study of Natural Philosophy (first published in 1831), and his text is quite explicit about the gradualist implications of Baconian inductivism. Experiments, he wrote, 'become more valuable, and their results clearer, in proportion as they possess this quality (of agreeing exactly in all their circumstances but one), since the question put to nature becomes thereby more pointed and its answer more decisive'.[13] That is, as we become better able to distinguish the different variations of circumstance that are possible in a given type of experimental situation, we can have greater confidence about which of these variations is in fact responsible for the phenomenon under investigation.

William Whewell republished the methodological part of his *Philosophy of the Inductive Sciences, Founded upon their History* (first published in 1840) under the title *Novum Organum Renovatum*, and was another admirer of Bacon's gradualism. 'By far the most extraordinary parts of Bacon's works are those in which, with extreme earnestness and clearness, he insists upon a *graduated and successive induction* as opposed to a hasty transit from special facts to the highest generalizations.'[14] And Whewell's own reflections led him to add that the most important kind of step in this progress to a higher level of generalization was what he called 'consilience'. Consilience occurs when inductions from altogether different kinds of facts are, quite unexpectedly, seen to share a common explanation. Thus Newton's theory of universal gravitation, 'which had been inferred from the *Perturbations* of the moon and planets by the sun and by each other, also accounted for the fact, apparently altogether dissimilar and remote, of the *Precession of the equinoxes*'.[15] In such a case, wrote Whewell, when the evidence in favour of our induction enables us to explain and determine facts of a kind different from those which were contemplated in the formation of our hypothesis,

---

[13] *A Preliminary Discourse on the Study of Natural Philosophy* (London: Longman, Rees, 1833), 155. John Frederick William Herschel (1792–1871) made important contributions to astronomy and chemistry, and wrote about the philosophy of science on the basis of his own experience as a scientist.

[14] *The Philosophy of the Inductive Sciences* (London: J.W. Parker, 1847), ii. 232 (Whewell's italics). William Whewell (1794–1866) wrote a history of science in preparation for his philosophy of the subject. He worked also in mineralogy, and was influential in reforming the teaching of mathematics at Cambridge University.

[15] Ibid. 66 (Whewell's italics).

'this evidence is of a much higher and more forcible character' than when the facts explained are of the same kind as those initially observed.[16] Or, as Bacon would have put it, our certainty increases as we progress up the pyramid of laws, embracing more and more 'natures' within the scope of our explanations. And Whewell was able to illustrate his epistemology with intuitively convincing examples drawn from the history of science since Bacon's day, whereas most of Bacon's own examples were necessarily speculative because his philosophy of science, formulated as it was in the early seventeenth century, had to be largely prospective and programmatic rather than retrospectively analytical.

Whewell saw also that Bacon had recognized, as Aristotle had not,[17] how important it was in inductive reasoning to operate with the right concepts as well as to perform the right experiments.[18] Indeed, Whewell himself thought that in every new inductive inference a new conception is invented and 'superinduced' upon the facts.[19] For example, according to Whewell, when Kepler discovered the laws of planetary motion he bound together particular observations of planets' positions by the conception of an ellipse 'which was supplied by his own mind'.[20] And on this point Whewell's quasi-Kantian idealism has naturally been opposed by realists like J. S. Mill (writing in the Lockean tradition) who insist that 'the ellipse was in the facts before Kepler recognised it'.[21]

But the issue is a complex one. Even if we set aside the metaphysical dispute between realism and idealism, we can still distinguish two rather different methodological claims, of unequal merit, which might be taken to be implicit in Whewell's remarks. First, there is the claim that conceptual innovation—the invention of a new concept—has always been, and

---

[16] Whewell, *The Philosophy of the Inductive Sciences*, 65.

[17] Ibid. 50.   [18] Ibid. 237–8.   [19] Ibid. 50–1.

[20] W. Whewell, *Of Induction, with especial reference to Mr J. Stuart Mill's System of Logic* (London: J. W. Parker, 1849), 28.

[21] J. S. Mill, *A System of Logic Ratiocinative and Inductive* (London: Longmans, Green, 1896), 193. John Stuart Mill (1806–73) sought to found his theory of induction on the practice of the natural sciences and then to apply it within his philosophy of the social sciences. He argued that the course of human history is subject to the operation of general laws, knowledge of which would assist in furthering the central objective of utilitarian ethics—human happiness.

is always likely to be, central to any major theoretical advance in natural science. Whewell produced plenty of historical data that illustrate this thesis, and Mill produced none that refute it. It is indeed integral to any understanding of what Whewell called 'consilience', as we shall see later (§ 20). (The importance of conceptual innovation for innovative inductive reasoning has also been noticeable recently[22] in knowledge engineering, whereby particular kinds of expertise are extracted from human practice and articulated in so-called expert systems for implementation on appropriate computers.) Secondly, there is the claim that conceptual innovation in this sense is necessary for any kind of inductive reasoning whatever, however humble. But such a claim would draw too tight a boundary around our notion of induction. Too much of the quite respectable causal reasoning that Mill discusses would then have to be rejected because it contained no conceptual innovation.

One other preliminary issue about induction needs some discussion: is it to be understood as a process in time? Bacon remarked that knowledge is not communicated in the same order as that in which it was discovered.[23] But he drew no sharp distinction between the concept of induction as a process of research or gradual discovery and the concept of induction as a pattern of proof or of graded justification, though the former is concerned with temporal sequences of events and the latter with timeless relations between propositions. Mill had approached this distinction by 1851, when he claimed, in the third edition of his *System of Logic*, that even if his inductive methods were not methods of discovery they were at least methods of proof.[24] And since Mill's day most writers on induction have concentrated on the logic of inductive proof rather than the methodology of inductive discovery. (Perhaps the only systematic exceptions to this tendency today are computer scientists writing about the construction of expert systems.) The present book, as an introduction to the contemporary state of the subject, will

---

[22] See e.g. N.M. Cooke, 'Modelling Human Expertise in Expert Systems', *New Mexico State University Memoranda in Computer and Cognitive Science*, 12 (1985).

[23] *Valerius Terminus*, ch. 18 (*Works*, iii. 248).

[24] *System of Logic*, p. 284.

necessarily follow the dominant trend.[25] It will therefore be mainly concerned with induction as a pattern of proof or graded justification. And in any case we need to have an adequate criterion of what is to count as well-supported before we can profitably begin to discuss how to discover well-supported generalizations.

Bacon has in fact often been criticized for urging scientists to collect facts before they form hypotheses, rather than vice versa. But we need not concern ourselves at all with this issue of temporal priority, if our concern is with the logic, not the heuristics, of induction. In our sense of the term induction is not in any kind of competition with the so-called hypothetico-deductive method, for instance, whereby a generalization is first propounded and then evaluated by deducing its consequences in a particular situation and checking whether they obtain. Rather, the hypothetico-deductive method may be said to be a heuristic that exploits our beliefs about the relationships of inductive support which obtain between some propositions and not between others, since it is those beliefs that justify the direction of enquiry which the method takes on any particular occasion of its employment. Certain consequences of a generalization are checked because the results of such checks reveal the extent of inductive support that exists for the generalization.

[25] Even a genetic epistemology (see R.F. Kitchener, 'Is Genetic Epistemology Possible?', *British Journal for the Philosophy of Science*, 38 (1987), 283–99) needs to postulate criteria for evaluating any particular stage of cognitive development. More detailed expositions and evaluations of Bacon's and Whewell's views are to be found in M. Hesse, 'Francis Bacon', in D.J. O'Connor (ed.), *A Critical History of Western Philosophy* (New York: Free Press of Glencoe, 1964), 141–52; L. Jardine, *Francis Bacon: Discovery and the Art of Discourse* (Cambridge: Cambridge University Press, 1974); P. Urbach, *Francis Bacon's Philosophy of Science* (La Salle: Open Court, 1987); G. Buchdahl, 'Inductive *Versus* Deductivist Approaches in the Philosophy of Science as Illustrated by some Controversies between Whewell and Mill', *The Monist*, 55 (1971) 343–67; M. Fisch, 'Whewell's Consilience of Inductions—An Evaluation', *Philosophy of Science*, 52 (1985), 239–55, and 'Necessary and Contingent Truth in William Whewell's Antithetical Theory of Knowledge', *Studies in History and Philosophy of Science*, 16 (1985), 275–314; and the papers in M. Fisch and S. Schaffer (eds.), *William Whewell: A Composite Portrait—Studies of his Life, Work and Influence* (Oxford: Clarendon Press (forthcoming)). For some medieval anticipations see J.R. Weinberg, *Abstraction, Relation and Induction* (Madison: University of Wisconsin Press, 1965), 121–53.

Not that it is easy to operate in this area with a vocabulary that tidily abstracts from all temporal or methodological considerations. Even the term 'hypothesis' is potentially misleading, since in ordinary speech it denotes not just a proposition or unit of logical analysis, but a person's working assumption. Indeed, the ordinary concept of a hypothesis may have an important role to play in the history and heuristics of natural science. But it is not intrinsic to the logic of inductive support. Similarly, though the term 'confirmation' is often used in place of 'inductive support', it has a temporal implication that may also be misleading. In ordinary usage a prediction needs to have been advanced, or a hypothesis entertained, before it can be said to be confirmed. What confirms normally comes later than what is confirmed. But it is only so far as inductive confirmation is conceived as a timeless relation that the question arises whether it is properly categorized as a form of probabilification that is subject to the principles of the mathematical calculus of chance.

We must now move further towards understanding the problem which that question formulates. As a start in that direction the present section has outlined the classical, Baconian tradition about inductive support. The other necessary preliminary is to sketch the fundamental features of Pascalian probability. And this task will also be approached initially, in the next section, from a historical point of view.

§ 3. THE RISE OF PASCALIAN PROBABILITY

The mathematics of Pascalian probability originated in the study of games of chance, and in the latter half of the seventeenth century it began to be applied to measurements of the credibility of a proposition. But, though aleatory probability always requires a complementational principle for negation and a multiplicative principle for conjunction, there are contexts in which credibility conforms to non-Pascalian principles. The mathematics of Pascalian probability has subsequently been enriched in many ways, not least by Bernoulli's Limit Theorem, by Bayes's Law, and by modern axiomatizations.

We have seen that in the Baconian tradition certainty was treated as a matter of degree. At least, the grade of certainty of one generalization about the cause of a particular physical property could be compared with that of another generalization about the same property, on the evidence to hand, or a generalization's grade of certainty on the basis of one set of evidential facts could be compared with its grade of certainty on the basis of another such set. Perhaps comparisons could also be drawn between generalizations about different properties, so far as they had been subjected to checks against the same kinds of evidence or could be assigned to particular levels in the pyramid of laws; and such comparisons might affect the choice of means to given ends. But that was as far as gradation could go. Certainty was not treated as a quantitative property that could be measured in terms of standard units, as length can be measured in terms of metres or yards, or time in terms of days or years. Nor was there any logical syntax for judgements of certainty, enabling anyone to infer, for example, the level of a proposition's certainty from the level of its negation's certainty, or the level of a conjunctive proposition's certainty from the level of its conjuncts' certainty (i.e. the certainty-level of $H_1\&H_2$ from the certainty-levels of H_1 and H_2). In fact J.S. Mill was the first to propose a more refined mode of gradation within a systematic treatment of variative induction. His proposal exploited what had by his day come to be known as 'the theory of probability': Pascal's legacy at last converged with Bacon's. But before we traverse Mill's ideas on the subject it will be useful to sketch, very briefly, the history of Pascalian probability.

The mathematics of probability originated in the discussion of rules for calculating the chances of specified kinds of outcomes or combinations of outcomes in dice-throwing and similar games of chance. Thus the great astronomer Galileo took an interest in the problem of calculating the number of different permutations in which three dice could be thrown so that the numerals on their topmost sides sum to a particular number. Similarly the Chevalier de Méré's famous questions put two problems to Pascal:[26] how should the stakes be divided when two players separate without finishing their game and how many tosses are needed, in throwing two dice, to have at least an even chance of

---

[26] Blaise Pascal (1623–62) was well known as a strong supporter of Jansen's theology as well as being an important mathematician.

getting a double six? And the discussion of such issues was further promoted by Pascal's 1654 correspondence on them with Fermat, by Christiaan Huygens's 1657 book on reckoning in games of chance and by the much-delayed publication of the mathematician and physician Cardano's mid-sixteenth-century writings on this subject in 1663.

But the study of games of chance has an epistemological ambiguity that is found in other branches of elementary mathematics also. On the one hand its problems are soluble a priori, by theorem-licensed calculation from the figures supplied, just as, if we are given the length of a square's side in Euclidean space, we can calculate the length of its diagonal on the basis of Pythagoras's theorem. On the other hand, to the extent that the dice used are unbiased and thrown at randon we expect the relevant calculations to be empirically confirmed by relative frequencies in the actual outcomes, just as we expect actual diagrams on paper or actual squares of wood to confirm our Euclidean calculations. The a priori calculations represent ideal cases, to which we expect the real world to be seen to conform within appropriate limits of approximation. If this conformity is not found, then either the calculations are incorrect or the dice-throws are biased. Not surprisingly, therefore, the observational experience of generations of dice-throwers seems sometimes to have acted as a historical check on the mathematics, as in the case of Galileo's claim that the outcomes of three dice-throws had been observed to have a greater chance of summing to 11 than to 12. To establish this result mathematically it was necessary to make sure that one assumed all the different permutations of outcomes, not the different combinations, to have equal chances of occurrence. (A 'combination' of possible outcomes specifies just which particular numbers are thrown and how often, irrespective of which throw produces which number, while a 'permutation' assigns a number to each particular throw. So the only combination of three throws that sums to 4, for example, is two 1's and a 2, but this combination has three different permutations: 1-1-2, 1-2-1 and 2-1-1.)[27]

[27] I. Hacking, *The Emergence of Probability: A Philosophical Study of Early Ideas about Probability, Induction and Statistical Inference* (Cambridge: Cambridge University Press, 1975), 51–3.

In this seminal period it was not just the mathematics that was developing, but also its range of applications. The crucially important step that had clearly been taken by 1662 was to apply the calculus of chance to other domains than the outcomes of aleatory games. Thus the agnostic, in Pascal's famous wager,[28] is supposed to treat the existence and non-existence of God as having equal chances and then to choose the religious life because of its infinitely superior expectations, much as in a fair toss we should put our money on heads if it had a higher pay-off than tails. In any case there are problems about the force of Pascal's arguments. For example, so far as it applies at all, it applies equally well to decisions about the existence of any other benevolent deity than the Judaeo-Christian one. But what is relevant in the present context is that Pascal's argument extends the concept of chance in an important way. The existence and non-existence of God are not types of repeatable event or alternative types of outcome in any kind of game, like a coin's falling heads or tails. So no relative frequencies among actual events can operate as a check on the assignment of equal chance to the two propositions, nor can we usefully characterize the particular issue at stake—the existence or non-existence of God—as an instance of a familiar kind of issue, in the way that the outcome of the next toss can be characterized as just another instance of the issue of a fair toss. Indeed, on this issue we seem not to be dealing at all with a measurable property of classes or kinds of events either in an ideal world or in the real one, but rather with a measurable property of propositions. It is a matter of the probabilities we assign in our reasonings, on the basis of the information that we have in our minds, rather than a matter of the chances that are objectively there to be counted.

Moreover, in the Port-Royal *Logic*,[29] first published in 1662, the fact that a certain type of event has happened more often than not when the circumstances are of such-and-such a kind is

---

[28] B. Pascal, *Pensées*, trans. H.F. Stewart (London: Routledge and Kegan Paul, 1950), 120–1.

[29] A. Arnauld, *The Art of Thinking: Port-Royal Logic*, trans. J. Dickoff and P. Jones (Indianapolis: Bobbs-Merrill, 1964), 350–1. Antoine Arnauld (1612–94) supported Jansen's theology against that of the Jesuits. He is generally credited with the authorship of the book *La Logigue ou l'Art de Penser*, which was published by Jansenists from Port-Royal in 1662.

said to warrant belief with a high degree of probability, on a particular occasion in which these circumstances are present, that an event of the kind in question occurred. For example, if 999 contracts out of 1,000, that have been signed by two notaries, have not been post-dated, it is very highly probable that the contract I see (which has been signed by two notaries) has not been post-dated. The validity of such an argument needs further discussion—see § 14 below. But it is clear that the measurement of a proposition's credibility is now being treated as having the same mathematical structure as the measurement of an aleatory chance and that the term 'probability' is now being used in both connections.[30]

Nor was this identification of structure as much of a truism as it may seem. The chance of a fair die's falling six uppermost ($\frac{1}{6}$) is obviously equal to one minus the chance of its falling with some other number uppermost (i.e. to $1 - \frac{5}{6}$). And in general, if the chance or relative frequency of A is n, the chance or relative frequency of not-A is the complement of n. However, credibility differs here from chance or relative frequency. It is not necessarily governed by a complementational principle for negation. Such a principle is certainly in operation if the negation we have in mind in connection with the credibility of A is the incredibility of A. As the credibility of A goes up, the incredibility of A goes down, and vice versa. But a complementational principle will not apply if the negation we have in mind in connection with the credibility (belief-worthiness) of A is not the incredibility of A, but the credibility (belief-worthiness) of not-A. On the basis of a rather jejune statement of supposed evidence the credibility of A and the credibility of not-A—that is, the justification for believing A and the justification for believing not-A—may both be rather low. For example, the report that a certain document has not been notarized at all may provide as little warranty to believe that it has not been post-dated as to believe that it has. In this sense of 'probability' the probability of its having been post-dated will not vary inversely with the probability that it has not been. And the everyday concept of certainty is similarly ambivalent. As the certainty of A goes up, the uncertainty of A goes down, and vice versa. But there may

30 *The Art of Thinking*, pp. 351, 355.

well be very little certainty that A and also very little certainty that not-A.

So the quantitative gradation of belief, credibility, etc. took one road initially with the Pascalian theory of probability and its aleatory model, although another mathematical road was also open. Later in the seventeenth century Jacob Bernoulli took some exploratory steps down that other road, and so did J.H. Lambert in the latter half of the eighteenth century.[31] And more recently this important issue has been reopened (see § 14 and §§ 22–24 below). Certainly the dominant mathematical doctrine has been that—in accordance with the aleatory model—probabilities are complementational or additive, as canonically declared by Abraham de Moivre in 1718. De Moivre wrote that 'If the Probability of Happening and Failing are added together, the Sum will always be equal to unity':[32] in modern terms

$$p(A) + p(\text{not-}A) = 1.$$

But it would be dangerously misleadng to regard this thesis as a truism.

Compare the Pascalian law for the probability of a conjunction of outcomes, which is easily established from an aleatory model. When the outcomes are independent of one another, as when each ball drawn at random from an urn is immediately replaced, we must just multiply together the probabilities of the separate outcomes. For example, if there are two white and two black balls in the urn, the chance of drawing a white ball on any one drawing is 2 out of 4, and, if there are two drawings, then, since each of the four possible outcomes of the first drawing may be followed by any of the four possible outcomes of the second drawing, the chances of drawing a white ball twice is $\frac{1}{4}$. Of course, the ball drawn first may not be replaced. If so, the second outcome will not be independent of

---

[31] See G. Shafer, 'Non-Additive Probabilities in the work of Bernoulli and Lambert', *Archive for the History of Exact Sciences*, 19 (1978), 309–70.

[32] A. de Moivre, *The Doctrine of Chances, or a Method of Calculating the Probability of Events in Play* (London: de Moivre, 1718), 1. Abraham de Moivre (1667–1754), a French Huguenot who emigrated to England, was one of the commissioners appointed by the Royal Society to arbitrate on the dispute between Newton and Leibniz about which of them invented the differential calculus.

the first, and we shall be concerned in its case with only the three outcomes left possible by the outcome of the first drawing. The chance of drawing a white ball twice will then be $\frac{1}{6}$. Symbolically, let A be the event of drawing a white ball first, and B the event of drawing a white ball second; and let the dyadic function $p(B|A)$ evaluate the probability of B given A. Then both cases will be covered by the same multiplication principle for conjunction,

$$p(A\&B) = p(A) \times p(B|A),$$

which says that the chance of drawing two white balls is the product of the chance of drawing a white ball first and the chance of drawing a white ball second, given that a white ball was also drawn first. According to that principle, where the ball is replaced after being drawn $p(A\&B)$ equals $\frac{1}{4}$, because the two outcomes are independent and $p(B|A)$ equals $p(B)$ and thus equals $\frac{1}{2}$; and, where the ball is not replaced after the first drawing so that the two outcomes are not independent, $p(B|A)$ equals $\frac{1}{3}$ and so $p(A\&B)$ equals $\frac{1}{6}$. (We say that $p(A)$ is a 'monadic' function of A, because its value depends on just one issue—the issue of whether A occurs or not. Similarly $p(A\&B)$ is a monadic function of $A\&B$. But $p(B|A)$ is a 'dyadic' function of A and B because its value depends on the two issues that it relates.)

All this is straightforward and incontrovertible if our model is an aleatory one. But suppose an art historian declares two pictures to be genuine Vermeers. He seems to have given you a warranty—the warranty of his expertise—to believe that the first is a Vermeer, a warranty to believe that the second is, and a warranty of just the same nature to believe that they both are. The warranty for the conjunction seems no less reputable, and no less thoroughly researched, than for either of the conjuncts. But this conflicts with Pascalian principles because the above-mentioned multiplicative law for the probability of a conjunction ensures that, except in limiting cases, the conjunction is less probable than either conjunct. If $p(A) > 0$ and $p(B|A) < 1$, $p(A\&B)$ must always be less than $p(A)$, since in accordance with the multiplication principle for conjunction $p(A\&B)$, as we have just seen, is equal to a proper fraction of $p(A)$, namely, $p(A) \times p(B|A)$. Of course, the *chance* of both pictures' being genuine may well be a lot less than the chance of just one's being genuine. But is the credibility of their genuineness to be judged in terms of such chances (which are presumably to be viewed metaphorically as chances in the lottery of life) or in terms of the reputation of the author of the warranties that have been given you? The dominant theory has treated such warranted credibilities as sharing the same mathematical structure as aleatory chances. But this assignment of mathematical structure is by no means as incontrovertible in the case of warranted credibilities as in that of aleatory chances.

So both in dealing with conjunction and in dealing with negation more than one structure is conceivable. And if there is more than one way of dealing with conjunction there must also be more than one way of relating dyadic to monadic probabilities. For it is a matter of elementary algebra, where $p(A) > 0$, that in accordance with whether $p(A\&B)$ is, or is not, equal to $p(A) \times p(B|A)$, correspondingly $p(B|A)$ is, or is not, equal to

$$\frac{p(A\&B)}{p(A)}$$

Moreover, when using Pascalian functions, we have to distinguish carefully between judgements of the form '$p(B|A) = n$', judgements of the form 'If A, then $p(B) = n$', and judgements of the form '$p(\text{If } A, \text{ then } B) = n$'. Pascalian principles are demonstrably insufficient to ensure that a judgement of one of these three forms entails a judgement of one or other of the other two forms.[33] For example, if the monadic Pascalian probability of a conditional statement, i.e. if $p(\text{If } A, \text{ then } B)$, is n, then the monadic Pascalian probability of its contrapositive, i.e. $p(\text{If not-}B, \text{ then not-}A)$, should also be n since a Pascalian function admits the replacement of an expression by a logically equivalent one.[34] But in a similar context, if the dyadic—often called

---

[33] See L. Jonathan Cohen, *The Probable and the Provable* (Oxford: Clarendon Press, 1977), 30 n. 21.

[34] The contraposability of conditional statements has been called into question by E. W. Adams, *The Logic of Conditionals* (Dordrecht: Reidel, 1975). But Adam's argument rests on the counter-intuitive, or at least controversial, assumption that the probability of a conditional 'If A, then B' has to be equated with the conditional probability $p(B|A)$, and that conditionals cannot be assigned dichotomous truth-values in a way that will always and necessarily equate the probability of a conditional with the probability of its being true. Indeed, we should be quite unnecessarily impoverishing our conceptual resources if we excluded ourselves from ever employing the expression 'if . . ., then

'conditional'—probability $p(B|A)$ is n, it does not follow that the contrapositive of this probability, namely $p(\text{not-}A|\text{not-}B)$, is also n. Though there is only a rather low probability that a person lives in Oxford given that he lives in England, there is quite a high probability that he does not live in England given that he does not live in Oxford. So when we want to use a kind of dyadic probability function that *is* invariant under contraposition, we must either apply some appropriate non-Pascalian principles or some appropriate refinement of Pascalian ones. And such a function does sometimes seem appropriate. It may be tempting, for example, always to equate the probability, in a particular case, that the accused is guilty, given that such-and-such evidence is before the court, with the improbability of that evidence's being before the court, given that the accused is not guilty. For this purpose we seem to need a way of judging probability according to which the dyadic probability $p(B|A)$ is necessarily equal to the monadic probability $p(\text{If } A, \text{ then } B)$.

Since its beginnings in the years around 1660 the Pascalian theory of probability has made enormous progress, both in the enrichment of its mathematics and in the extension of its range of application. Indeed, these two types of progress have constantly reinforced one another. But it will suffice to cite here only three major developments in the mathematics of probability that will be mentioned in later discussions of the philosophy of induction.

In 1692 Jacob Bernoulli proved an important theorem[35] about any countably infinite set of chance outcomes. Let n be the number of outcomes in a finite subset of this set; let r be the relative frequency with which members of that subset have a certain feature; and let p be the probability of that feature's occurring in a member of the superset. Then Bernoulli proved that as n increases without bound, the probability that r is within

---

. . .', or an equivalent, in a necessarily contraposable sense or in a sense in which the probability of the conditional 'If A, then B' is not necessarily equivalent to the conditional probability $p(B|A)$. See also D. Lewis, 'Probabilities of Conditionals and Conditional Probabilities', *Philosophical Review*, 85 (1976), 297–315.

[35] Later published in pt. IV, ch. 5 of his *Ars Conjectandi* (Basle: Thurnisii Brothers, 1713). For an exposition of the proof see W. Kneale, *Probability and Induction* (Oxford: Clarendon Press, 1949), 136–9, or J.R. Lucas, *The Concept of Probability* (Oxford: Clarendon Press, 1970), 73–83. Bernoulli (1654–1705) opened a public seminary for teaching experimental physics in Basle after returning in 1682 from travels in England, France, and Holland. In 1687 he became Professor of Mathematics at the University of Basle and later its Rector.

a specifiable, small interval of p, increases towards 1. That is to say, the larger we make the subset, the higher the credibility that the relative frequency of the feature in the subset approximates p, given that p is the true probability of the feature's occurring in a member of the superset. (As a corollary, for any specified level of credibility, the interval within which r may be said, with that level of credibility, to approximate p, will decrease as n increases.) This result, known as 'Bernoulli's limit theorem' or, more colloquially, as 'the law of large numbers', has numerous applications. For example, where the superset consists of random drawings—with replacement—from an urn containing 9 black and 3 white balls, we can determine a priori a value for the true probability of drawing a black ball, namely, $\frac{3}{4}$. Bernoulli's theorem then allows us to predict, with a credibility not too far from 1, that in a long sample-sequence of actual drawings the empirically ascertainable relative frequency of black balls' being drawn should approximate this figure. Again, if a large insurance company knew that the true probability with which a man of certain age, life-style, and medical condition will die within a year is $\frac{1}{8}$, it could use Bernoulli's theorem to derive, with credibility not too far from 1, the approximate proportion of its own clients in that category who will die within the year.

But how can the company determine the true probability? In the case of the urn, we obtained this probability a priori, on the assumption that the drawings were random ones But mortality rates are facts of nature and need to be discovered empirically. It is tempting, therefore, to invert the inference and to derive (with sufficient credibility) an approximate figure for the true probability from a year's relative frequency of deaths in some sufficiently large sample of the appropriate category of men. But this inverse inference was not established by Bernoulli's mathematics. And we can easily see that the credibility (i.e. Pascalian probability) of B, given A, is not necessarily identical with the credibility (i.e. Pascalian probability) of A, given B, if we compare the probability (namely, $\frac{1}{2}$) of a dice-throw's being even, given that it is greater than 2, with the probability (namely, $\frac{2}{3}$) of a dice-throw's being greater than 2, given that it is even.

So how can Bernoulli's theorem be usefully applied when the true probability is an empirical fact that needs to be estimated? Bernoulli himself claimed that even though an approximate value for the true probability does not follow inversely, with high credibility, from the size of the relative frequency in a large sample, at least the existence of that value for the true probability is the simplest possible explanation of the size of the relative frequency.[36] A different manœuvre is adopted by the various statistical procedures that derive from the work of R. A. Fisher, E. Pearson, or J. Neyman in the earlier part of the present century.[37] There the underlying idea is that the investigator is invited to agree some conventional value for a specified parameter—for example, a 'significance level'—such that if that value is attained, in respect of a sample of specified size, then the true probability may be taken not to differ from the observed relative frequency by more than some stated interval. For example, it might be unacceptably improbable that a relatively large sample with that relative frequency in the sample had been observed unless the true probability was reasonably close to the relative frequency. It might be unacceptably improbable that 80 per cent of a 10,000-membered sample of tuberculous patients recovered after treatment with a certain drug unless the long-run expectancy was reasonably close to that percentage. This conventionalist idea emerges in a variety of sophisticated forms in many modern statistical textbooks, and very many probabilities have been estimated on its basis in various fields of scientific research.

But some statisticians, often called 'Bayesians', prefer instead to exploit the mathematical law that governs the inversion of a probability and relates the probability of B given A to the probability of A given B. This law is widely known as Bayes's law, because awareness of it is implicit—although not explicit—in a paper of Thomas Bayes (1763).[38] In its simplest

---

[36] Letter to Leibniz of 20 April 1704, in *Leibnizens mathematische Schriften*, ed. C. I. Gerhardt, iii (Halle: H. W. Schmidt, 1855), 87–8.

[37] See esp. R. A. Fisher, *Statistical Methods for Research Workers*, 7th edn. (Edinburgh: Oliver and Boyd, 1938), 120 ff.; J. Neyman, 'Outline of a Theory of Statistical Estimates Based on the Classical Theory of Probability', *Philosophical Transactions of the Royal Society of London*, ser. A, 236 (1937), 333 ff.; E. Pearson, 'On the Criteria that a given System of Deviation from the Probable in the case of a Correlated System of Variables is such that it can be reasonably supposed to have arisen from Random Sampling', *The London, Edinburgh, and Dublin Philosophical Magazine and Journal of Science*, 5th ser. 50 (1900), 157–75, and 'The Fundamental Problem of Practical Statistics', *Biometrika*, 13 (1920), 1–16.

[38] T. Bayes, 'Essay towards Solving a Problem in the Doctrine of Chances', *Philosophical Transactions of the Royal Society of London*, 53 (1763), 371–418.

form the law states that, where $p(B) > 0$,

$$p(A|B) = \frac{p(B|A) \times p(A)}{p(B)}.$$

And in that form the law is very easily derived within the calculus of Pascalian chance. It results, by elementary algebra, from putting equal to each other the two basic ways of spelling out (in accordance with the multiplication principle for conjunction) the probability of the conjunction of two outcomes, A and B, namely, $p(A|B) \times p(B)$ and $p(B|A) \times p(A)$. But Bayes's law obviously does not solve all the problems here. When you know the value of $p(A|B)$, Bayes's law can be used to derive $p(B|A)$ only if you also know the values of $p(A)$ and $p(B)$ or accept some conventional procedure for determining them. So whether you think of Bayes's law as a supplement to Bernoulli's theorem that is useful in relation to the inverse inference, or wish to exploit it in some other way, you must be able to evaluate these monadic probabilities (see further § 9 and § 19).

In the present century the mathematics of Pascalian probability have been studied systematically by means of axiomatization, with varying thoroughness of formalization. Thus A. Kolmogorov in 1933[39] produced six axioms for the monadic probability function that are demonstrably consistent and independent, plus a definition of the dyadic function in terms of the monadic, one that, where $p(B) > 0$, puts $p(A|B)$ equal to

$$\frac{p(A\&B)}{p(B)}$$

Of course, except in certain limiting cases, such as $p(A\&\text{not-}A) = 0$, this axiomatization gives us, as theorems, only laws governing relations between probability-judgements. It does not enable us to assign determinate probability-values to specified outcomes. Indeed, axiomatization has made it possible

---

[39] See A. Kolmogorov, *Foundations of the Theory of Probability*, trans. N. Morrison (New York: Chelsea Publishing Company, 1950).

thus to distinguish between problems about the syntax of probability-functions and problems about their semantics, in a way that was impossible in previous centuries.

Kolmogorov's treatment assumes probabilities to be real-number-valued functions of sets. That is, the expressions that are to occupy the argument-places in his functors 'p(. . .)' or 'p(. . .|. . .)' are expressions of a Boolean algebra that designate sets, and when the functors are thus filled out they designate real numbers. So, though his axiomatization has several mathematical advantages, it is not as neutral as it might be between different interpretations of the Pascalian structure. Since truth-functional operations on propositions, such as negation, conjunction, and disjunction, obey the same formal principles as Boolean operations on sets, such as complementation, intersection, and union, respectively, an interpretation of Boolean algebra in terms of propositions is as legitimate as an interpretation in terms of sets. But Kolmogorov's treatment excludes probabilities from being functions of propositions, unless we are willing to identify each proposition with some corresponding set, such as the set of possible worlds in which it is true. And this creates an unnecessary, technical obstacle to any analysis of inductive support in terms of mathematical probability. If inductive support is a relation between one proposition (stating evidence) and another (stating a hypothesis), Kolmogorov's theory of probability seems to rule out any Pascalian analysis of inductive support *ab initio*, unless you are willing to introduce controversial assumptions about the nature of propositions.

One should note, therefore, that it is also possible to axiomatize the structure, or logical syntax, of Pascalian probability in a way that imposes less restriction on the application of its principles. This more thoroughly formalized axiomatization of the Pascalian theory was achieved by K. R. Popper in 1938.[40] The expressions that occupy the argument-places in his monadic functors may designate *any* elements of a Boolean algebra. Moreover, Kolmogorov's definition of the dyadic probability functor in terms of the monadic one was restricted to cases where one of the monadic functions involved had a non-

[40] K. R. Popper, 'A Set of Independent Axioms for Probability', *Mind*, 47 (1938), 275 ff.

zero value (see above), and this too was unnecessarily restrictive. Popper later[41] replaced his 1938 axiomatization by a system of demonstrably independent and consistent axioms in which the dyadic functor is taken as primitive in place of the monadic one, and the latter is defined in terms of the former. In this system $p(A)$ is put equal to $p(A|B)$ if for every C $p(A|A)$ is equal to $p(B|C)$. (The point here is that, since $p(A|A)$ must equal 1, the requirement that, whatever C may be, $p(B|C)$ should equal $p(A|A)$ compels B to have the probability 1 on any condition whatever, and if B is thus necessary there can be no difference between $p(A)$ and $p(A|B)$.

Another important advance in the mathematics of Pascalian probability has been the development of interval-valued functions. Probabilities are then conceived as intervals between upper and lower limits, instead of as points, and it becomes possible to reflect the intuition that, especially in relation to single outcomes, precise estimates of probability often seem artificial and unrealistic. Alternatively we can say in such cases that point-valued judgements are idealizations of interval-valued ones.[42]

---

[41] *The Logic of Scientific Discovery* (London: Hutchinson, 1959), 326-48.

[42] For the history of the earlier period in the mathematics of probability see I. Todhunter, *A History of the Mathematical Theory of Probability from the Time of Pascal to that of Laplace* (Cambridge: Macmillan, 1865). For a variety of views about the interrelations between the origin and development of probability theory and its social context see L. E. Maistrow, *Probability Theory: A Historical Sketch*, trans. S. Kotz (New York: Academic Press, 1974); I. Hacking, *The Emergence of Probability*; D. Garber and S. Zabell, 'On the Emergence of Probability', *Archive for the History of Exact Sciences*, 21 (1979), 33-53; and I. Schneider, 'Why Do We Find the Origin of a Calculus of Probabilities in the Seventeenth Century?', in J. Hintikka, D. Gruender, and E. Agazzi (eds.), *Probabilistic Thinking, Thermodynamics and the Interaction of the History and Philosophy of Science: Proceedings of the 1978 Pisa Conference on the History and Philosophy of Science* (Dordrecht: Reidel, 1981), ii. 1-24. There are also some interesting historical remarks in J. M. Keynes, *A Treatise on Probability* (London: Macmillan, 1921), 79-91, and in addition a useful bibliography, 431-58. R. Jeffrey, 'De Finetti's Probabilism', *Synthese*, 60 (1984), 73-90 emphasizes, against Hacking, the influence of the Sceptic philosopher Carneades (214-129 BC), via Sextus Empiricus and Montaigne, on the development of the concept of probability. But this is poor historiography. It crucially underrates the importance of later mathematical developments (Cardano, Galileo, Pascal, Fermat, Huyghens) which were essential to give a gradational structure to the concept of probability. No doubt some concept of probability existed long before Carneades even. What are historically important are the events that triggered off a rich new development in its structure. These events took place mainly in the seventeenth century. Carneades and the other Sceptics merely encouraged the use of the concept, whatever its structure, in contexts where certainty would otherwise be taken for granted. For the history of probability in nineteenth-century science see L. Krüger et al. (eds.), *The Probabilistic Revolution* (Cambridge, Mass: MIT Press, 1987) i and ii. On the contribution of legal notions of fairplay to the aleatory

But it would be out of place to comment at greater length on the mathematics of Pascalian probability. Enough has now been said about its principles to give a fairly clear sense to the philosophical question: does such a probability afford an appropriate measure for Baconian induction?

§ 4. THE COMBINATION OF BACONIAN AND PASCALIAN THEMES

Leibniz, Bernoulli, Hume, and Herschel made no attempt to grade the strength of variative induction by Pascalian probability. But, when Mill developed a theory of variative induction in terms of his Methods of Agreement, Difference, Residues, and Concomitant Variations, he implicitly or explicitly sanctioned the use of Pascalian probability in the evaluation of some relevant parameters.

What we have seen in § § 2–3 is that in the seventeenth century the gradation of certainty began to develop along two apparently different lines. On the one hand, Bacon explored the role of evidential variety as a basis for ampliative induction, and gave no indication of any kind that he would have accepted an aleatory model for the gradation of inductive support. He does not even seem to have conceived a generalization's degree of certainty as a ratio of any kind. On the other hand, Pascal, Fermat, Huygens, and others explored the mathematics of chance as a syntax for judgements of probability, but did not apply it to the evaluation of variative inductions. Nor did these two lines of enquiry begin to converge for about a couple of centuries. Thus Leibniz called one scientific hypothesis more probable ('probabilior') than another if it was simpler and yet it explained a larger variety of phenomena from a smaller number of postulates, and especially if it allowed the prediction of as yet unknown phenomena.[43] But he apparently never tried to represent or elucidate these thoroughly Baconian criteria within the mathematics of chance, despite his readiness to apply the calculus of chance to other kinds of probability-judgement.

[43] Letter to Conring, 19 March 1678, in *Die philosophische Schriften von Gottfried Wilhelm Leibniz*, ed. C.I. Gerhardt. (Berlin: Weidmannsche Buchhandlung, 1865), i. 195–6. Leibniz (1646–1716) originated many important ideas in logic, philosophy, and mathematics, and was the first president of the Berlin Academy of Sciences.

Bernoulli certainly thought that his own theories about mathematical probability had important implications for the
evaluation of scientific hypotheses. But he spoke of the number,
not of the variety, of evidential instances as being relevant for
the purposes of this evaluation.[44]

Hume explicitly recognized the issue. Probabilities arising
from chance, as in a game of dice, he evaluated by the ratio of
favourable outcomes among a class of outcomes that are all
indifferently possible.[45] And probabilities arising from a causal
tendency that does not operate in every instance Hume
evaluated by the same rule as that applied in the Port-Royal
Logic (see § 3 above) to the authenticity of notarized contracts.
In Hume's example, if I have found by long observation that of
twenty ships which go to sea only nineteen return, then $\frac{19}{20}$
measures the strength of my belief that a ship which goes to sea
in the future will return.[46] Indeed, Hume did not just *assume* the
appropriateness of an aleatory model for such judgements: he
argued it. On his view

> Every past experiment may be consider'd as a kind of chance; it being
> uncertain to us, whether the object will exist conformable to one
> experiment or another: And for this reason every thing that has been
> said on the one subject is applicable to both.[47]

But this kind of probability is concerned with the numbers of
evidential instances, not their variety. And Hume treated
probabilities 'arising from analogy' as a third, quite distinct
category, which he never suggested measuring by a numerical
ratio. He maintained that reasoning from causes or effects
requires not only the conjunction of two objects in all past
experience but also the resemblance of a present object to any
one of them. He inferred that

> as this resemblance admits of many different degrees, the reasoning
> becomes proportionably more or less firm and certain. An experiment
> loses of its force, when transfer'd to instances which are not exactly
> resembling; 'tis evident it may still retain as much as may be the foun-
> dation of probability, as long as there is any resemblance remaining.[48]

[44] Letter to Leibniz of 20 April, 1704, in *Leibnizens mathematische Schriften*, ed.
Gerhardt, iii. 87–8.

[45] *A Treatise of Human Nature*, ed. L. A. Selby-Bigge (Oxford: Clarendon Press, 1888),
125 ff. David Hume (1711–76) was born in Edinburgh and eventually became librarian
to the Faculty of Advocates there. His sceptical epistemology has constituted an
important challenge to many subsequent philosophers.

[46] Ibid. 134–5.   [47] Ibid. 135.   [48] Ibid. 142.

So, since some closer resemblance between selected evidential and predictive instances may be expected when a generalization is confirmed by a greater *variety* of evidential instances, it is clear that what Hume called 'probability arising from analogy' is closely connected with the gradation of variative induction. But, though he uses the term 'probability' here, he makes no suggestion that it is a probability subject to the mathematics of chance.

Similarly Herschel was well aware of the theory of Pascalian probabilities and applied it in the resolution of problems about accuracy of measurement in the physical sciences.[49] But he made no reference to this theory when he used the term 'probability' elsewhere in talking about the 'probability of success' in discovering correct explanations of natural phenomena or when he enunciated a gradualist approach, like Bacon's, to variative induction.[50]

In fact, it seems to have been J. S. Mill who first attempted to combine a Baconian emphasis on the importance of variative induction with Pascalian convictions about the mathematics of probability, while withdrawing in the second edition of his *System of Logic* (1846) the somewhat sceptical view about the overall foundations of the calculus of chance that he had taken in the first edition of that book.[51]

For the most part, and despite criticism of Bacon in respect of some details, Mill's inductive logic is an elaboration and extension of Bacon's ideas on the subject. He too assigns an inferior value to induction by simple enumeration. 'The tendency of unscientific enquirers', he says, 'is to rely too much on number, without analysing the instances; without looking closely enough into their nature, to ascertain what circumstances are not eliminated by means of them.' Like Bacon, Mill insists on the superior value of a single falsifying instance that excludes some feature from being causally relevant to the occurrence of a particular phenomenon, as against any multitude of verifying instances that are evaluated purely by their number.[52] And, as in Bacon's inferences from his tables of presence and absence, Mill acknowledges two main principles to

[49] Herschel, *The Philosophy of the Inductive Science*, p. 217.
[50] Ibid. 148, 155.
[51] *System of Logic*, p. 351. Compare the preface to the second edition, pp. vii-viii.
[52] *System of Logic*, p. 287.

be at work. One, called 'the Method of Agreement' compares together different instances in which the phenomenon under investigation occurs. By this method, on its own, we may establish only what Mill calls 'empirical laws', that is correlations or connections between phenomena that are not the ultimate laws of causation.[53] The other method, however, is capable, on Mill's view, of leading us to ultimate causal laws. It is called 'the Method of Difference' and compares instances in which the phenomenon does occur with instances in other respects similar in which it does not.

The principle regulating the Method of Agreement, according to Mill, was that

If two or more instances of the phenomenon under investigation have only one circumstance in common, the circumstance in which alone all the instances agree is the cause (or effect) of the given phenomenon.[54]

Or, schematically, if circumstances A&B&C issue in $a\&b\&c$, and circumstances A&not-B&not-C issue in $a\&$not-$b\&$not-c, then a is the effect of A because its occurrence is unaffected by the presence or absence of B or of C. For example, if an alkaline substance is combined with an oil in several otherwise different varieties of circumstance, and in each case a soap results, then 'the combination of an oil and an alkali causes the production of a soap'.[55] So the Method of Agreement may be said to stand on the ground that whatever can be eliminated, because the phenomenon under investigation occurs whether or not it is present, is not connected with the phenomenon by any causal law. And an experimenter's object will normally be to eliminate a number of such factors by 'controlling' for them, as it is now called. (The 'control' situation is the one where supposedly just the suspect factor is absent.)

Clearly there is also room for a complementary method whereby whatever can *not* be eliminated, because the phenomenon under investigation does not occur when it is absent, must be connected with the phenomenon by some causal law. Mill calls this complementary method the Method of Difference, and regards its regulative principle as being that

If an instance in which the phenomenon under investigation occurs, and an instance in which it does not occur, have every circumstance in

---

[53] *System of Logic*, pp. 338–43.   [54] Ibid. 255.   [55] Ibid. 254.

common save one, that one occurring only in the former; the circumstance in which alone the two instances differ is the effect, or the cause, or an indispensable part of the cause, of the phenomenon.[56]

Schematically, if circumstances A&B&C issue in *a&b&c* and circumstances not-A&B&C—the control—in not-*a&b&c*, then *a* is the effect of A because its presence is adversely affected by the absence of A. For example, says Mill,[57] 'when a man is shot through the heart, it is by this method we know that it was the gunshot which killed him: for he was in the fulness of life immediately before, all circumstances being the same except the wound'.

Thus both methods are eliminative, in that they guide investigators as to which factors can or cannot be eliminated from the enquiry. And neither is enumerative, because neither exploits the mere accumulation of instances irrespective of those instances' circumstances. Moreover, both methods assume that there is always a uniformity to be found. As Mill puts it, in every induction we assume that 'the universe, so far as known to us, is so constituted, that whatever is true in any one case, is true in all cases of a certain description; the only difficulty is, to find what description'.[58] Or, more precisely, we assume that this type of regularity pervades 'the particular class of phenomena to which the induction relates'.[59] So, for example, an induction concerning the motions of the planets would not be vitiated if we supposed that wind and weather are the sport of chance, provided it be assumed that astronomical phenomena are under the dominion of general laws.

But what ground can there be for supposing the truth of this assumption about a universal 'law of causation', as Mill called it? Mill's answer to that question is to claim that here induction by simple enumeration has a legitimate field of application.[60] The assumption has been found true in a very large number of cases and has never been found false. It is therefore justifiable to treat apparent counter-instances (cases where apparently no causal law operates) as due merely to human ignorance. Mill is careful to qualify his thesis in relation to circumstances that are unknown to us and beyond the possible range of our experience. The law of causation, on his view, must not be received as a law

---

[56] Ibid. 256.   [57] Ibid.   [58] Ibid. 201.
[59] Ibid. 203.   [60] Ibid. 372-6.

of the universe but as a law 'of that portion of it only which is within the range of our means of sure observation, with a reasonable degree of extension to adjacent cases'.[61] But he does not seem to have appreciated that even when formulated in these modest terms his law of causation is not easily substantiated. To say that it is supported by enumerative induction is just to raise the further question: what is the rational warranty for assuming that enumerative induction is a justifiable procedure?

Mill pointed out that induction by the Method of Agreement is subject to a special kind of uncertainty because a particular kind of phenomenon *may* be produced by more than one kind of cause. For example, two great philosophers might both have been educated at the same school and be otherwise different in background: yet their philosophical abilities might be due to different causes.[62] Mill saw two ways of reducing such an uncertainty. One was by the observation of very numerous and sufficiently various instances, so that coincidental similarities between all observed instances are gradually eliminated, and it then becomes clear whether evidence for a unique cause persists in being present in the data or whether the apparent uniqueness of cause was just an illusion created by insufficient variation of circumstances. And the other way of reducing uncertainty, in Mill's view, was by attempting to confirm the results obtained from the Method of Agreement, either by using the Method of Difference in combination with it or by connecting its results deductively with some law or laws ascertained by the latter method. But Mill apparently did not see that even the Method of Difference may not reveal a unique cause. For example, even though in some cases where there is no bacterial infection the presence or absence of an ulcer is responsible for the presence or absence of a stomach-ache, there may be other, ulcer-free, cases in which the presence or absence of bacterial infection is responsible for the presence or absence of a stomach-ache.

Scientists often need to build on previously acquired knowledge. So Mill proposed also a Method of Residues, and enunciated its principle as follows:

---

[61] *System of Logic*, p. 376.   [62] Ibid. 286.

Subduct from any phenomenon such part as is known by previous inductions to be the effect of certain antecedents and the residue of the phenomenon is the effect of the remaining antecedents.[63]

Schematically, if circumstances A&B&C issue in *a&b&c*, and if B is already known to cause *b* and C to cause *c*, then A must be the cause of *a*. For example, said Mill (following J.F.W. Herschel),[64] if the movements of a comet cannot be wholly accounted for by its gravitation towards the sun and planets, the residual feature must be explained by the resistance of the medium through which it moves. But in such a case Mill recognized that in practice we could not be certain that A is the only antecedent to which the residual phenomenon *a* may be referred. So any induction by the Method of Residues needs to be confirmed by obtaining A artificially and trying it separately, or by deriving its operation from otherwise known laws.[65]

Finally, Mill drew attention to the fact that some kinds of circumstance cannot be varied experimentally. For example, we cannot remove the seas from the presence of the moon. Nevertheless we can discover the influence of the moon on tidal flows by the Method of Concomitant Variations. This method operates in accordance with the principle that

Whatever phenomenon varies in any manner whenever another phenomenon varies in some particular manner, is either a cause or an effect of that phenomenon, or is connected with it through some fact of causation.[66]

Mill acknowledged that it may be dangerous to predict the same numerical rates of variation for quantitative phenomena that are outside the limits within which our own observations have been conducted. But he claimed—ignoring altogether the possibility of sustained coincidences—that the Method of Concomitant Variations could always establish at least the existence of some causal connection between the two kinds of phenomena investigated.[67]

Mill's writings on induction can easily give the impression that he oversimplified the issues, because he tended to introduce his theses initially in a rather dogmatic and unqualified form.

---

[63] Ibid. 260.   [64] Ibid. 280.   [65] Ibid. 261.
[66] Ibid. 263.   [67] Ibid. 266.

But the requisite qualifications are often found elsewhere in the text. Thus after giving examples in which the Method of Agreement seems to work smoothly and uncomplicatedly he points out that 'it is hardly ever possible to ascertain all the antecedents' of a phenomenon and that even when we can produce the phenomenon artificially this difficulty is merely lightened and not removed.[68] In other words we have to distinguish between the highly tangled actual situations that we encounter when we apply his inductive methods in practice and the ideally simplified situations in terms of which Mill formulated the principles that underlie those methods. Inevitably, therefore, to the extent that we have not ascertained all the antecedents of a phenomenon under investigation, some uncertainty must remain attached to our conclusion about which of those antecedents is causally connected with the phenomenon. And that source of uncertainty must affect the Method of Difference, though Mill apparently failed to see this, just as much as it affects the Method of Agreement. We cannot be absolutely sure, when we operate the Method of Difference, that the two canonical instances have *every* circumstance in common save one. We therefore cannot be sure that some unnoticed difference is not the true cause.

Again, Mill initially speaks of causes as invariably followed by their effects.[69] But later he insists that all causal laws 'require to be stated in words affirmative of tendencies only',[70] because he recognizes that any one causal factor may be counteracted in its operation by another. For example, a body may be kept in equilibrium by two equal and opposing forces, each of which on its own tends to move the body in a certain direction and each of which would suffice to move it if circumstances were otherwise favourable. Now obviously this doctrine does not cohere well with Mill's formulation of the principle underlying the Method of Difference. According to that principle what would cause the body in equilibrium to move would be the absence of one of the two mutually counteracting forces, whereas, if causal processes are viewed as tendencies, what causes it to move is the presence of a force. But on the latter view there will clearly be room for uncertainty on any particular occasion about whether such a tendency will actually be realized.

---

[68] *System of Logic*, p. 255   [69] Ibid. 214.   [70] Ibid. 293.

How is inductive uncertainty to be measured? Mill dealt with this issue in at least three connections. And in all three he came to evaluate uncertainty in broad conformity with the mathematical calculus of chance or in terms of a ratio or relative frequency that could be treated as a Pascalian probability.

First, he argued that inductive reasoning by the Method of Agreement is to be evaluated in accordance with the mathematical probability that the observed correlation is due to causation rather than to chance. But in order to have the data for such an evaluation 'it would be necessary to know what proportion of all the individual sequences or co-existences occurring in nature are the result of law, and what proportion are mere casual coincidences'.[71] And Mill thought it evident that we cannot form even a plausible conjecture as to the size of these ratios. That is why we have to fall back, in any particular case, on the assurance afforded by observing the correlation in a large number of appropriately varied instances. But such assurance may itself be a matter of degree and Mill made no suggestion how *it* might be measured.

Secondly, Mill, like Bacon, held that as empirical laws rise in their degree of generality they become more certain. But Mill, unlike Bacon, sought an explanation of this fact. On his view, when an empirical law derives somehow from causal laws, this is because relatively few changes in the combination of causal factors could counteract it 'since the greater number of possible combinations must have already existed in some one or other of the instances' in which the law has been found to operate. So apparently a hitherto unrefuted empirical law's degree of generality should be measurable in terms of the proportion of possible combinations of potentially counteractive causal factors that have already existed in its instances. And even if the law is just 'an ultimate co-existence', and not a causal connection, the more general it is the greater is the probability that if exceptions had existed some would already have presented themselves. For example, we are readier to accept the possibility of an error in our beliefs about the properties shared by all crows than in our beliefs about the properties shared by all birds.[72] However, Mill's argument here assumes that different combinations of

---

[71] Ibid. 359.   [72] Ibid. 384.

potentially counteractive causal factors tend to occur uniformly and homogeneously throughout human experience. And this assumption is scarcely tenable in the context of scientific enquiry.[73] The design of an experiment is often motivated by the desire to produce combinations of circumstances that do not occur naturally in observable human experience. So the actual probability that exceptions to a generalization have already occurred will in practice depend on the decisions of research-workers and those who fund their researches. It is certainly important to gauge the impact of increased generality on the inductive standing of a hypothesis. But Mill's proposal for a method of measuring this is not successful.

Thirdly, Mill insisted that there is no intrinsic difference between inductive and analogical reasoning.[74] By ordinary induction we infer that anything resembling certain known items in being A resembles them also in being B. By analogy, according to Mill, we can infer that anything resembling a known item in a certain proportion of its hitherto observed properties will have a probability, equal to that proportion, of resembling the item in any other of its properties.

If we discover, for example, an unknown animal or plant, resembling closely some known one in the greater number of the properties we observe in it, but differing in some few, we may reasonably expect to find in the unobserved remainder of its properties a general agreement with those of the former, but also a difference corresponding proportionately to the amount of the observed diversity.[75]

So analogical reasoning is another form of induction that, on Mill's view, has gradations of certainty that conform to the mathematics of chance. Mill clearly assumes here, as elsewhere, that there is only a finite number of mutually independent observable properties for a thing to have or not to have. But, unlike Bacon, he never acknowledged this assumption. Also, unlike Bacon, he made the rather implausible assumption that every feature in which one item may or may not resemble

---

[73] See also § 16 below.

[74] *An Examination of Sir William Hamilton's Philosophy and of the Principal Philosophical Questions Discussed in his Writings* (London: Longmans, Green, 1865), 402.

[75] *System of Logic*, p. 367.

another is of equal importance in relation to any kind of prediction about it. Yet the fact that two patients resemble one another in literary interests, for example, would normally be much less important for medical prognosis than that they have the same viral infection in their bloodstreams.

Thus Mill's philosophy of induction, though it agreed with Bacon's in the importance it attached to eliminative procedures as distinct from enumerative ones, took at least one important new step within the eliminativist tradition. Whenever Mill thought that criteria for the gradation of inductive certainty are called for, he applied criteria that, however crudely, exploited a conception of probability which conforms with the mathematics of chance.

Bernard Bolzano, like Mill, assigned a central role in science to the discovery of causes, and in a book published in 1837[76] he had already advocated methods of ampliative induction that were very similar to those that Mill advocated independently in 1843. He differed from Mill, however, in holding that, when one investigates the reliability of a hypothesis, one should take multiplicity of confirmatory evidential instances to be as 'important a ground for confidence as variety'.[77] Moreover, variative induction, he thought, could sometimes be rendered particularly difficult because the number of circumstances that accompany every event is not finite[78] (as Bacon and Mill apparently supposed it to be). And, though Bolzano thought, like Mill, that the gradation of inductive certainty could be accomplished in terms of Pascalian probability, he relates this measure to the number of evidential instances[79] rather than to their variety.[80]

[76] B. Bolzano, *Wissenschaftslehre* (Sulzbach: J. E. von Seidelchen, 1837), trans. and ed. R. George, under the title, *The Theory of Science* (Oxford: Blackwell, 1972). Bernard Bolzano (1781-1848) was appointed professor of religious instruction in Prague Univeristy in 1805 and was dismissed for heterodoxy in 1819.

[77] *The Theory of Science*, p. 378.

[78] Ibid.

[79] Ibid. 380-1.

[80] Useful discussions of J.S. Mill's ideas about induction may be found in L.S. Stebbing, *A Modern Introduction to Logic*, 7th edn. (London: Methuen, 1950), 331-43; G. H. von Wright, *A Treatise on Induction and Probability* (London: Routledge and Kegan Paul, 1951), 84-166; R.P. Anschutz, *The Philosophy of J.S. Mill* (Oxford: Clarendon Press, 1953), 78-123; K. Britton, *John Stuart Mill* (Harmondsworth: Penguin Books,

Several twentieth-century philosophers, like J.M. Keynes and Mary Hesse, have followed Mill's example here, though with a considerably more sophisticated appreciation of the problems that affect such an application of probability theory to variative induction. However, though the historical fact of Mill's innovatory move is clear enough, it is quite another question whether he was making a move in the right direction. Three other moves are co-ordinate possibilities that have been much discussed in the analysis of ampliative induction. One such move is to retain a Pascalian framework but treat multiplicity, not variety, of evidential instances as crucial, as Bernoulli did. Another is to retain a Baconian emphasis on evidential variety, but develop an intrinsically non-Pascalian system of gradation. And a fourth move is to construct a Pascalian system of gradation that amalagamates support from evidential multiplicity with support from evidential variety. These four philosophical options will be referenced, explored, and evaluated in § § 16–24 below.

But as a foundation for that exploration and evaluation we need first to enquire rather more deeply into the nature of Pascalian probability. So far we have merely noted a few facts about the history of its mathematics, which have introduced the reader to some basic principles of logical syntax governing the constraints that one judgement of Pascalian probability imposes on another: the complementational principle for negation, the multiplicative principle for conjunction, and so on. It is clear that an axiomatization of those syntactic principles serves to define the concept of a Pascalian function, in the sense that any functor which satisfies the axioms is to be considered capable of expressing such a function. So what makes a judgement of probability Pascalian is its logical syntax. But what is the semantics of such a judgement? What makes it a judgement of *probability*? What are we measuring when we measure a Pascalian probability? And how is that measurement actually

1953), 147–85; and J.L. Mackie, *The Cement of the Universe* (Oxford: Clarendon Press, 1974), 297–321. Bolzano's views are discussed in L. Jonathan Cohen, 'Bolzano's Theory of Induction', in *Bernard Bolzano (1781–1848)*, special issue 13 of *Acta Historiae Rerum Naturalium nec non Technicarum* (Prague: Czechoslovak Academy of Sciences, 1982), 443–57, repr. in M.H. Salmon (ed.), *The Philosophy of Logical Mechanism* (Dordrecht: Reidel, forthcoming).

carried out? Only when these issues have been resolved shall we be in a position to investigate whether ampliative induction is best graded in terms of Pascalian probability. And the topic is in any case an important one since, whether or not Pascalian probability has a central role to play in the gradation of induction, it certainly has many other valuable uses in contemporary culture.

II

The Controversy about the Nature of Pascalian Probability

Widely different theories have been proposed for the semantics of probability judgements that have a Pascalian syntax. We can distinguish roughly, but only roughly, between theories concerned to argue how such probabilities are actually conceived and theories concerned to argue how they ought to be conceived, and also between theories that adopt a realist point of view and theories that adopt an idealist one.

Pascalian mathematics, as we saw in § 3, provides a system of syntactic constraints that judgements of probability impose on one another—the complementational law for negation, and so on. It thus allows us to formulate an axiomatic definition for the concept of a Pascalian function. A function may then be said to determine a Pascalian probability only if it satisfies the axioms of that mathematical system. But this does not tell us, except in certain limiting cases (e.g. $p(A\&\text{not-}A) = 0$), how to evaluate that function in particular cases, or what the truth-conditions are for such evaluations. Nor does it even provide an adequate definition of a probability-function, since it does not exclude non-standard—i.e. non-probabilistic—interpretations of the Pascalian system, such as in terms of area-ratios.

Many philosophers have therefore produced theories about the epistemology or semantics of Pascalian probability, and there is an extensive polemical literature on the subject. In order to show the dimensions of the problem, the present chapter seeks very briefly to sketch the main types of theory that have been produced and the main considerations that weigh for or against them. No attempt is made here, however, to argue that any one such theory is superior to the rest. Instead, it will be argued later (§§ 12–15) that this eristic approach to the subject may profitably be replaced by a more eirenical strategy in which we explain and justify the existence of a variety of legitimate types of probability judgement by exploring the wide range of syntactic and semantic factors that are relevant to the taxonomy and employment of such judgements. Only when this task has been adequately carried out will we be in a proper position to discuss (§§ 16–21) what types of probability-judgement are suitable —and under what conditions—for employment as a mode of inductive evaluation.

No one achieves even a one-sided philosophy of probability, however, by making a few dogmatic, off-the-cuff statements about the concept in the course of developing some system of mathematical calculations or statistical procedures. At the least arguments have to be given—arguments that support or oppose some analysis of the concept. And even well-argued analytical theories about the nature of probability are not always targeted at exactly the same objective. One polar aim for such a theory is to describe, analyse, and explain how probability is actually conceived in human judgements. The alternative polar aim is to prescribe how probability should be conceived and, in particular, how the formalism of the mathematical calculus should be interpreted. But those two objectives, though quite different from one another in principle, are often difficult to hold apart in practice. On the one hand, it is natural for philosophers of science to prefer to describe what they take ideally to be implicit in the best usage that they can find among reputable scientists and mathematicians, rather than whatever is actually implicit in the imprecise and inexpert thoughts of the man-in-the-street. On the other hand, anyone who prescribes how probability should be conceived presumably thinks of himself as understanding and answering a question that relates to the familiar existing practice of judging probabilities: the question is about how this practice is to be executed, and so any answer to it must presuppose at least some description of the presumed aims of the practice and of the factors that constrain it. Accordingly, though it is important to keep the descriptive–prescriptive polarity in mind here, I shall not try to identify in every case exactly which type of objective has been dominant in the minds of those proposing a particular kind of theory. (It will be evident enough, however—see pp. 64–5 below—that the 'guarded assertion' theory, for example, is content to be descriptive in purpose, while Bayesian personalism, with its criterion for rationality, is determinedly prescriptive. So at least those two theories are not in serious competition with one another. They answer different questions—though their adherents may well disagree about which question is the more important one.)

Another distinction that cannot in practice always be drawn very sharply is that between realist and idealist theories. In the context of the philosophy of probability a theory may be classified as a realist one if it treats probability as assessable primarily in relation to events, objects, classes of events, classes of objects, natural kinds, physical properties, or other similar elements, groupings, or features of reality. A theory may be classified as an idealist one if it treats probabilities as assessable primarily in relation to arguments, propositions, beliefs, assertions, or other similar elements, groupings or features of our thoughts about reality. Here again the difference is evident enough in some cases. To identify probabilities with the relative frequencies of events is clearly a realist move, while to identify it with strength of belief is clearly an idealist one. Such theories are necessarily in conflict with one another. But the theory that is based on the so-called 'principle of indifference', as we shall see, has both realist and idealist versions.[1]

---

[1] A useful survey of different mathematical ideas about probability, within the Pascalian mainstream, is to be found in T. L. Fine, *Theories of Probability: An Examination of Foundations* (New York: Academic Press, 1973). See also, for a comprehensive textbook on the mathematics of Pascalian probability, W. Feller, *An Introduction to Probability Theory and its Applications*, 3rd edn. (New York: J. Wiley, 1968). A pluralist approach to the semantics of probability, within Pascalian limits, is to be found in E. Nagel, 'Principles of the Theory of Probability', in O. Neurath, R. Carnap and C. Morris (eds.), *Foundations of the Unity of Science*, (Chicago: Chicago University Press, 1939), i. 341–422; J. J. Mehlberg, 'Is a Unitary Approach to Foundations of Probability Possible?' in H. Feigl and G. Maxwell (eds.), *Current Issues in the Philosophy of Science* (New York: Holt, Rinehart and Winston, 1961), 287–301; H. Freudenthal, 'Realistic Models in Probability', in I. Lakatos (ed.), *The Problem of Inductive Logic* (Amsterdam: North-Holland, 1968), 1–23; and J.L. Mackie, *Truth, Probability, and Paradox* (Oxford: Clarendon Press, 1973), 154–236.

§ 6. INDIFFERENCE THEORIES

Indifference theories define the probability of an outcome as the ratio of the number of favourable cases to the total number of equally possible cases. They vary in their implications according to whether equal possibility is understood in realist or idealist terms. They avoid circularity only where this equal possibility is supposed to be established a priori or to be demonstrable within a well-supported theory.

What an indifference theory claims is that the probability of an outcome may be defined as the ratio of the number of favourable cases to the total number of equally possible cases. Such a theory, strictly speaking, quantifies over a domain of outcome-types, not of individual outcomes. So the probability of throwing a four in a game of dice is $\frac{1}{6}$, since a dice-throw has six possible types of outcome, of which only one is favourable for the throw in question. Indeed, though an indifference theory obviously cannot allow probability-functions to include irrational numbers among their values, it seems particularly well suited to the aleatory models with which the earliest mathematics of probability was mainly occupied. Also we can easily see why, if some form of indifference theory is correct, the mathematics of probability must be what it is: the calculus of chance is just the arithmetic of rational numbers.

But by what principle are equally possible cases to be enumerated? The principle of indifference, as it has come to be called, states that any cases are equally possible if there is no reason for one such case rather than for another. And this principle admits of both realist and idealist interpretations.

On a realist interpretation, it means, if a monadic probability—i.e. a one-place function $p(A)$—is at issue, that outcomes are equally possible if and only if there is nothing to cause one type of outcome rather than another (as perhaps with certain movements of a sub-atomic particle). Or, if a dyadic probability—i.e. a two-place function $p(B|A)$—is at issue it means, as William Kneale proposed,[2] that outcomes are equally possible in relation to such-or-such a specified property if and

[2] W. Kneale, *Probability and Induction* (Oxford: Clarendon Press, 1949), 116.

only if nothing is caused by that property to have one type of outcome rather than another.

On an idealist interpretation, however, the principle of indifference is concerned not with gaps in the causal determination of reality, but with gaps in our knowledge about it. The principle then means, in regard to monadic probabilities, either that cases are equally possible if and only if there is no humanly available knowledge why any judge of the probability at issue should expect one type of outcome rather than another, or that, for the present judge of the probability at issue, cases are equally possible if and only if he or she knows no reason to expect one type of outcome rather than another. The former of these two idealist interpretations for the monadic function, apparently favoured by Laplace,[3] still implies, like a realist interpretation, that on each issue there is a uniquely true probability to be discovered. The latter interpretation, defended by Jevons[4] and Mill,[5] has no such implication. It implies that even on the same issue different judgements of probability may be correct for different people. It is thus a subjective rather than an objective idealism. And in regard to dyadic probabilities the tension between a subjective and an objective idealism is preserved. An objective idealist version of the indifference principle for the dyadic function would state that, within such-or-such specified evidence, there is nothing to justify expecting one type of outcome rather than another, whereas a subjective idealist version would state that within such-or-such specified evidence the present judge finds nothing to justify expecting one type of outcome rather than another.

The idealist form of indifference theory has long been accused of 'professing to evolve knowledge out of ignorance',[6] and the realist version might with equal justice be accused of professing to discern something evolved out of nothing. But some may

---

[3] P.S. de Laplace, *A Philosophical Essay on Probabilities*, trans. F.W. Truscott and F.L. Emory (New York: Dover, 1951), 4 ff. Laplace (1749–1827) is famous for his work on gravitational mechanisms as well as for his work on probability.

[4] W.S. Jevons, *The Principle of Science: A Treatise on Logic and Scientific Method* (London: Macmillan, 1883), 198 ff. Jevons (1835–82) was an economist as well as a logician.

[5] *System of Logic*, p. 351: Mill took this view in the second edition (1846), having held a more realist view in the first (1843).

[6] See Jevons, *Principle of Science* p. 199.

think it interesting if we *could* evolve knowledge out of ignorance or discern something evolved out of nothing. A more powerful complaint against any indifference theory is therefore that, while professing to let us do this, the theory provides no unambiguous instructions on how we are to do it and in practice licenses mutually contradictory conclusions.

For example, such a contradiction arises when an attempt is made to answer the question: what is the probability of getting heads in both of two tosses of the same coin? One line of inference here from the indifference theory would conclude that the answer is $\frac{1}{4}$ because there are four equally possible outcomes: two heads, two tails, first heads and then tails, and first tails and then heads. Another line of inference would conclude instead that the answer is $\frac{1}{3}$ because there are three equally possible outcomes; two heads, two tails, and the combination of heads and tails. But this kind of objection can be met by insisting that the circumstances are not indifferent, because there is in fact a reason to expect the heads and tails combination rather than the two heads (or two tails) combination. The reason is that the heads and tails combination can occur in two different ways, depending on whether heads or tails comes first. So, if we break down the set of possibilities into all the ultimate permutations (see p. 15 above), a uniquely correct answer of $\frac{1}{4}$ seems to be inferable.

Even so, that answer might still be challenged. We have established only that there is no a priori reason to expect any one of the four possibilities rather than any other. The possibility remains, in the case of any particular coin or tossing procedure, that there is an empirically detectable reason to expect one of the four ultimate permutations rather than another. On the subjective idealist version of the indifference theory for monadic probabilities—the Jevons-Mill version—this possibility does not matter at all to a judgement of probability so long as the author of the judgement does not know any such reason. Only his or her actual knowledge at the time is relevant. But on any other version of the theory for monadic probabilities, the possibility does matter: the existence of such a reason has to be excluded. So, to exclude the existence of such a reason, we need to be able to judge that no factor is present—like, for example, the existence of more wear on the heads side—that makes one of the four permutations more probable than the others. And clearly, if we do need to be able to judge that, the indifference theory would be circular. With respect to any one issue, it would define the probability of a particular type of outcome in terms that presuppose an appropriate set of comparative judgements of probability, on available evidence, over all the possible types of outcome.

At best, therefore, an indifference theory applies only where it is either assumed or demonstrable that no such set of individually researched judgements of comparative probability is needed. For example, in a game like coin-tossing or dice-throwing this is assumed by calling it a game of chance. Every game has rules that regulate how it is played, and the rules of a game of chance must therefore determine a priori its range of mutually exclusive and mutually co-ordinate outcome-types. In a normal game of dice-throwing, for example, the rules determine a priori six possible types of outcome for any one throw depending on which side is uppermost: a die's being poised on an edge or a corner is not a recognized type of outcome and voids the throw. Also in certain areas of natural science it may be demonstrable within a well-supported theory that ideally there is nothing to cause one type of outcome (within a certain set of possible outcome-types) rather than another. This is the situation in, for example, Boltzmann's interpretation for the law of entropy (the second law of thermodynamics[7]).

But there will be a wide variety of judgements to which the indifference theory is inapplicable. Sometimes this will be because the various possible outcomes are not equally probable, as with a biased coin. Sometimes it will be because the number of possible outcomes is infinite and therefore the ratio of favourable outcomes cannot be calculated. And sometimes, indeed often, it will be because there is no relevant constraint on the range of alternative possibilities. In judging the probability of heads on the toss of an unbiased coin to be $\frac{1}{2}$ a person assumes that the coin is restricted to falling either heads or tails and will not fall on its edge. But in judging the probability that the main course of any student you pick out at random on the campus is in the history of the bassoon you need not assume anything about the number of

[7] See A. Pap, *An Introduction to the Philosophy of Science* (London: Eyre and Spottiswoode, 1963), 210 ff.

main courses available. The relevant ratio seems to be that of the number of bassoon-historians to the total number of students, rather than that of the number of bassoon-history courses to the total number of courses. The probability has to be established by an empirical enumeration of students' actual choices, not by relatively a priori research into the curriculum catalogues. It is a ratio within a domain of individual entities, not within a domain of types of individual entities.[8]

§ 7. FREQUENCY THEORIES

If the probability $p(A|B)$ is understood as the relative frequency of As among Bs, it becomes impossible to give an account of the probabilities of individual events or of the probability of As where there are infinitely many Bs. Attempts have been made to deal with the problem of infinite reference-classes by equating probabilities with mathematical limits (in a sequence of cumulative relative frequencies). But this makes probabilities depend on an ordering of outcomes that is arbitrary or irrelevant. It may also be objected that some sequences of outcomes are accidentally cut short, before a significant relative frequency establishes interval-valued conception of probability.

Because the indifference theory fails to cope with judgements of probability that are supported by empirical enumerations, it is tempting to suppose instead that probabilities are empirically estimatable relative frequencies. The supposition then is not merely that observed relative frequencies normally constitute the evidence on the basis of which we estimate probabilities, but that there is nothing more to the probability of a B's being an A than the overall relative frequency of As among Bs. If the probability of any randomly selected student's being a bassoon-historian, for example, is evaluated at $\frac{1}{500}$, this means just that the

[8] The principle of indifference is discussed in J. M. Keynes, *A Treatise on Probability* (London: Macmillan, 1921), 41–64 (where the name of the principle originates) and 81–3; B. Russell, *Human Knowledge: Its Scope and Limits* (London: Allen and Unwin, 1948), 391–7; K. R. Popper, *The Logic of Scientific Discovery* (London: Hutchinson, 1959), 168–9; G. H. von Wright, *A Treatise on Induction and Probability* (London: Routledge and Kegan Paul, 1951), 228–34; and S. Blackburn, *Reason and Prediction* (Cambridge: Cambridge University Press, 1973), 116–35.

relative frequency of bassoon-historians among the students is 1 in 500. Probability-judgements thus count individual outcomes, not outcome-types.

And on such a view probabilities are essentially dyadic, since they will always be concerned with the frequency of some specified feature (such as that of being a bassoon-historian) in some independently specified or specifiable reference-class (such as the class of students enrolled on our local campus in 1986). They will also be essentially objective, constituting a touchstone against which human thoughts and reasoning can be impartially evaluated. Indeed, a frequency conception of probability was used by Galileo when he cited the observed results of long runs of dice-throws as a check on a priori calculations of aleatory probabilities.[9] It is also a great convenience that for finite reference-classes, according to a relative frequency analysis, the mathematics of probability reduces to the arithmetic of rational numbers.

But the frequency approach has at least three weak points. The first one is that it can offer no account of the probabilities of individual events. In a game of chance the indifference theory authorizes a value of $\frac{1}{2}$ for the probability that heads is the next toss's outcome-type, because in the case of any toss it authorizes a value of $\frac{1}{2}$ for the probability that the toss's outcome-type will be heads. But the frequency analysis cannot authorize a value of, say, $\frac{1}{500}$ for the dyadic probability that George is a bassoon-historian, given that he is a student. One reason for this is that such a purported judgement of probability can have no literal meaning on that analysis.[10] It is features, not propositions—whether about individuals or about anything else—that have frequencies of occurrence relative to a reference-class. And another reason is that the probability of *George*'s being a bassoon-historian, given that he is a student, may not be at all the same as the general probability that anyone is a bassoon-historian, given that he or she is a student. George may be very much a special case, since his father is a well-known bassoon-player. So that the probability of *his* being a bassoon-historian, if

---

[9] I. Hacking, *The Emergence of Probability: A Philosophical Study of Early Ideas about Probability, Introduction and Statistical Inference* (Cambridge: Cambridge University Press, 1975), 53.

[10] As admitted by R. von Mises, *Probability, Statistics and Truth*, 2nd edn. (London: Allen and Unwin, 1957), 11.

it is to be equated with any relative frequency at all, can be equated only with the relative frequency of bassoon-historians among students whose fathers are well-known bassoon-players. And then, since George is the only such student, we can apparently not learn the probability that he is a bassoon-historian without learning whether or not he is in fact a bassoon-historian. But this would be unacceptably paradoxical, because we should obtain a reliable probability for George's being a bassoon-historian if and only if we are 100 per cent certain that he is one or that he is not one. In short, a frequency analysis not only allows no literal meaning to judgements of individual probability but also creates difficulties for any attempt to treat them systematically as covertly general judgements.

Nor is it open to a frequency theorist to claim that all important probabilities are indeed general, not singular. It often seems very important to be able to calculate the probability of success for your own child's appendectomy, the probability of a bull market in equities next spring, or the probability of rain tomorrow.

The frequency approach's second weak point is that it encounters serious problems in dealing with infinite reference-classes. If a coin were tossed for ever, and the tosses remained fair throughout, then not only would the number of tosses be infinite but also the number of tosses that landed heads. (If, instead, in an infinite sequence of tosses the number that landed heads were finite, then, however large that number was, the probability of heads would be infinitely small—which conflicts with our assumption of fair tosses.) So the probability of a toss's landing heads, which is presumably $\frac{1}{2}$, cannot be equated with the relative frequency of heads *simpliciter*, i.e. with $\frac{\infty}{\infty}$. And analogously, if student enrolments go on for ever, while the usual variety of courses are favoured, the probability of a student's being a bassoon-historian cannot be equated with the relative frequency of bassoon-historians. There is a risk that this fact may be obscured by the use of ambiguous expressions like 'in the long run'. In one sense this means 'in a very large, but finite, set of cases', in another it means 'in an infinite set of cases'. In the former sense, a relative frequency in the long run may exist, in the latter it cannot.

In the case of endlessly repeated trials at a game of chance, where such repetition is assumed to have no effect on the physical state of the coin, die, etc., there is a plausible way out of the difficulty, adopted by S.D. Poisson[11] and others. If the reference-class consists of the outcomes of such trials, it is well-ordered by their succession in time: each member of the reference-class has a unique position in the temporal ordering. So there is an infinite succession of outcomes, and the probability of a certain kind of outcome can apparently be equated, as the number of outcomes goes to infinity, with the mathematical limit of the sequence of relative frequencies of that kind of outcome. That is, the probability $p(A|B)$ can be equated with the limit of the sequence of cumulative relative frequencies of As among Bs that consists of the frequency (which will be 0 or 1) in the first outcome, the frequency (which will be 0, $\frac{1}{2}$, or 1) in the first two outcomes, the frequency in the first three outcomes, and so on. (An infinite sequence of functions r_1, r_2, r_3 . . . has a limit r_L if and only if for as small a positive real number as you please, ϵ, there is for each member of the sequence r_i a later member r_j such that r_j does not differ by more than ϵ from r_L.)

However, as Bertrand Russell pointed out,[12] the same infinite set of fractions can be arranged into different infinite sequences that converge to different limits. Russell took as his example the probablity that an integer chosen at random will be a prime. If we take the integers in their natural order, then, as we go to infinity, the limit of the sequence of cumulative relative frequencies of primes is zero. But suppose we rearrange the integers by putting first the first 9 primes, then the first number that is not a prime, then the next 9 primes, then the second number that is not a prime, and so on indefinitely. When the integers are arranged in this order, the limit of the sequences of cumulative relative frequencies of primes is $\frac{9}{10}$. And Russell also

[11] S.D. Poisson, *Recherches sur la probabilité des jugements en matière criminelle et en matière civile précédées des règles générales du calcul des probabilités* (Paris: Bachelier, 1837). Poisson (1781–1840) was a friend of Laplace. His most important work was in the application of mathematics to physics. See also H. Reichenbach, *The Theory of Probability*, trans. E.H. Hutten and M. Reichenbach, 2nd edn. (Berkeley: University of California Press, 1971), 68–9.

[12] B. Russell, *Human Knowledge* pp. 384–5 A. Pap, *Introduction to the Philosophy of Science*, pp. 180–1, contradicted Russell, but his argument is not cogent.

showed how by yet another arrangement of the integers the limit in question would be 1. So it is clear that, if a probability is defined in terms of the limit to a sequence of relative frequencies, it might differ under certain rearrangements of the underlying set of outcomes. But the probability that a B is an A should be unique. So Poisson's procedure makes the probability p $(A|B)$ depend on there being only one relevant ordering for the class of Bs, which is the reference-class for the probability.

Now the trouble is that the members of some reference-classes do not all obviously belong to some set that is well-ordered by temporal succession or by some other uniquely appropriate relation. Thus, if the class of student enrolments is an infinite one, some of its members may be simultaneous with one another, so that it is certainly not well-ordered by temporal succession. Moreover, even when the reference-class is well-ordered by some supposedly appropriate relation, the sequence of cumulative relative frequencies may not in fact converge to a limit. Or—and this is the commonest situation—there may be infinitely many other equally appropriate well-orderings of the class, each of which determines a different limiting value for the sequence of relative frequencies in question.

A possible way of dealing with those difficulties would be to identify the probability with the limit to which the relative frequencies converge within an infinite-membered sub-class of the reference-class that satisfies appropriate conditions for randomness and convergence, as proposed by von Mises.[13] But this proposal still raises the question why *any* ordering should be relevant to the value of the probability, within a set of outcomes that are independent of one another. If the outcome of a toss is supposed to be unaffected by its position in a sequence of tosses, because repeated tosses are assumed to have no effect on the state of the coin or of the tossing mechanism, why should the ordering of the sequence be relevant to the probability of heads as against tails? Moreover, a statement evaluating the limit of a sequence of relative frequencies hypothetically continued to infinity implies nothing whatever that is empirically testable about any initial segment of the sequence, however large,

---

[13] See R. von Mises, *Probability, Statistics and Truth*, 2nd edn. (New York: Dover, 1957), 24–5.

because such a segment can be replaced by any arbitrary sequence of the same length without affecting the limit of the sequence as an infinite whole.

It might be thought that these problems about infinite reference-classes at least leave the frequency analysis safely available in the case of finite reference-classes. And, after all, very many of the probabilities with which we are concerned in the natural or social sciences are probabilities in supposedly finite classes, although such classes are often indeterminately large. But a third weakness of the frequency analysis seems to be clearly displayed in certain cases where the reference-class is certainly finite in size. One may well believe that a nicely produced coin, fresh from the mint, has a probability of falling heads that is correctly evaluated at $\frac{1}{2}$. But suppose it is tossed three times, landing heads twice and tails once, and is then melted down for scrap. A crude relative frequency theory would apparently evaluate the probability of its falling heads at $\frac{2}{3}$, which cannot be correct. Perhaps a frequency theorist has therefore to say instead in such a case that the probability of heads is not to be identified with the actual relative frequency of heads, but with what that relative frequency would have been in the long run. But then either that means 'in an infinite set of tosses', in which case the difficulties already mentioned apply; or it means 'in a very large, but finite, set of actual or potential tosses', in which case the probability would still be altered a bit if the coin were tossed just one more time, since the relative frequency of heads would inevitably increase or decrease, depending on the actual outcome of that additional toss. So where the reference-class is finite the frequency analysis seems to make the exact value of a probability depend on some quite accidental fact about the precise number of instances that are supposed to belong to the reference-class, just as where it is infinite the probability is made to depend on some quite accidental fact of ordering.

Of course, where the reference-class is finite we can escape introducing such a dependence on irrelevant contingencies if we are willing to take the probability-statement in question to be saying that the actual or potential relative frequency falls within a specified interval (e.g. 0.5 plus or minus 0.16). But the difficulties about individual events and about infinite reference-classes cannot be so easily dodged.[14]

§ 8. PROPENSITY THEORIES

If $p(A|B)$ is to be thought of as a propensity, this cannot in every case be the propensity of B to cause A. But a propensity interpretation of the probability calculus does allow probabilities to be assigned to individual outcomes. The main weakness of such an analysis is that it does not supply any intrinsic guidance in regard to the actual evaluation of probabilities or any obvious rationale for the principles derivable within the calculus of chance.

If probabilities are indeed objective features of reality, but are not to be identified with some collective property of the reference-class, like the property of having a certain relative frequency of members that have such-or-such a characteristic, perhaps instead they are related distributively to each member of this class. The $\frac{1}{2}$ probability that a coin-toss will fall heads is then a physical propensity that is operative in each coin-toss rather than a relative frequency that characterizes the totality of coin-tosses.[15] On this view probabilities are displayed in, or evidenced by, the relative frequencies observed in appropriate samples, but are not to be identified with them or with relative frequencies 'in the long run'. Relative frequency analyses are to be looked on as the outcome of empiricist prejudice, confusing the meaning of a statement with its evidential warranty.

Indeed, unless we think of a coin's objective probability of falling heads as a measurable propensity rather than as a relative frequency, it would not seem reasonable to assign a point-value

[14] Analyses of probability in terms of relative frequency are expounded or discussed in J. Venn, *The Logic of Chance*, 2nd edn. (London: Macmillan, 1876); Reichenbach, *Theory of Probability*; Pap, *Introduction to the Philosophy of Science*; W.C. Salmon, *The Foundations of Scientific Inference* Pittsburgh: University of Pittsburgh Press, 1966), 83–108; R.B Braithwaite, *Scientific Explanation* (Cambridge; Cambridge University Press, 1953), 115–95; and D. Gillies, *An Objective Theory of Probability* (London: Methuen, 1973).

[15] D.H. Mellor, *The Matter of Chance* (Cambridge: Cambridge University Press, 1971), 63–82.

(as distinct from an interval-value) to such a probability in the case of a coin that is melted down very soon after manufacture, perhaps after only three tosses. Nor would it seem possible to assign an irrational number as the value of a probability within a finite reference-class, unless we think of that probability as a propensity rather than a relative frequency. Yet irrational numbers enter very easily into our reasonings about probabilities. For example, when we judge the joint occurrence of two independent and equiprobable events to have a probability of $\frac{1}{2}$, we imply that the probability of each event on its own is $1/\sqrt{2}$, because of the multiplicative principle for conjunction.

Sometimes, where dyadic probabilities are at issue, it may be tempting to treat such propensities as measurable degrees of causal power. For example, this looks appropriate in the case of the probability that a match will light, given that it is struck. Striking the match may be thought of as having a certain degree of efficacy in regard to the match's lighting. But there are also many kinds of case where probabilities cannot be conceived in this way. For example, when we speak of the probability that a person elected to Parliament was educated at a university, or of the probability that the accused is guilty given his demeanour in the witness-box, we are certainly not in either case measuring the power of one event to cause another, since, if we were, we should be supposing that a later event can cause an earlier one.

So what are propensities? Popper has argued that they are a kind of physical property. He explicitly compares a field of propensities, as 'a dispositional property of singular physical experimental arrangements', with a field of forces.[16] He thinks of his account of propensities as 'a new physical hypothesis (or perhaps a metaphysical hypothesis), analogous to the hypothesis of Newtonian forces'.[17] Such a conception might be used, for example, in measuring the probability of a radioactive particle's decaying within some specified period. And it associates naturally with a rejection of determinism. If physical dispositions of this kind exist in nature, some events are inherently unpredictable.

---

[16] K.R. Popper, *Realism and the Aim of Science* (London: Hutchinson, 1983), 351.
[17] Ibid. 360.

But, if this were the only appropriate way to conceive propensities, there would be very many kinds of probability-judgement to which the propensity account would not apply. For example, we could not conceive thus the backward-looking probability that a person elected to Parliament was educated at a university or even the forward-looking probability that a fifty-year-old politician will survive to the age of seventy. Many issues in probabilistic reasoning are not concerned with fundamental physical properties or their inherently unpredictable manifestations, but with statistically evidenced tendencies that are taken to result from the operation of just some out of the many different causal factors that combine to determine the actual outcome. In such cases to declare the probability of A given B is merely to evaluate the contribution or significance towards A of some potentially operative factor or set of factors, B.

Indeed, we have here an analogy between the indifference theory, in its realist presentation (see pp. 43–4), and the propensity theory. On causal issues both kinds of theory have a strong, monadic version that takes the occurrence of one outcome rather than another, with a probability less than 1, as a manifestation of indeterminism, and both theories have a weaker, dyadic version that is compatible with treating the actual outcome as a fully determined one.

All versions of the propensity theory have two important features that no relative frequency account can have. They apply just as well to infinite populations as to finite ones. And they all allow probabilities to be assigned to specified individual events, since propensities may be treated as properties either of what Popper calls 'singular physical experimental arrangements' or of individual set-ups of some other kind. More strictly, perhaps, we can say that, as a conditional probability, propensity is a second-order relation—a relation of probabilification that links one first-order property to another. In virtue of that fact we can express a general probability—a probability that does not refer to any individual object, event, or set-up—as a propensity, like the propensity of a fifty-year old politician to survive to the age of seventy. But, because individuals have first-order properties, we can also express many singular judgements of probability in terms of propensities, such as the propensity that Smith will survive to the age of seventy in virtue of his being at present fifty years old. The propensity then measures the strength of the link between one first-order property that Smith might have and another. And singular judgements of *unconditional* probability lend themselves to a similar form of analysis. If there is a 0.8 probability of such a kind that Smith will survive to the age of seventy, we must suppose a 0.8 propensity in Nature for this to happen. Propensities are then being treated either as properties of properties or as properties of events.

The main weakness of a propensity analysis is that it does not intrinsically carry with it any distinctive type of guidance in regard to the actual evaluation of probabilities. The indifference theory tells us to calculate the ratio of the favourable to the equally possible cases. It may sometimes be difficult to determine the implications of this requirement coherently and unambiguously. But at least in standard games of chance the theory can be made to work as a basis for assigning probability-values, and it also provides an obvious rationale for the principles that are derivable within the calculus of chance—the multiplication law for conjunction, the complementational law for negation, and all the other principles that fit an aleatory model. Again, the relative frequency theory states a ratio that we need to estimate. It may sometimes be difficult to do this reliably because of the large size of the reference-class and the small size of the available sample. But at least the theory tells us in numerical terms what we ought to find out (where the reference-class is finite), and it too provides us with an obvious rationale for the mathematics of probability. The propensity analysis, on the other hand, speaks the language of causality or of physics, not of ratios. Correspondingly, since the talk about propensities has no distinctive numerical implications, it provides no inherent basis for the assignment of actual probability-values. And it also provides no wholesale rationale for the principles derivable within the calculus of chance.[18]

---

[18] Propensity analyses of Pascalian probability are further defended or discussed in C.S. Peirce, *Collected Papers*, ed. C. Hartshorne and P. Weiss (Cambridge, Mass.: Harvard University Press, 1932), 409–14 (paras. 2. 662–8); Popper, *Realism and the Aim of Science*, pp. 281–401; I. Hacking, *Logic of Statistical Inference* (Cambridge: Cambridge University Press, 1965), 1–26; A.R. White, 'The Propensity Theory of Probability', *British Journal for the Philosophy of Science*, 23 (1972), 35–43; T. Settle, 'Propensity Theories of Probability Unscathed: A Reply to White', *British Journal for the Philosophy of Science*,

Indeed, a propensity theory may even be seen, in certain contexts, to suggest one or two non-Pascalian principles. For example, it is not at all obvious that propensities have to obey the complementational law for negation, if we just think of them intuitively and forget for the moment what we know about the mathematics of Pascalian probability. Drinking a cup of tea a day may have only a small propensity (or a slight tendency or a weak disposition) to make a person well, but it certainly does not have a correspondingly large propensity (or a big tendency, or a strong disposition) to make him or her unwell: it just has very little effect on health in either direction. No doubt we can regiment our thoughts about propensities, so that they always conform to the mathematics of probability. But in its naïve and unreconstructed form the concept of a propensity will not necessarily lead us to draw inferences that are isomorphic with those which the Pascalian concept of probability leads us to draw. Conversely, the crucial issue is whether in comparing $p(A|B)$ with $p(\text{not-}A|B)$ we take ourselves to be comparing the extent of B's propensity for A with the extent to which B has no propensity for A or with the extent to which B has a propensity for not-A. In the former case our logic of propensity needs an additive, complementational principle for negation, in the latter it needs to avoid such a principle.[19] Compare what was said earlier about credibility (pp. 17–18).

This important issue will be discussed more fully in § § 14 and 15 below. But one possible objection to what has just been said needs to be considered here. It might be claimed that there is a mathematically consistent way of describing two weak, yet opposing propensities in terms that are both Pascalian and non-additive: we can just say that $p(A|B)$ does not differ much from

23 (1972), 331–5; L. Sklar, 'Is Probability a Dispositional Probability?', *Journal of Philosophy*, 67 (1970), 355–66; H.E. Kyburg, 'Propensities and Probabilities', *British Journal for the Philosophy of Science*, 25 (1974), 358–75; T. Settle, 'Induction and Probability Unfused', in P.A. Schilp (ed.), *The Philosophy of Karl Popper* (La Salle: Open Court, 1974), 722–49; P. Suppes, 'Popper's Analysis of Probability in Quantum Mechanics', ibid. 760–74; P. Clark, 'Determinism and Probability in Physics', *Proceedings of the Aristotelian Society*, supplementary vol. 61 (1987), 185–210; and J. Butterfield, 'Probability and Disturbing Measurement', ibid. 211–34.

[19] See also P. Humphreys, 'Why Propensities Cannot be Probabilities', *The Philosophical Review*, 94 (1985), 557–70.

p(A) and that p(not-A|B) does not differ much from p(not-A). The strength of the propensity-type connection between B and A is thus viewed as the difference between the conditional and unconditional probabilities of A—often called the 'relevance' of B to A—and the strength of the propensity-type connection between B and not-A is viewed analogously as the difference between the conditional and unconditional probabilities of not-A. And obviously these two differences can both be quite small without any transgression of Pascalian mathematics. (For example, let p(A|B) = 0.55 and p(not-A|B) = 0.45, while p(A) = p(not-A) = 0.5.) However, the price paid for this manœuvre is that, since propensities are defined by it only in terms of the difference between dyadic and monadic probabilities, no sense is given to statements that are just about monadic probabilities or just about dyadic ones, and not about the difference between the former and the latter. And an analogous argument applies to any other attempt to treat propensities as complex functions of probabilities rather than as probabilities *simpliciter*. The original purpose of the propensity theory—to provide an adequate interpretation for all well-formed formulae of the Pascalian calculus of probability—is not attainable when propensities are treated in that kind of way.

§ 9. PERSONALIST THEORIES

Ramsey held that a person's judgement of probability measured his degree of rational belief, where degree of belief is manifested by the lowest betting-odds on A that he would accept within a coherent system of wagers. But Ramsey was mistaken in thinking that p(A|B) can then be interpreted as expressing the lowest odds at which the person would now bet on A, with the bet only being valid if B is true. Moreover, someone who holds that a person's judgement of probability measures his degree of rational belief may hold one or other of several different views about the linguistic function of sentences that evaluate probabilities. A Ramsey-type analysis of probability-judgements is in practice often combined with endorsement of a Bayesian strategy for evaluating them. But problems arise about the extent to which different persons' evaluations can then be expected to converge.

On a realist account probabilities concern events, classes of events, properties, or other features of reality. Yet in the ordinary speech of both scientists and laymen there is often talk about the probability with which a certain proposition or belief is true or a certain inference valid. A realist may wish to claim that all probability-judgements that are formulated in this way could just as well be formulated in terms of the corresponding features of reality that underlie them. But there are idealist theories that offer a more idiosyncratic set of truth-conditions for statements of probability-assignments—that is, a set of truth-conditions that has no equivalent in realist terms.

Thus Ramsey[20] held that a person's judgement of probability measures his or her degree of rational belief, where the measurement relates not to any kind of introspected feeling of belief-intensity but to the kind of action that would in suitable circumstances result from the belief. Roughly, a person's belief that p is to be measured by the lowest odds he will accept on a bet that p. If the lowest odds he will accept are n to m, his degree of belief is to be measured by the relative size of what he is prepared to lose if he is wrong, that is, by the ratio of his own stake to the sum of both stakes, $m/(n + m)$. Thus if George will accept the offer of a bet at 3 to 1 that it will rain tomorrow, but not at 2 to 1 or at any other odds lower than 3 to 1, then he must have a $\frac{1}{4}$ degree of belief that it will rain then. Or, to put it another way, George is so doubtful about there being any rain tomorrow that he will risk losing £1 in a bet on it only if he stands to gain at least £3 if there is no rain. But Ramsey recognized that such a bet should not be assumed to be made in monetary units, partly because of the diminishing marginal utility of money (an extra £3 is not worth as much to a millionaire as to a pauper) and partly because a particular person may be abnormally attracted, or abnormally averse, to monetary gambles. He therefore specified that the bet should be supposed to be made in terms of whatever measurable values or utilities the bettor ultimately desires, and he was willing to accept that it might be an idealization to suppose the actual existence of such ultimate values.

Ramsey also recognized that degrees of belief, measured thus

[20] F.P. Ramsey, *The Foundations of Mathematics and other Logical Essays* (London: Routledge and Kegan Paul, 1931), 156–98.

in terms of a policy of conduct, are not necessarily degrees of rational belief. For example, perhaps someone will try to get me to take bets both on its raining tomorrow and on its not raining. I am to take a bet at odds of 1 to 2 that it will rain and at the same odds that it will not rain. Then, if it rains, I shall gain only one unit on the first bet and lose two on the second, and, if it does not rain, I shall lose two on the first and gain only one on the second. What is called—in race-track jargon—a 'Dutch book' will have been made against me. That is, a set of bets is registered on which, whatever happens, I am bound to make an overall loss. So because a rational person would not wish to behave in such a way as to ensure a loss in relation to his or her ultimate values, Ramsey inferred that a person's system of beliefs at any one moment is rational only if it is such that a Dutch book cannot be made against it. And he showed that a set of degrees of belief that satisfied this condition would also satisfy the laws of the mathematical calculus of probability—a theorem that was later independently proved by Bruno de Finetti (who described such a set of probability-judgements as 'coherent').[21]

Ramsey's analysis was the archetype of a group of theories that are sometimes called 'personalist', sometimes 'subjectivist', and sometimes (for reasons that will emerge) Bayesian. Such an approach applies most naturally to the interpretation of monadic probability-functions. Those functions can readily be supposed to evaluate degrees of belief unconditionally by reference to lowest acceptable betting odds. But what about dyadic functions? Ramsey himself at one point interprets a person's dyadic probability $p(A|B)$ as expressing 'the odds at which he would now bet on A, the bet only to be valid if B is true'.[22] And an obvious trouble, unnoticed by Ramsey, is that this interpretation in terms of a conditional bet would allow a Dutch book to be made against certain otherwise unexceptionable assignments of equal values to $p(A|B)$ and $p(\text{not-}A|C)$, if B and C both turn out to be true. Consider, for example, a case in which A is 'It will rain tomorrow', B is 'The barometer is fall-

---

[21] See B. de Finetti, 'Foresight: Its Logical Laws, Its Subjective Sources (1937)', in H. E. Kyburg and H. E. Smokler (eds.), *Studies in Subjective Probability* (New York: John Wiley and Sons, 1964), 99–158.

[22] Ramsey, *Foundations of Mathematics*, p. 180. Ramsey's full definition here is too complex to be enlightening.

ing', and C is 'The wind is in the east', where the bets would be 1 to 2 on A, if B is true, and 1 to 2 on not-A, if C is true. And there would also be trouble if, as might well be the case, $p(A|B)$ were said to be not equal to $p(A|C)$. For then what would be asserted on Ramsey's interpretation would be, if B and C were both true, a self-contradictory statement about what are the lowest acceptable odds in a bet on the truth of A. Those odds on A would be said to be not equal to those odds on A.

We must therefore in any case reject Ramsey's interpretation for dyadic probability functions. It has devastatingly counter-intuitive consequences. Indeed Ramsey here seems to have been confounding statements of the form '$p(A|B) = n$' with statements of the form 'If and only if B is true, then $p(A) = n$', and to have been interpreting the former kind of statement in a way suited only to the latter. Nor have other personalist philosophers of probability, working independently of Ramsey, always been at their most clear-headed on this issue. Parts of de Finetti's writings, for example, are hit by the same paradoxes as Ramsey's analysis,[23] though L.J. Savage was more careful.[24]

Someone might try to defend the Ramsey–de Finetti interpretation of dyadic probability-functions by pointing out that it will work quite satisfactorily in practice if the proposition upon which the validity of the bet is made conditional is required not only to be true, but also to state the *only* additional fact that must become known,[25] if the condition's fulfilment is to be warranted to be assertable. This manœuvre will certainly preclude generating the kind of incoherence or contradiction to which Ramsey's analysis was shown above to be exposed. You cannot have B and C stating different things and yet both, as premisses, stating the only additional facts to become known. It may still seem pradoxical, however, that the determination of betting-odds relating to a conditional probability is made dependent on such an unrealistic assumption as that in ordinary life items of knowledge can come one at a time in neatly packaged separation from one another, so as to allow only B to be known additionally, or only C. The world in which we

[23] De Finetti, 'Foresight', p. 108.

[24] L.J. Savage, *The Foundations of Statistics* (New York: Dover, 1972), 44.

[25] This is the analysis adopted by de Finetti in his *Theory of Probability*, trans. A. Machi and A. Smith, i (London: J. Wiley, 1974), 134.

actually make bets is not like that and, if it were, so much might be different that it is very difficult to predict how we should be inclined to bet on a particular issue. What perhaps one wants to be able to say here, therefore, is that $p(A|B)$ is the probability assigned to A where B states the only *relevant* additional fact to become known. But any reference to relevant evidence makes the interpretation circular, since relevance must itself be defined in this context in terms of dyadic or conditional probabilities. A true proposition B states all the evidence relevant to another proposition A only if there is no true proposition C, such that C does not logically entail A and $p(A|B)$ is not equal to $p(A|B\&C)$.

However, there is an obviously safe way out of these difficulties. We have in any case, on a personalist view, to treat $p(A|B)$ as measuring the ratio of the lowest odds acceptable on $A\&B$ to the lowest odds acceptable on B alone, since (as we have seen in § 3) the mathematics of the Pascalian calculus gives us

$$p(A|B) = \frac{p(A\&B)}{p(B)}$$

where $p(B) > 0$. We can, if we like, treat this ratio as evaluating the strength of a person's belief in the truth of A, given just B as evidence, that is, the strength of belief in the truth of A that is attributed to the truth of B, and the ratio would thus constitute a measure of conditional belief. Both monadic and dyadic judgements would then express belief-intensity—unconditional and conditional, respectively. But, whether conditional or unconditional, belief-intensity would on this interpretation always be measured in terms of *un*conditional bets.

We should note here an important shift in the question that is being answered, when we compare a subjective idealist theory, like Ramsey's or de Finetti's, with a realist theory, like those discussed in § § 6–8. Both types of theory purport to analyse the concept of probability. But, whereas the realist theories offer analyses that might help to answer the question 'How am I to reason about probabilities?', a Ramsey–de Finetti type of personalist theory is directed rather towards the question 'How am I to reason about a person's probability-judgements?' Realist theories aim to clarify the truth-conditions for assigning particular values to the probability-function in relation to particular events or kinds of events. But a Ramsey–de Finetti theory tells us the truth-conditions for statements about what values a particular person actually assigns to his probability-function. If you want to know instead what a man's probability-assignment *means*, Ramsey and de Finetti can tell you only that, if sincere and prudent, it expresses the man's degree of rational belief, and that answer supplies no reason at all why two different people ought properly to have the same degree of rational belief about the same issue if given the same evidence. So far as the Ramsey–de Finetti theory goes, two people could be equally rational and yet assign very different probabilities to the same event, on the same evidence, provided that each person's system of probability-judgements was internally coherent (in the sense that a Dutch book could not be made against him). Correspondingly, there can be no valid arguments that one assignment of this type is correct and others incorrect, whereas the objectivist theories do—each in its own way—allow such arguments.

It follows that a belief-theoretical account of probability-judgements could be combined with a realist one, although this possibility was not envisaged by Ramsey himself and was explicitly rejected by de Finetti.[26] The realist theory could be taken to disclose the *meaning* of a person's probability-statements, while the belief theory could be taken to show how we may test the sincerity and prudence with which those statements are asserted. Of course, a person may pretend to have beliefs or partial beliefs that he does not have, by accepting wagers in public that run counter to his own private judgement. But, if he is not so pretending, and is sufficiently clear-headed, then, if the lowest odds he will accept on the outcome *A* (in a coherent system of bets) are 3 to 1, this could be taken by belief-theorists as showing the strength of his belief in *A* when he says, according to a realist interpretation, that the (probabilistic) propensity for *A*, for example, is $\frac{1}{4}$.

There are, however, at least three possibilities open to someone who rejects a realist analysis of probability-judgements and wishes to treat Ramsey's type of theory as providing an

[26] De Finetti, 'Foresight', p. 154.

account not just of partial belief but also of the way in which sentences about probability function in human discourse.

One possibility is to treat the utterance of these sentences not just as an indication of what the speaker believes, and of how strongly he believes it, but as purporting to describe this. To say 'The probability of A is $\frac{1}{4}$' is then equivalent to saying 'My own degree of belief that A is $\frac{1}{4}$'. Such a view is rather similar to Hume's analysis of moral judgements:

> When you pronounce any action or character to be vicious, you mean nothing, but that from the constitution of your nature you have a feeling or sentiment of blame from the contemplation of it.[27]

But this type of analysis, analogously to Hume's, suffers from an obvious disadvantage. It implies that in disputing a person's spoken judgement of a probability one must be disputing the accuracy or correctness with which he reports his own state of belief. And that cannot be what advocates are arguing about in court, for example, when they differ about the probability of the defendant's having fired the fatal shot, any more than a dispute about the alleged viciousness of blood sports is a dispute about the actual feelings or sentiments of the disputants.

A second possibility is to suppose that mental states of partial belief are matched by speech-acts of partial commitment. The analysis is now a contribution to the pragmatics, rather than the semantics, of word-use. To say that there is a $\frac{2}{3}$ probability of rain on any day in April is now just to hedge one's prediction, as Toulmin claims,[28] and describes neither the speaker's internal state of mind nor the relative frequency with which rain occurs in April, though willingness to bet at the corresponding odds would again be a test of sincerity. And such a view too has a counterpart in the analysis of moral discourse, when it is urged, as by Hare,[29] that words of moral evaluation, like 'good' and 'bad', should be understood in terms of the characteristic speech-acts that they perform. 'Good', for example, is to be analysed as an adjective of commendation. But it is easily objected that this kind of analysis does not work satisfactorily

[27] D. Hume, *A Treatise of Human Nature* (London: J. Noon, 1739–40), bk. III, pt. 1, sect. 1, ed. L.A. Selby-Bigge (Oxford: Clarendon Press, 1888), 469.

[28] S. Toulmin, *The Uses of Argument* (Cambridge: Cambridge University Press, 1958), 44–93.

[29] See R.M. Hare, *The Language of Morals* (Oxford: Clarendon Press, 1952), 79–150.

when the words in question, like 'probable' or 'good', occur in the antecedents of conditional sentences or in any other sentential context in the utterance of which no speech-act of the relevant kind is normally performed.[30] Nor can the speech-act be replaced in such contexts by its own description, since the statement 'If I were to assert guardedly that it will rain this afternoon, then I should be excessively cautious in my weather predictions' may well be true when the statement 'If it were probable that it will rain this afternoon, then I should be excessively cautious in my weather predictions' was false.

There is also a third way in which judgements of probability may be treated as a measure of partial belief. Instead of treating a person's willingness to accept certain betting-odds as an indication of his belief-strength, or as what he is asserting, or as the expectable associate of a guarded commitment, one might suppose that judgements of probability are intended to measure the lowest odds that a rational bettor *should* accept. Sentences about probability are then characteristically normative or prescriptive in relation to partial belief.[31] Indeed, this version of a Ramsey-type theory is the most defensible one, though perhaps it should not be called a 'personalist' analysis, as Ramsey-type theories are often called. It is an objective idealism, rather than a subjective idealism. It avoids the difficulties that face the self-descriptive and speech-act analyses, without reverting to a realist semantics. But it still has at least three important limitations which it shares with all Ramsey-type theories.

First, it cannot apply to that aspect of belief in which (as we saw on pp. 17–18 above) a person's degree of belief that not-*A* is not necessarily the complement of his degree of belief that *A*. The commonest kind of situation in which this non-complementationality seems to operate is when a person thinks himself to be rather short of relevant evidence and is therefore inclined to have only a weak belief that *A* along with only a weak belief that not-*A*. The immediately available evidence may even be strongly in favour of one conclusion rather than another, but also contain so small a number of the relevant facts that no

---

[30] Compare J. R. Searle, 'Meaning and Speech Acts', *Philosophical Review*, 71 (1962), 423–32.

[31] See e.g. P. Horwich, *Probability and Evidence* (Cambridge: Cambridge University Press, 1982), 32–5.

strong belief is justified. In that kind of situation a rational person may well be reluctant to accept any bet at all that *A* or that not-*A*. It is not just that he would not, or should not, accept a bet of £1 to £1 on a coin's falling heads if he does not have reason to believe that the coin would be unbiased and the toss would be fair. In such circumstances he would not, or should not accept a bet on heads at any other odds either. So, where the weakness of justified belief is due to the overall inadequacy of the given evidence rather than to the fact that some of it favours one conclusion and some another, one cannot measure degree of justified belief by the lowest acceptable odds. (Note that this limitation on the scope of a Ramsey-type theory operates both in regard to monadic probability-functions, which the theory takes to evaluate unconditional degrees of belief, and also in regard to dyadic ones, which the theory takes to evaluate conditional degrees of belief.)

The second limitation affects the strength of beliefs that may be evaluated by reference to the lowest acceptable odds on their truth. Clearly betting odds cannot be used to measure either of the two limiting cases. Where a person supposes a probability of 1, or a probability of 0, that such-or-such is the case, the strength of his justified belief cannot be represented by appropriate betting odds, because both sides to a wager need to have something at stake. And it is no good objecting that a person's certainty about an outcome is adequately indicated by his unwillingness to risk any wager on it, since as we have just seen, such unwillingness is also appropriate where relevant evidence is in short supply.

The third limitation affects the context of beliefs. A rational person does not accept bets on issues that can never be settled. So beliefs about the past present a special problem for Ramsey-type theories. Knowing that literary or archaeological evidence would eventually be available to settle the issue, a rational person might bet on whether or not a Roman legion once marched along Fleet Street. But suppose that all the relevant evidence which there will ever be is already available. Then one could never settle a bet that was conditional on this evidence. We have no time-machine to take us back to look at the actual event. Yet there does seem to be a determinate probability, on the evidence, that such an event actually occurred. And a similar difficulty arises in regard to any beliefs that such-or-such a generalization states a law of nature. An open-ended generalization of that kind might be conclusively falsified (though even this is doubtful: see pp. 181–2 below). But it could certainly never be conclusively verified. So a bet on its truth could never be won (and perhaps never lost either). Of course, you could imagine the existence of an omniscient umpire who would kindly arbitrate between human bettors. But would it be rational to undertake any commitment on the assumption that such a being exists? If not, it would be irrational to bet about issues that humans cannot settle. Yet it does not seem irrational to have partial beliefs about at least some such matters.

The term 'Bayesianism' is often used as a name for some version or other of what I have here been calling a 'Ramsey-type' theory. Ramsey himself did not introduce any reference to Bayes's law (p. 23 above) into his writings on probability. But de Finetti and Savage have exploited Bayes's law in the attempt to develop a methodology for any coherent pattern of probabilistic reasoning that employs a personalist analysis of probability-judgements. Their thesis is, roughly, that if the recommended procedure is followed people's personal probabilities, even if very different at the outset, will converge towards identity, because differences in personal probability must be largely due to differences of knowledge and experience. The claim is not that there is an objectively true value, or an objectively valid system of measurement, for the probability of a particular outcome, but that, if people are constrained by their awareness of more and more of the evidence and by the need to avoid a Dutch book's being constructable against them, they will gradually develop a consensus. For a pure, unmixed Bayesian this kind of convergence replaces the estimation of propensities or relative frequencies from statistical samples, and constitutes a research strategy of wide application. The end-product thus has at best the status of social convention rather than of knowledge or discovery. But Bayesians can point out that standard Fisher or Neyman–Pearson procedures for estimating probabilities (p. 23) also involve an irreducibly conventional element about the acceptability of results with certain significance-levels, confidence-intervals, and so on.

The term 'Bayesianism' thus comes to name championship of

a certain procedure for reasoning about probabilities, rather than just the acceptance of a personalist analysis of probability-judgements. In its simplest form the basic Bayesian procedure is as follows. Suppose the question at issue to be the probability, on all available evidence, of the hypothesis H—for example, the proposition that it will rain within an hour. The investigator begins by assigning a prior value to the probability of H (that is, he decides his lowest acceptable betting-odds) in advance of any consideration of the evidence, and he also asigns a value to the conditional probability of E_1 (his first piece of evidence) given the truth of H. For example, if E_1 reports the presence of dark clouds, $p(E_1|H)$ might be quite high. If a probability is also assigned to $p(E_1)$, or to its equivalent $p(E_1|H) + p(E_1|\text{not-}H)$, it is then possible to calculate $p(H|E_1)$ by means of Bayes's theorem, since that theorem puts $p(A|B)$ equal to

$$\frac{p(B|A) \times p(A)}{p(B)}$$

where $p(B) > 0$. The investigator next updates his value for the monadic probability $p(H)$ by putting it equal to $p(H|E_1)$, and he takes the *next* piece of evidence available into account— perhaps E_2 reports a rising barometer—by evaluating $p(E_2|H)$ and $p(E_2)$. It is then possible to calculate $p(H|E_2)$ by a fresh application of Bayes's theorem, and the whole procedure is repeated again and again until all available items of evidence have been taken into account. At each stage—that is with each E_i on which H is conditionalized—the probability-function employed is properly regarded as a different one, expressing the investigator's state of mind at just that stage of the investigation. After the last piece of evidence, E_n, has been taken into account and a corresponding value obtained for a penultimate dyadic function $p(H|E_n)$, a final monadic probability-function emerges, which expresses the investigator's state of mind in the light of all the available evidence, and $p(H)$ according to this function is put equal to $p(H|E_n)$ according to the penultimate function.

In practice, of course, the investigator may often come to know the truth of E_i before he has had an advance opportunity to decide his lowest acceptable betting-odds on that proposition. In such a case he presumably has to imagine what these odds would be in the ideal situation in which the truth of E_i is not yet known. But there is a more serious problem about the procedure of successive re-conditionalization. Does it really tend to produce consensus? This looks at first sight like being a question that can be settled by psychological experiment. But it has certainly not yet been so settled. On the one hand, sharp controversy exists as to whether people who are untutored in probability-theory are inclined to make certain systematic kinds of mistake when confronted with Bayesian tasks.[32] For example, do they tend to overestimate, or to underestimate, the importance of prior probabilities? On the other hand, if instead the experiment is carried out on instructed and informed investigators, it may reveal nothing more than the results of imparting such instruction and information in a particular way. Moreover, any apparent failure of Bayesian reasoners to converge towards consensus can always be put down to their having stopped too soon in the process of seeking out, and assimilating, evidential facts. So on a wider view the convergence thesis looks as though it may be unfalsifiable.

It is sometimes claimed that the eventual convergence of Bayesian reasoners needs no empirical confirmation. The argument is that de Finetti has proved the applicability of Bernoulli's limit theorem (the so-called 'law of large numbers'—see pp. 21–2) to sequences of what de Finetti calls 'exchangeable' events. So that in the case of such sequences, whatever be the opinion with which a person starts out, he must, if he is to be coherent in his beliefs and has made a sufficient number of observations, come to assign a probability to the type of event in question that is sufficiently close to its observed relative frequency.[33] But the trouble is that what makes a sequence of events—such as a sequence of coin-tosses —exchangeable, in de Finetti's sense, is that their order of

---

[32] For the view that they do make such mistakes, see R. Nisbett and L. Ross, *Human Inference: Strategies and Shortcomings of Social Judgement* (Englewood Cliffs: Prentice-Hall, 1980), and D. Kahneman, P. Slovic, and A. Tversky (eds.), *Judgment under Uncertainty: Heuristics and Biases* (Cambridge: Cambridge University Press, 1982). For the view that they do not, see L. Jonathan Cohen, 'Can Human Irrationality be Experimentally Demonstrated?', *The Behavioral and Brain Sciences*, 4 (1981), 317–31, 359–70, and *The Dialogue of Reason* (Oxford: Clarendon Press, 1986), 157–92.

[33] See Kyburg and Smokler, 'Introduction', in Kyburg and Smokler, (eds.) *Studies in Subjective Probability*, pp. 12–15.

occurrence does not affect the probabilities in which we are interested. So even exchangeability depends, in the end, on subjective judgements of probability, and if two people differ in such judgements, or on what to count as evidence, the events in a particular sequence may seem exchangeable to one and not to the other. As de Finetti himself has said 'the condition of "exchangeability" itself has, from the beginning, only a subjective value'.[34] Inevitably, therefore, the possibility remains open, where there is no *ad hoc* agreement on the exchangeability of a particular sequence, that two people who are fully rational by Bayesian standards may differ in their initial judgements of probability and never converge to a consensus, despite the internal coherence of both sets of beliefs and the extensive observations that give rise to them.[35]

§ 10. MULTI-VALUED LOGIC THEORIES

The conception of probability as a truth-value in a multi-valued logic has three disadvantages. It fails to imply any guidelines for the measurement of probability, it seems inapplicable to dyadic probability, and it requires our multi-valued logic to be non-truth-functional.

We have seen that the Ramsey–de Finetti–Savage philosophy of probability is primarily directed towards the question 'How

---

[34] De Finetti, 'Foresight', p. 153.

[35] Personalist analyses are discussed further in D. Gillies, 'The Subjective Theory of Probability', *British Journal for the Philosophy of Science*, 23 (1972), 138–57; G.H. von Wright, 'Remarks on the Epistemology of Subjective Probability', in E. Nagel, P. Suppes, and L. Tarski (eds.), *Logic, Methodology and Philosophy of Science: Proceedings of the 1960 Congress* (Stanford: Stanford University Press, 1962), 330–39; R.C. Jeffrey, *The Logic of Decision* (New York: McGraw-Hill, 1965); E. Eells, *Rational Decision and Causality* (Cambridge: Cambridge University Press, 1982), 1–86; I. Hacking, 'Subjective Probability', *British Journal for the Philosophy of Science*, 16 (1966), 334–9; and K. Heilig, 'Carnap and de Finetti on Bets and the Probability of Singular Events: The Dutch Book Argument Reconsidered', *British Journal for the Philosophy of Science*, 29 (1978), 325–46. In regard to exchangeability see also B. de Finetti, 'On the Condition of Partial Exchangeability', in R.C. Jeffrey (ed.), *Studies in Inductive Logic and Probability* ii (Berkeley: University of California Press, 1980), 193–205. In regard to convergence see also G. Shafer, 'A Subjective Interpretation of Conditional Probability', *Journal of Philosophical Logic*, 12 (1983), 453–66, B. Skyrms, *Pragmatics and Empiricism* (New Haven: Yale University Press, 1984), 20–92, and K. Lehrer, 'Consensus', in R.J. Bogdan (ed.), *Keith Lehrer* (Dordrecht: Reidel, 1981) 63–75.

does a person assign values to his probabilities?' rather than towards the question 'What are the correct values to assign to one's probabilities?' According to such a personalist theory a judgement of A's probability consists in its author's degree of belief that A is true. But many people take their own degree of belief to be the inter-subjectively correct one, as in the normativist version of a Ramsey-type theory. So for such people, if a probability is attached to a proposition, it can be regarded as the inter-subjective truth-value of that proposition rather than as the degree of justifiable mental commitment to it. Accordingly it is possible to interpret the Pascalian calculus of chance as a multi-valued logic. To judge that the proposition A has zero probability is to judge that it is false; to judge that it has probability 1 is to judge that it is true; and to judge that it has some intermediate degree of probability is to assign it one from an infinite set of intermediate truth-values.

At first sight this conception of probability seems to have the great advantage of simplifying our conceptual system. A familiar branch of mathematics turns out to instantiate a familiar species of logic. Also, as Lucas points out,[36] the conception of probability as a partial truth fits particularly well with Toulmin's idea (p. 64) that in voicing a judgement of probability one utters a speech-act of partial commitment. If anybody who asserts a proposition unguardedly is thereby claiming its truth, anybody who asserts it guardedly may be regarded as thereby claiming an intermediate truth-value for it.

But, even apart from the objections to Toulmin's idea that have already been noted (pp. 64–5), there are at least three reasons why a multi-valued logic analysis is less useful than it may seem.

The first reason is that, considered on its own, the analysis gives us no hint as to how we should in practice measure probabilities. In that respect it is similar to a propensity analysis. Its distinctive feature is that it introduces gradations into the evaluation of propositions, rather than of natural tendencies. But, whether you say that the calculus should be interpreted in objective-idealist style as a multi-valued logic or in a realist style as a theory of natural tendencies, you imply no guide-lines for

---

[36] J.R. Lucas, *The Concept of Probability* (Oxford: Clarendon Press, 1970), 1–22.

carrying out conscious measurements of probability. Such measurements are normally rooted in something quite different—most often in an examination of the evidence provided by observed relative frequencies. And in fact Reichenbach showed how the conception of probabilities as truth-values could be mapped on to a Pascalian-structured calculus of relative frequencies in the special case in which the reference-class is always identical with the universe. Roughly, the truth-value of 'This is an *A*' is equated with the relative frequency of *A*s in the contextually assumed universe.[37] Even then we are left with the problem of how to measure the truth-value of 'This is an *A*' where we know the relative frequency of *A*s only within a reference-class that is smaller than the relevant universe as a whole.

Secondly, though a propensity analysis can interpret dyadic judgements of probability as statements of conditional tendencies (and a personalist analysis can relativize strength of belief to awareness of particular items of evidence), a multi-valued logic account sits easily only with monadic judgements, because each proposition is naturally assumed to have just one truth-value, whether or not we know it. The proposition that it will rain soon may be probable on the evidence of dark clouds, and improbable on the evidence of increasing atmospheric pressure. But this proposition presumably has only one truth-value, which is determined by the actual event, when it happens, and is not relative to some other, quite different events. No doubt we could restrict ourselves to a monadic judgement here by identifying the conditional probability with the probability of the corresponding conditional—that is, we could identify $p(A|B)$ with $p(\text{If } A, \text{ then } B)$. But there would be a price to pay for this. It would reduce the variety of different facts that our judgements of probability are capable of expressing, as we have already seen (pp. 20-1). The better course would be just to define $p(A|B)$ as

$$\frac{p(A\&B)}{p(B)}$$

where $p(B) > 0$.

---

[37] Reichenbach, *Theory of Probability*, pp. 395-7.

Thirdly—and this is perhaps the most important point —standard multi-valued logics are truth-functional, in the sense that the truth-value of a logically compounded proposition, like a conjunction or a disjunction, always depends solely on the truth-values of the propositions compounded. But the probability of a conjunction depends solely on the probabilities of the conjuncts only in the special case where these probabilities are independent of one another. For example, if we replace the ball after each drawing (see pp. 18–19 above) we can calculate in this way the probability of drawing a white ball twice from an urn containing two black balls and two white ones; but, if the first ball drawn is not replaced, we cannot do this. Indeed, the general law for conjunction—$p(A \& B) = p(A) \times p(B|A)$—shows clearly that, if the Pascalian calculus is interpreted as a multi-valued logic, that logic must be non-truth-functional, in the sense that the probability of a compound proposition, like $p(A \& B)$, is not necessarily a function of the probabilities of the propositions compounded, $p(A)$ and $p(B)$. So instead of being able to treat the mathematics of the calculus as just another instance of a familiar kind of logic we have in fact to extend our conception of such a logic in order to embrace a new, non-truth-functional type of system. Such an extension is more acceptable to some logicians than to others, and this has inevitably affected the extent to which it has been thought helpful or illuminating to conceive of probability as an intermediate truth-value.[38] So in one important respect the conception of probability as a truth-value within a multi-valued logic is like the conception of probability as a propensity. It is compatible with a Pascalian structure but does not demand one, as does any conception that takes probabilities to be ratios, whether these be ratios of the permutations of chances (as in § 6), of the cardinalities of sets (as in § 7), of the sizes of betting stakes (as in § 9), or of quantities of logically possible worlds (as in § 11). Indeed the normal[39] principle for conjunction in a multi-valued logic (equating the value of a conjunction with its least-valued conjunct) is in fact shared by the non-Pascalian

---

[38] N. Rescher, *Many-valued Logic* (New York: McGraw-Hill, 1969), 186–8.
[39] Ibid. 131.

system of inductive and probabilistic reasoning that is discussed in § 21 below.[40]

§ 11. LOGICAL RELATION THEORIES

If probability is thought of as a logical relation, we can take the ratio of the quantity of logically possible worlds in which $A\&B$ is true to the quantity of logically possible worlds in which B is true as determining the extent to which A is a logical consequence of B and thus as defining the probability of A given B. Carnap constructed a systematic version of this analysis, but pointed out in effect that there is an infinite number of different ways of measuring quantities of logically possible worlds.

If the mathematics of Pascalian probability is to be treated as a kind of generalized logic, the conception of probabilities as the truth-values of a multi-valued logic is not the only option. That analysis in any case, as we have already seen, sits easily only with monadic probabilities. And there is another logical option that sits more naturally with dyadic probabilities, namely the conception of $p(A|B)$ as the degree to which B entails A. On this view, as Keynes put it in 1921, no proposition is probable, or improbable, in itself but only relative to certain premises, and this relation is a logical one.[41] So we shall have $p(A|B) = 1$ if and only if $B\&\text{not-}A$ is self-contradictory, and $p(A|B) = 0$ if and only if $B\&A$ is self-contradictory. The argument from B to A is certain—has maximum probability—when A is a logical consequence of B. But how are the intervening values to be determined?

Keynes thought that some probabilities are just not comparable at all with one another. Most others, in his view, are not measurable, despite being intuitively comparable in terms of 'greater than', 'lesser than', or 'equal to'. And he thought that only in a very special type of case (suitably constrained and qualified inferences from statistical data) are probabilities

---

[40] On the multi-valued logic analysis see further A. A. Zinov'ev, *Philosophical Problems of Many-valued Logic* (Dordrecht: Reidel, 1963), 107–9; and A. R. White, *Modal Thinking* (Oxford: Basil Blackwell, 1974), 59–74.

[41] J. M. Keynes, *A Treatise on Probability* (London: Macmillan, 1921), 7. Keynes (1883–1946) is perhaps better known for his work in economics than for his philosophy of probability.

numerically measurable.[42] But Carnap showed, in 1950, that it is possible to develop numerical measures for Pascalian probability that apply whenever this probability is conceived as a logical relation between sentences in a particular kind of artificial language.

Unlike Keynes, Carnap did not claim a monopoly of truth for the logical relation theory. Rather, he argued that there were two primitive or presystematic concepts of probability, which he called 'probability'$_1$ and 'probability'$_2$, respectively. Probability$_1$ is a relation between conclusion and evidence, broadly describable as degree of confirmation. A function that assesses probability$_1$ takes sentences as fillers of its argument-places. Moreover, judgements of probability$_1$, assigning numbers as values of such a function for particular fillers of its argument-places, are either analytically true or analytically false: their truth-value depends on the rules of the language in which they are formulated. Probability$_2$, on the other hand, is a relation of relative frequency between properties, classes, or kinds of events. Judgements of probability$_2$ are therefore factual and empirical. Carnap fully acknowledged the utility of probability$_2$ for many purposes. He accepted that in statistical enquiry judgements of probability characteristically relate properties, classes, or kinds of events, and should be analysed as empirically assessable statements about relative frequencies. Later he also worked with a Ramsey-type analysis of probability.[43] But his 1950 theory of probability as a relation between propositions was concerned only with a priori judgements of the extent to which a particular statement of evidence would logically confirm a particular hypothesis at issue. And Carnap acknowledged[44] that the germ of his theory of logical probability derived from Waismann's elaboration[45] of an idea originally formulated in Wittgenstein's *Tractatus*.[46] Indeed,

---

[42] Ibid. 34.

[43] R. Carnap, 'Inductive Logic and Rational Decisions', in R. Carnap and R.C. Jeffrey (eds.), *Studies in Inductive Logic and Probability*, i (Berkeley: University of California press, 1971), 5–31.

[44] R. Carnap, *Logical Foundations of Probability* (Chicago: Chicago University Press, 1950), 299

[45] F. Waismann, 'Logische Analyse des Wahrscheinlichkeitsbegriff', *Erkenntnis*, 1 (1930-1), 228–48, repr. in English as 'A Logical Analysis of the Concept of Probability', in F. Waismann, *Philosophical Papers* (Dordrecht: Reidel, 1977), 4–21.

[46] L. Wittgenstein, *Tractatus Logico-Philosophicus* (London: Kegan Paul, Trench,

there are also some anticipations of Carnap's approach to the problem in the writings of Leibniz.[47]

If A is a logical consequence of B, then $A\&B$ is true in every logically possible world in which B is true. But if A is neither a logical consequence of B nor inconsistent with it, then $A\&B$ is true only in some, not all, logically possible worlds in which B is true (namely, those in which A also happens to be true). If, therefore, we have a measure for possible worlds, we can take the ratio of the quantity of logically possible worlds in which $A\&B$ is true to the quantity of logically possible worlds in which B is true as determining the extent to which A is a logical consequence of B and thus as defining the probability of A given B (if we conceive degree of probabilification as degree of logical consequence).

That is the nub of the Wittgenstein–Waismann–Carnap analysis. But in keeping with the prevailing nominalism of the period, Carnap formulated it in terms of expressions in an artificial language rather than in terms of possible worlds. Specifically, Carnap began by supposing a standard type of artificially composed logical language, with a finite number of monadic, first-order predicates F, G, H, . . . (like 'is red', 'is square', 'is male', etc.) and a finite number of individual constants a, b, c, . . . (like uniquely assigned proper names). An atomic sentence is then defined as an assignment of an individual constant to a predicate, e.g. Fa (like 'Tom is male'). A state description is defined as a conjunction of sentences containing every atomic sentence or its negation but not both. (So a state description describes a distinct possible world, within the limits of the language's descriptive potential.) The range of a sentence may then be defined, roughly, as the class of state-descriptions in which that sentence holds. More precisely, the range of a sentence is the class of state-descriptions such that, for each of these state descriptions, the sentence would be true if individuals had just those properties attributed to them by the state description.

Trubner, 1922), 111 (para. 5.15). Some sketchy remarks survive which suggest that Wittgenstein later changed his mind on this issue. See e.g. his *Philosophical Remarks*, ed. R. Rhees, trans. R. Hargreaves and R. White (Oxford: Blackwell, 1975), 227–47, and *Wittgenstein and the Vienna Circle*, ed. B. McGuinness, trans. J. Schulte and B. McGuinness (Oxford: Blackwell, 1979), 93–6, 98–9.

[47] See I. Hacking, *The Emergence of Probability*, pp. 134–142.

Each state-description is then assumed to have a measure which is a positive real number such that the sum of all the state-descriptions' measures is equal to 1; and the measure of a sentence's range is said to be the sum of all the measures of the state-descriptions in which that sentence holds. Carnap abbreviates 'the measure of the range of *h*' to 'm(*h*)' and defines the extent to which *e* confirms *h* (abbreviated to c (*h,e*) as the ratio

$$\frac{\mathrm{m}(e\&h)}{\mathrm{m}(e)}$$

—in effect, as the ratio of the quantity of logically possible worlds in which both *e* and *h* are true to the quantity of logically possible worlds in which *e* is true. Finally, for languages with an infinite number of individual constants m(*h*) is defined as the limit of its values in a sequence of languages with ever increasing finite numbers of individual constants, and c(*h,e*) is defined analogously. And Carnap proves that any confirmation-function, thus defined, conforms to the standard mathematics of conditional probability, while any such measure-function conforms to the standard mathematics of unconditional (i.e. monadic) probability.

Carnap then concentrates his attention on a particular type of confirmation-function which he calls 'symmetrical'. A symmetrical confirmation-function is one that treats all individuals alike and thus allows any uniform replacement of one individual constant within its scope by another, provided that this preserves existing relations of sameness and difference between occurrences of those constants. For example, if c is a symmetrical confirmation-function c(*Fa,Fb*) will have the same value as both c(*Fa,Fc*) and c(*Fc,Fb*), but not the same value as c(*Fa,Fa*). The theory of symmetrical confirmation-functions derives from assuming, not unreasonably, that two state descriptions have the same measure if they differ only in respect of which individuals have the particular set of properties described. Indeed Carnap believed that there was general agreement among writers on probability₁ that any analysis of logical probability should attribute to it this property of symmetry, just as all individuals have equal rights before the tribunal of deductive logic. When we infer from 'All men are mortal' and 'Socrates is a man' to 'Socrates is mortal', the validity of our inference is unaffected if we replace each occurrence of 'Socrates' by an occurrence of 'John Doe' or of any other proper name. (Compare the account of de Finetti's idea of 'exchangeability, on pp. 69–70 above.)

But no unique measures emerge in this way. For example, one possible option would be to assign the same real number to each state-description of any kind (with all these numbers summing to 1). After all, there seems to be no reason, prior to actual experience, why one state-description should be regarded as less probable than another. The principle of indifference seems to be applicable here. And Carnap assigned the name '$c\dagger$' to the symmetrical confirmation-function that is evaluated in this way in any language. Yet it would also be possible to apply the principle of indifference in another way. Specifically, we might suppose that what were ultimately to be put on a level with one another were *patterns* of state-description, rather than individual state-descriptions, on the ground that what mattered were the particular predicates instantiated or not instantiated, rather than which particular individuals instantiated them. Carnap called such a pattern a 'structure-description', defining it as a disjunction of isomorphic state-descriptions. If each structure-description is assigned—for its measure—the same real number as every other structure-description (with all these numbers summing to 1), a measure can then be assigned to each of the n disjoined state-descriptions within a particular structure-description by dividing the measure of that structure-description by n. And Carnap designates a confirmation-function that is evaluated in this way by the symbol c^*. In terms of the distinction between permutations and combinations that was noted on p. 15 above, (compare p. 45) $c\dagger$ treats the different permutations of predicates and individual constants as the fundamental units of account whereas c^* treats the different combinations of them as the fundamental units.

Waismann had already made the general point that no uniquely correct range-measure is possible. But it was Carnap who first took this problem seriously. He not only drew the explicit distinction between $c\dagger$ and c^*, but also emphasized that they have importantly different properties, as a simple example will illustrate. Consider a language with only one atomic predicate H (which could mean 'falls heads uppermost') and only three individual constants a, b, and c (which could designate a particular coin's first, second, and third tosses, respectively).

There are then eight different state-descriptions of which one is *Ha&Hb&Hc*, two include *Ha* and *Hb*, two include *Ha* and *Hc*, and four include *Ha*. It follows that, using Carnap's system of measurement, we shall have c† $(Hc,Ha) = \frac{1}{4}/\frac{1}{2} = \frac{1}{2}$ and also c† $(Hc,Ha\&Hb) = \frac{1}{8}/\frac{1}{4} = \frac{1}{2}$. But there are four different structure-descriptions (all heads, two heads, one heads, and no heads). So m*$(Ha\&Hc) = \frac{1}{4} + \frac{1}{12} = \frac{1}{3}$, because *Ha&Hc* holds good in one state-description that is the only member of its structure-description (the structure-description where all tosses are said to fall heads) and in one state-description that is a third of the membership of its structure-description (the structure-description where only two tosses are said to fall heads). Similarly m* $(Ha) = \frac{1}{4} + \frac{2}{12} + \frac{1}{12} = \frac{1}{2}$. So c*$(Hc,Ha) = \frac{2}{3}$; and, when calculated analogously, c*$(Hc,Ha\&Hb) = \frac{3}{4}$. In other words, when measured by c† the logical probability of *Hc*, on the evidence of *Ha*, is not increased by the additional evidence that *Hb* provides. But, when measured by c*, the probability *is* thus increased. Clearly c† might be a suitable measure when successive outcomes are assumed a priori to be independent of one another and empirical evidence about past outcomes is taken to be irrelevant to the probabilities of future ones, as in an acknowledged game of chance; whereas c* might be suitable when no such assumptions are made and empirical evidence about past outcomes is allowed to affect the probabilities of future ones.

In both cases the sentence evaluating the function—for example, the equation c†$(Hc,Ha) = \frac{1}{2}$ or c*$(Hc,Ha) = \frac{2}{3}$—is to be regarded as an a priori truth, since it is derivable from the principles of the system and does not require looking and seeing, as does the measurement of a relative frequency. But in the case of c† it is an a priori truth about the value of a probability that is not conditional on the evidence's consisting of any particular number of resembling items, whereas in the case of c* it is an a priori truth about the value of a probability that is conditional on such evidence. In the latter case, if anyone gives us both the hypothesis and the evidence, we can work out a priori the probability of the one on the other: in the former case, if anyone gives us just the hypothesis we can work out a priori its probability on any number—from zero upwards—of distinct but resembling evidential items. And it is clear that, in addition to c† and c*, an infinite number of other symmetrical c-functions could be designed, so as to provide other bases for the a priori measurement of probability when conceived as a logical relation. As different kinds of inequality are introduced into the measure of state-descriptions, according to the weighting attached to the number of state-descriptions isomorphic with a given state-description, probabilities are made sensitive to evidence to varying extents. Also, c-functions are possible that share with c^* its sensitivity to additional evidence but avoid making the degree of confirmation for any sentence depend in part, as c^* depends, on the choice of primitive predicates within each family of primitive predicates in the language,[48] which seems to be a purely conventional issue. But any true statement assigning a specified value to a c-function for specified fillers of its argument-places—like '$c(Fa,Fb) = \frac{1}{2}$'—is always analytic. In any treatment of probability as a logical relation intermediate uses of that relation are just as much an issue for a priori assessments as are the limiting cases of entailment and contradiction.

Carnap's theory of logical probability was intended to provide a system of gradation for inductive inference, and its adequacy for this purpose will be discussed in § 17 below. But, within the constraints of an artificial language where primitive predicates are monadic in structure and finite in number, Carnap's theory certainly provided a rigorously developed method of interpreting the Pascalian calculus along idealist lines. And it inspired a number of other philosphers, in particular Hintikka (see § 17 below), to seek to improve on Carnap's formulations. But, though Carnap's analysis generated different probability-functions as the size or content of the language is altered or a different measure-function adopted, he explicitly denied that the choice of one measure-function rather than another could ever be justified by empirical evidence.[49] So judgements of probability$_1$ inevitably contain, on Carnap's view, an element of intuitive or conventional arbitrariness, when compared with judgements of probability$_2$.[50]

---

[48] I. Hacking, 'Linguistically Invariant Inductive Logic', *Synthese*, 20 (1969), 25–47.

[49] *Logical Foundations of Probability*, p. 299.

[50] On the logical relation analysis see further H. Jeffreys, *Theory of Probability* (Oxford: Clarendon Press, 1948); R. Swinburne, 'The Probability of Particular Events', *Philosophy of Science*, 38 (1971), 327–43; and the references given in nn. 6–15 for ch. IV below.

III

The Foundations of Pluralism in the Analysis of Probability

§ 12 SOME LOGICAL DISTINCTIONS EXPLOITED BY DIFFERING ANALYSES OF PASCALIAN PROBABILITY

Different analyses of Pascalian probability have different implications in regard to certain important issues about the logic of
probability-judgements. One such issue concerns whether a
probability-judgement is at best necessarily true or contingently
true. A second concerns whether the judgement is sentence-
related or predicate-related. A third concerns the substitutivity
conditions for A and B in a judgement of probability $p(A|B) = n$.
A fourth concerns whether or not a given judgement of probability is counterfactualizable.

The previous chapter distinguished at least six different kinds of
theory about the semantics and epistemology of Pascalian probability. One kind of theory evaluated probabilities with the
help of a principle of indifference, a second by reference to
relative frequencies, a third by natural propensities, a fourth by
actual or appropriate strength of belief, a fifth by multi-valued
logic, and a sixth by ratios of logical ranges. What are we to
make of this embarrassingly rich diversity of philosophical
analyses? None of the analyses considered seemed altogether
without a rationale. But neither did any seem universally
applicable.

Of course, not all philosophical analysts of probability have
claimed that their own analysis is the only correct one. For
example, though indifference theorists[1] and Bayesians[2] have

---

[1] e.g. P.S. de Laplace, *A Philosophical Essay on Probabilities* (1814), trans. F.W.
Truscott and F.L. Emry (New York: Dover, 1951), 4 ff.
[2] e.g. B. de Finetti, 'Foresight: Its Logical Laws, Its Subjective Sources (1937)', in
H.E. Kyburg and H.E. Smokler (eds.), *Studies in Subjective Probability* (New York: John
Wiley and Sons, 1964), esp. 111–18.

often done this, Carnap[3] originally thought that probability could be conceived either as a logical relation or as a relative frequency and others, like Nagel[4] and Mackie,[5] have been even more open-minded and have acknowledged the existence of four or five different concepts of Pascalian probability. But a tolerant pluralism leaves many questions unanswered. In particular, we need to understand how it is that several very different concepts of probability are possible; we need to know which concepts are most appropriate to which contexts of employment; and we also need to discover whether there is reason to suppose that the six kinds of theory examined in § § 6–11 are the only philosophical analyses of probability that are possible, or whether the underlying problem-situation admits a wider space of possible solutions.

It will not do to tell us here, as Mackie does, quoting with approval from J.S. Mill, that 'names creep on from subject to subject until all traces of a common meaning sometimes disappear',[6] unless there is historical evidence that some such gradual process of linguistic expansion accounts for all the differences under examination. But Mackie offers no historical evidence to support his thesis. Indeed, we have seen (§ 3) that some diversity of conception was present at the outset. Even in the earliest years of work on the mathematical principles of Pascalian probability those principles were already being applied both to judgements of aleatory chance and also to judgements of evidenced credibility. Compare judgements of goodness. Most philosophers would agree with Aristotle[7] that the various uses of the word 'good' in 'good man', 'good health', 'good pen', etc. are not due to chance homonymy. No more should we simply assume that the various available senses of the word 'probable' (and of its equivalents in other languages) are due to accidents of linguistic history.

---

[3] *Logical Foundations of Probability* (Chicago: Chicago University Press, 1950), 23–36.

[4] E. Nagel, *Principles of the Theory of Probability*, in O. Neurath, R. Carnap, and C. Morris (eds.), *Foundations of the Unity of Science* (Chicago: Chicago University Press, 1938), i. 342–422.

[5] J.L. Mackie, *Truth, Probability and Paradox* (Oxford: Clarendon Press, 1973), 154–236.

[6] Ibid. 155, quoting from J.S. Mill, *A System of Logic* (London: Longmans, Green, 1896), 24.

[7] *Nicomachaean Ethics* 1096^{b}, 26–27.

Nor is any light cast on the problem by Mackie's claim[8] that probability should be seen as a 'family-resemblance' concept in Wittgenstein's sense,[9] since that approach to the understanding of conceptual pluralism is inherently unrewarding. For example, men ride petrol-tankers, horses, and tractors, but not oxen; oxen, horses, and tractors, but not petrol-tankers, are used on farms for pulling things; petrol-tankers, tractors, and oxen stay on the ground, while horses sometimes jump; and all petrol-tankers, oxen, and horses have their front and rear means of locomotion approximately the same height, while most tractors do not. But no one supposes it appropriate to mark this particular nexus of family resemblance by carrying over the name of one of the four sorts of objects to describe the other three sorts. The fact is that some groups of four or more sorts have common names, and some do not, even when the sorts exhibit family resemblance to one another. So unless the exponent of a family-resemblance approach to probability tells us why *his* supposed nexus of family-resemblance generates a common name, in contrast with others that do not, he has not explained anything. But if he does do this, and does it adequately, he has to go beyond a merely family-resemblance account. It will certainly not be adequate to say that a common name is generated when the resemblances are sufficiently close, if the only criterion of sufficient closeness is the use of a common name.

A deeper level of philosophical understanding is clearly necessary here. To achieve it we must begin by paying some attention to the fact that the different kinds of analysis of Pascalian probability that philosophers have proposed differ not only in the substance of their central message, but also in what they imply about certain important logical issues. Not all of these differences of implication have been adequately recognized in discussions of the relevant analyses. But when they are recognized they help us to see that behind the different kinds of philosophical analysis lie quite a variety of different conceptions of Pascalian probability that are available for human reasoning. For example, let us consider first the modality of probability-judgements, then whether they are

8 Mackie, *Truth, Probability and Paradox* p. 155.
9 L. Wittgenstein, *Philosophical Investigations* (Oxford: Blackwell, 1953), 32–3.

sentence-related or predicate-related, then their substitutivity conditions, and then what may usefully be termed their 'counterfactualizability'.

Thus, if you adopt an indifference analysis for a particular judgement of probability, and assume the value of the probability to be determined ultimately by the rules of a game, that judgement is made out to be either necessarily true or necessarily false. If in a valid throw, a die can fall only on one or other of its six sides and if there is assumed to be an equal chance of its falling on any one side, there is no possible world in which, when such a game is played, the licit probability of its falling twice with the same side uppermost is anything other than $\frac{1}{36}$. Similarly Carnap's logical range theory imposes necessary truth or necessary falsehood on any evaluation of a particular probability-function for a particular pair of sentences, such as $c^*(h,e) = \frac{1}{3}$ or $c\dagger(h,e) = \frac{1}{2}$. But relative frequencies, natural propensities, or strengths of belief (or empirically established indifference-dependent chances) could be different in other logically possible worlds than the actual one. So judgements of probability in those terms can at best be contingently—not necessarily—true.

Again, we commonly take the overall structure of a probability-judgement to be represented by the symbolism $p(A) = n$ or $p(A|B) = n$. It is understood here that the letter n stands in for a real number, or for a rational one, such that $1 \geqslant n \geqslant 0$. But what do the letters A and B stand in for—whole sentences, expressing fully determinate propositions, or just sentence-schemata or parts of sentences? Carnap's analysis requires the letters A and B to stand in for sentences, since it is concerned with probability as a confirmatory relationship between propositions, and the multi-valued logic analysis also is obviously sentence-related rather than predicate-related. But the relative frequency theory requires A and B to stand in for terms designating classes, since it is concerned with the relative frequency with which members of one class are also members of another. And the indifference, propensity, and personalist kinds of theory seem in principle to be compatible with both options, though particular versions of these analyses may not be. For example, you can speak in general about any game of drawing a card at random from a well-shuffled pack, and then A in $p(A) =$

$\frac{1}{13}$ will signify a type of outcome, namely, the drawn card's being an ace; so A will stand in for a sentence-part. Or you can speak specifically of the very next round of playing that game and say that there is a probability of $\frac{1}{13}$ that the next card drawn here this afternoon will be an ace, in which case A will stand in for a whole sentence. Again, you could measure both the strength of my belief, for any person, that he will survive to the age of seventy, given that he is a lorry-driver, and also the strength of my belief that our friend John Doe, specifically, will survive to the age of seventy given that he is a lorry-driver. In the former case A would stand in for a sentence-schema, in the latter for a fully determinate sentence.

Another important issue is that of substitutivity. Under what conditions of relationship between A and A' and between B and B' is the truth of $p(A|B) = n$ sure to be unaffected if we replace A by A' and/or B by B'?

We have already seen (pp. 72–3) that, when the mathematics of Pascalian probability is treated as a multi-valued logic, the logic is not truth-functional. So it is clear that propositions with the same truth-value cannot always be safely substituted for one another within a judgement of probability.

In certain other analyses of probability further restrictions on substitutivity also operate. For example, Carnap's analysis makes $p(A|B)$ depend on the ratio of the range of $A\&B$ to the range of B (§ 11). This ratio is 1 where B logically implies A (because then the range of $A\&B$ is identical with the range of B). Now consider the Carnapian representation of the case where B is a conjunction of atomic sentences (p. 76) that logically implies A, and B' differs from B only in so far as one of the atomic conjuncts in B' has a predicate that differs from the corresponding predicate in B but is co-extensive with that predicate in its application within the actual world. Under these conditions the ratio of the range of $A\&B'$ to the range of B' will not be 1, because $A\&B'$ and B' will not be true in just the same possible worlds. So $c(A|B) = 1$ will be true, but $c(A|B') = 1$ will be false. For example, though it is certain that this man is George's sibling, given that he is George's brother, it may be only probable that the man is George's sibling, given that he is George's partner, even though it is in fact the case that all and only George's brothers are his partners. Thus only those predicative expressions that are analytically equivalent can be safely substituted for one another within Carnapian c-functions. And some restriction on substitutivity, albeit a lesser one, applies also to a propensity theory, because accidentally co-extensive predicates do not attribute the same property or natural tendency. For example, there may be a strong natural tendency—equalling a probability of, say, 0.8—for persons elected to Parliament to have been educated at a university. But even if it were accidentally the case, through a surprising set of coincidences, that all and only Parliamentarians turn out to have names with eight vowels we should not suppose this feature of people's names to *depend* to any extent on their having been to a university: the probability that such a person had been to a university would be a relative frequency, not a propensity. For predicative expressions to be safely substitutable for one another within a statement of a propensity-type probability, their equivalence must be guaranteed by such laws as those of nature, logic, mathematics, or language.

Other kinds of substitution are less restricted.

For example, on a relative frequency account it obviously makes no difference to the value of a probability if we use a different expression to designate the same class. If the passengers on a particular train have return tickets if and only if they intend to return the same day, then the relative frequency of passengers with return tickets is just the same as that of passengers intending to return the same day. So on a relative frequency account co-extensive predicates—predicates satisfied by all and only the same individuals—can be substituted for one another within a judgement of probability without any risk of altering the judgement's truth-value. And the same holds good for the realist form of indifferentist account (§ 6), since the actual ratio of favourable to equally possible cases should be quite unaffected by a change in the expression used to designate the outcome of which the probability is at issue.

Even on a personalist analysis probability-judgements are by no means as resistant to substitution as personalist talk about probability's measuring strength of belief might lead one to suppose. In everyday descriptions of people's beliefs not even logically or mathematically equivalent expressions may safely be substituted for one another, let alone expressions that refer to the same individuals or predicate the same properties.[10] And the same holds good for probability-judgements if we accept a personalist analysis that does not insist on what de Finetti (p. 60) called coherence. But, where coherence is required, the restriction on substitutivity has to be discarded: the context needs to be referentially transparent. Anyone whose probability-judgements are to be taken as declarations of the lowest odds that he is prepared to accept will guard himself adequately against a Dutch book only if he treats all his ordinary probability-judgements as being open to the mutual substitution of terms that have the same reference or meaning as one another. You cannot allow yourself to lose a bet just because the person you bet with uses a different designation for the same outcome: a horse runs just as fast (like a rose smells just as sweet) under another name. The only wagers in which such substitutivity is restricted are those on the truth of propositions that are resistant to substitution even when they are not the subject of a wager: for example, certain propositions about a person's fears, hopes, desires, beliefs, or other mental states.

Important questions of substitutivity may also arise even where the two expressions that are candidates for inter-substitution do not designate the same thing. Consider a monadic or dyadic judgement about a specified individual, such as John Doe (as distinct from an explicity general judgement about 'any' person). We might say, for example, that the probability of John Doe's surviving to the age of seventy, given that he is a lorry-driver, is 0.8. Now does this statement refer to John Doe as just one individual among many others, so that if the probability holds for John Doe it must hold also for Richard Roe or for anyone else? Or does it refer to John Doe in all his singularity of circumstances (healthy exerciser, cautious eater, non-smoker, etc.), so that the probability of Richard Roe's survival to the age of seventy, given that he is a lorry-driver, may be quite different? In the former case the name 'John Doe' may be replaced by any other expression that designates a particular

---

[10] See R. Carnap, *Meaning and Necessity* (Chicago: Chicago University Press, 1947), 59–64, and W.V.O. Quine, *Word and Object* (Cambridge: Massachusetts Institute of Technology Press, 1960), 143–7.

individual, in the latter it may not. So let us use the term 'implicitly general' to describe those grammatically singular judgements of probability about a specified individual which necessarily remain true whenever expressions denoting that individual are uniformly replaced by expressions denoting any other individual within the same domain of discourse. And let us use 'implicitly singular' to describe a grammatically singular judgement of probability in which such an expression is not necessarily replaceable without affecting the judgement's truth-value. Then an indifference theory will impute implicit generality to grammatically singular judgements of probability. Also singular judgements made with the use of any of Carnap's symmetrical confirmation-functions (pp. 77–8) will be implicitly general, though singular judgements made with the use of non-symmetrical confirmation-functions will be implicitly singular. Again, a propensity theory will require grammatically singular judgements of probability to be implicitly general, in so far as the characteristic evidence for claiming the existence of a conditional propensity is an observed relative frequency. The observed ratio of As among Bs is just as good evidence for the strength of the tendency for any one particular B to be an A as it is for the strength of any other B's tendency to be an A. But a personalist theory need not require grammatically singular judgements of probability to be implicitly general unless the theory is confined to dealing with what de Finetti calls 'exchangeable' events (pp. 69–70). Certainly my belief that John Doe will survive to the age of seventy may well be stronger than my belief that Richard Roe will, and the lowest odds that I would accept on the one outcome might well be lower than the lowest that I would accept on the other, just as I might expect often to bet at different odds on different horses in the same race. So on a personalist analysis grammatically singular judgements of probability are implicitly singular also, unless otherwise stated.[11]

Yet another important logical issue concerns what is best called 'counterfactualizability'. This issue arises only in regard to those judgements of probability that are both dyadic and

---

[11] *Pace* Carnap, who claimed that 'all authors on probability$_1$, both classical and modern' must be taken to have accepted the implicit generality of grammatically singular judgements of probability: *Logical Foundations of Probability* (Chicago: Chicago University Press, 1950), 488.

implicitly or explicitly general. Such judgements typically concern the probability that an entity is *A* given that it is *B*. But does such a judgement apply even to entities that are not actually *B*, in which case it may be said to be 'counterfactualizable', or only to entities that are actually *B*, in which case it may be said to be 'non-counterfactualizable'? For example, to accept that, on the assumption that he is a forty-year-old asbestos worker, a man has a 0.8 probability of death before the age of sixty, is to accept an explicitly general conditional probability that applies not only to any person in the history of the universe who is actually a forty-year-old asbestos worker but also to any individual who is not. That is, the same judgement of probability would presumably hold good even if the number of asbestos workers were larger than it in fact is. Only thus might someone legitimately infer a reason for not going to work in a asbestos factory. But to accept a 0.6 probability, for any person picked out at random at a certain conference, that he is staying in the Hotel Excelsior is not to accept a probability that could be relied on to have held good if more people had been at the conference. Perhaps the additional participants would all have had to stay elsewhere because the Hotel Excelsior had no more unoccupied rooms. Such a probability-judgement states an accidental fact and is non-counterfactualizable, whereas the judgement about mortality among asbestos workers reflects a causal connection and is therefore counterfactualizable.

Just as some universal truths are counterfactualizable and some are not—compare 'Everyone who drinks cyanide is poisoned by it', with 'Everyone at this session is staying in the Hotel Excelsior'—so too some probability-judgements are counterfactualizable and some are not. But (in regard to probability-judgements that are both dyadic and general) a propensity analysis seems applicable only to counterfactualizable judgements. If a natural tendency exists for a certain kind of event to occur in such-and-such circumstances, it would normally still have existed even if those circumstances had occurred more often than they actually occurred. Similarly a relative frequency analysis imputes counterfactualizability where the reference-class has an infinite number of members, since any relevant convergence to a limit might be expected to maintain itself even if additional members joined the reference class. And an interval-valued relative frequency analysis (p. 52) also imputes counterfactualizability where the reference-class has an indeterminately large number of members, since the impact of any additional members might be expected to be accommodated within the specified interval. But where probability is conceived of as point-valued and the reference-class is of finite size, a relative frequency analysis does not impute counterfactualizability since in that case the probability-judgement is normally supposed just to report actual ratios of occurrence. Similarly the indifference theory does not impute counterfactualizability, because it supposes a probability-judgement to state the ratio of the number of outcome-types of a certain specified kind to the total number of mutually co-ordinate outcome-types and to say nothing about what this ratio might have been if there had been an additional co-ordinate outcome-type over and above the actual totality of them.

Thus (though the point is often unnoticed) different theories about the analysis of probability may in effect attribute different logical properties to probability-judgements. And we shall have to bear this in mind when we consider the relevance of different analyses to the various different purposes for which probability-judgements are required.

§ 13 THE APPROPRIATENESS OF DIFFERENT CONCEPTIONS OF PASCALIAN PROBABILITY TO DIFFERENT PURPOSES

The Pascalian calculus permits a wide range of variation in the logical properties of probability-judgements, which are then useful for correspondingly different purposes. For example, to judge a purely aleatory probability we require a conception of probability, like the indifference-theory's one, that makes correct judgements of probability necessary, extensional, implicitly general, and non-counterfactualizable. But where outcomes cannot be assumed to be determined by pure chance, we need probability-judgements that are contingent, extensional, implicitly general, and counterfactualizable or ones that are contingent, non-extensional, implicitly general, and counter-factualizable. There are good reasons for supposing that a variety of different conceptions of probability are operative here, rather than just a variety of different ways of measuring the same underlying parameter.

Different conceptions of Pascalian probability are suitable for different purposes, depending partly on the epistemology and partly on the logic of the judgements employing those conceptions. Indeed, by taking into account *all* the possible combinations of logical micro-features, we might conceivably obtain a greater potential diversity of probability-judgements than the catalogue (§§ 6–11) of six standard Pascalian analyses suggests. Different analyses of probability, it has already been shown (§ 12), have different implications about whether judgements of probability are necessary or contingent, sentence-related or predicate-related, extensional or non-extensional, implicitly general or implicitly singular, counterfactualizable or non-counterfactualizable. Yet the Pascalian mathematics of probability is quite neutral in regard to preferring a particular alternative on any of these five logical issues. The classical calculus admits of interpretation in any of the numerous different senses that can be generated by combining the various alternatives in the different ways that are possible. Clearly, if a probability-judgement had to be contingent, extensional, and predicate-related, for example, some kind of relative frequency interpretation would have to be accepted, while if it had to be necessary, non-extensional, and sentence-related, some kind of interpretation in terms of logical relations would be required. But there is no mathematical reason—no reason inherent in the uninterpreted calculus—to argue on such grounds in favour of any particular interpretation or semantical analysis.

Nor could one argue thus on the basis of ordinary linguistic usage or of current scientific practice. Even if in ordinary usage, or current practice, only one particular interpretation were assigned to the Pascalian calculus, it would still be possible to query whether that interpretation was the only useful one or even whether it was as useful as this or that available alternative. Moreover, what is useful for one purpose may be useless for another. It follows that the appropriate question is not 'What is the correct semantical analysis of probability-judgements?' Rather we should ask 'Which semantical analysis of probability-judgements is best suited to which kind of context?'

For example, in a context in which the probabilities being judged relate to a game that is assumed a priori to be one of pure chance, an objective idealist (p. 44) version of the indifference theory is appropriate. In specifying the nature of the game we have to postulate a domain of statutorily basic outcome-types, such as the two sides on which a presumably perfect coin can fall on any one randomly executed toss or the six sides on which a presumably perfect die can fall on any one randomly executed throw. And from that postulate the principle of indifference allows us to derive, as a necessary truth, the probability of any particular basic outcome-type or the probability of a particular compound outcome-type (such as the probability of two tosses' both landing heads). Correspondingly we can say that the establishment of these probabilities is an a priori, not an empirical task. In this context any claim to be measuring propensities of the gaming-device would appear to be misrepresenting an a priori issue as an empirical one.

So, since the probability, in this sense, of a particular outcome-type is determined by the rules that legitimate the range of basic outcome-types, it risks being affected if in our own judgements we choose to name the outcome-type in some other way than the rules do. If the rules mention a side named '5', but not a side named 'my favourite side', then the probability of throwing my favourite side is not derivable a priori from the rules and certainly cannot be equated on their authority with the probability of '5'. In short, because true judgements of probability in the relevant indifferentist sense are necessarily true, they are also non-extensional—i.e. resistant to the inter-substitution of accidentally co-extensive terms. Moreover, so long as the set-up considered continues to be one of pure chance, any unconditional evaluation for the probability of, say, a throw's being '5' will be implicitly general and apply also to the probability of a throw's being '6', and so on. But the probability of an outcome-type's being '5', given that it is nameable by an odd number, would not be the same if a more-than-six-sided die were in play. So judgements of aleatory probability are non-counterfactualizable. In sum, a purely aleatory context requires a conception of probability that satisfies an indifferentist analysis and makes correct judgements of probability necessary, non-extensional, implicitly general, and non-counterfactualizable.

Suppose, however, the game is not assumed a priori to be one of pure chance, but the question whether the game is one of pure chance is treated as an open, empirical issue, perhaps because there are reasons to think the coin or dice might be biased (although the bias may be a stable one). Clearly that issue may be put in the form: how closely does the empirically estimated probability of a particular outcome approximate to the probability of that outcome which is calculated a priori in indifferentist terms? So in order to take the issue seriously we need to operate here with another, *non*-indifferentist conception. We want to know how closely the value of the one function approaches the value of the other in regard to the same outcomes. More specifically, alongside the indifferentist conception we need here also a conception of probability that allows judgements of probability to be contingent and based on observed trials or samples, as in the calculation of life-expectancies for an annuity. These judgements must still be implicitly general, but, as they now quantify over a domain of outcomes, not of outcome-types, they would now be counter-factualizable (so far as any bias or absence of bias is stable). Such a conception fits either a relative frequency or a propensity account, depending on whether or not there is a requirement for extensionality and finitude.

Perhaps someone will be tempted to object that what is at stake here, in the issue whether the game is one of pure chance, is not the closeness with which the value of one probability-function approaches the value of another but rather the closeness with which results from one method of measuring the value of a particular probability-function approximate results from another method of measuring the value of the same function. Indeed, that would presumably be the gloss that a personalist, belief-theoretical account would wish to put on the situation. But what is this single parameter, then, that is allegedly being measured in two different ways? Clearly it is not the *actual* strength of a person's belief that is being measured in such cases: no *actual* betting behaviour is being observed (p. 64). At best a personalist might claim that what is being measured—in two different ways—is the strength which his belief *ought* to have. And then a realist could still rejoin that the propriety of a particular belief-strength must depend here, as elsewhere, on its correspondence with some objective correlate like a ratio of chances or a relative frequency, so that, if two different measurements are both correct, two different parameters are being measured.

Moreover, in yet another situation we might be dealing neither with an assumed game of pure chance nor with the accidental vagaries of a man-made gambling device, but with the physical properties of a particular example of this or that natural kind. For example, we might need to judge the probability that a neutron will decay in six minutes, where the assertion of a connection between physical property and natural kind imposes a requirement of non-extensionality. Since such a judgement will also be contingent, grammatically singular, implicitly general, and counterfactualizable, it operates with a concept of probability that satisfies a propensity analysis. Indeed, the physical tendencies of natural kinds are paradigm cases for that analysis. If you want to warn a non-smoker against the dangers of smoking, you need to be able to cite counterfactualizable probabilities. And that brings out another reason why the apparent plurality of probability-concepts cannot be reduced to a plurality of modes of measurement that are used in connection with a single probability-concept. We have to think of probability-judgements not only as conclusions that may be reached by different methods of calculation or measurement, but also as premises from which different kinds of conclusion may be drawn in accordance with differences in their logical structure. Issues about extensionality, implicit generality, counterfactualizability, and so on are crucial here. For example, the conception of probability on which we can base a warning about smoking or about working in an asbestos factory is not the same as that which relates only to accidental issues like the probability that a member of a certain conference is staying in a specified hotel (pp. 88–9).

§ 14 THE NEED TO SUPPLEMENT PASCALIAN JUDGEMENTS BY NON-PASCALIAN ONES

Various unsatisfactory proposals have been made, such as those by Hume and Laplace, for inferring the probability that a particular individual of a specified kind has a certain characteristic from evidence about the relative frequency with which individuals of that kind have the characteristic. We need here to attend to the factors affecting inferability from an implicitly general conditional probability to a singular unconditional probability. This inferabilty is a matter of degree, which Keynes called 'weight'. The weight of an argument is quite independent of its probability and has a non-Pascalian structure. There is a role for the concept of weight on more than one analysis of Pascalian probability, but weights can at best be ranked, not measured, within a particular category of judgement.

It is unnecessary, and perhaps impossible, to give a plausibly complete list of the ways in which different analyses of Pascalian probability are appropriate in different contexts. Different possible combinations of underlying logical distinctions (such as the distinctions examined in § 12) may well generate a wider spectrum of possible analyses than the six familiar ones that were discussed in §§ 6–11. But all that is required here is to have shown (in § 13) how different analyses, out of those discussed in §§ 6–11, may be appropriate in different contexts: the need for pluralism is deeply rooted. After all, we think of quantities of apples as volumes for the purpose of storage, as weights for the purpose of cooking, or as numbers for the purpose of distribution among children, and we evaluate people differently if we are considering them as athletes, as philosophers, or as friends. Why should we not also conceive probabilities differently for different purposes? Just as my harvest of apples may be smaller than yours by one criterion and larger by another, so too the probability of this coin's falling heads on the next two tosses may be 0.25 as a calculation in a game of chance but 0.5 as a measure of the tosser's subjective belief.

It will also be worth while enquiring whether there are even some contexts of probabilistic reasoning to which no analysis of probability is appropriate that imputes a Pascalian structure. We have seen already (pp. 17–21) that some logically possible ways of assessing evidentially warranted credibility have a non-Pascalian structure. They do not conform to an additive principle for negation. Or they do not conform to a multiplicative principle for conjunction. So the question arises whether those logically possible ways of assessing credibility have any real value. For, though they certainly occur sometimes in ordinary speech, it does not follow from this that their use is necessary or valuable for any important purposes.

It turns out that there is at least one important use for a non-Pascalian criterion of evidential strength—Keynes's concept of 'weight'—that is ancillary to the use of any Pascalian judgement for one particular type of purpose. You cannot make the Pascalian judgement without raising the non-Pascalian issue. So in this context the argument for a non-Pascalian analysis is not aimed at recommending the use of a non-Pascalian judgement in place of a Pascalian one in certain inferences but at elucidating what further kind of evaluation needs to be made when we do use a Pascalian judgement in such an inference. We shall come later (§§ 20–26) to consider the case for using a non-Pascalian conception of probability *in place of* a Pascalian one in certain contexts. And that rather bolder enterprise may seem less shocking if we first consider the use of a non-Pascalian conception *in alliance with* a Pascalian one.

Consider first some of the difficulties that arise where the probability that a particular individual of a specified kind has a certain characteristic is to be judged on the basis of evidence about the relative frequency with which individuals of that kind have the characteristic.

One of the earliest ideas about this—discussed by Hume, for example[12]—is the so-called 'straight rule'.[13] Where the evidence is that in an observed sample of Bs the relative frequency of As is r, the straight rule authorizes a conclusion that, on the evidence, the probability of the next B's being A is also r. If 19 out of the previous 20 ships to put to sea have returned safely, there is according to the straight rule a $\frac{19}{20}$ probability on that evidence that the next ship will do so also.

But there are two strong objections to allowing any general validity for this rule. The first is that it attaches no importance to the absolute size of the evidential sample, so that an observed relative frequency of, say, $\frac{19}{20}$ in a sample of 20 individuals justifies a predictive probability of $\frac{19}{20}$ just as much as does an observed relative frequency of $\frac{19}{20}$ in a sample of 2,000 individuals. And the second objection to the straight rule is that it attaches no importance to the representativeness of the evidential sample, so that an observed relative frequency of, say, $\frac{19}{20}$

---

[12] D. Hume, *A Treatise of Human Nature*, ed. L.A. Selby-Bigge (Oxford: Clarendon Press, 1888), 134 ff.: see § 4 above.

[13] The name is due to Carnap, *Logical Foundations of Probability*, p. 227.

in a sample of ships that were all in sound condition can apparently provide evidence for a prediction about a ship that, as it turns out, has a rotten hull. These two objections are particularly strong where the observed relative frequency is 1 and the straight rule, by therefore authorizing a prediction with probability 1, makes no allowance for the uncertainty of the future or the risk of error, even when the evidence consists of a very small and unrepresentative sample.

Laplace's 'rule of succession'[14] seems at first sight to be much more suitable. According to this rule, where E reports evidence that in a sample of n Bs the number of As is m, we may infer that, on the evidence E, the probability of the next B's being A is

$$\frac{m + 1}{n + 2}.$$

Hence, even when m/n—the relative frequency of As among the Bs—is equal to 1, the probability of the prediction is still less than 1. And this probability will also then be sensitive to the absolute size of the sample and approach asymptotically to 1 as the size of the sample increases without limit. Thus the rule of succession seems to be an intuitively plausible way of grading the importance of sample-size in relation to certainty of prediction by enumerative induction, where the evidence is uniformly favourable.

But, although it is an improvement on the straight rule in this respect, the rule of succession attaches no more importance than the straight rule does to the representativeness of the sample. Even a very large sample may in practice be heavily biased. And the rule of succession generates some obvious paradoxes when applied to empirical issues. Thus it implies that observably rare events are less rare than, rather than as rare as or rarer than, they are observed to be. For example, if only 1 out of 99 ships has already come to grief the rule of succession tells us that on this evidence, the probability that the next ship to sail will come to grief is $\frac{2}{101}$. Again, if there is no evidence, we have $m = n = 0$. So according to the rule of succession there is then a probability of $\frac{1}{2}$

---

[14] Laplace, *A Philosophical Essay on Probabilities*, p. 19. The rule is discussed by, among others, J. Venn, *The Logic of Chance*, 2nd edn. (London: Macmillan 1876) 171–83, and J.M. Keynes, *A Treatise on Probability* (London: Macmillan, 1921), 372–83.

that the next B will be A. But, since this probability derives from the absence of any evidence, and holds good whatever A and B are, it can hardly constitute an empirically learned fact about the actual world. Indeed there is analogous trouble even when evidence is not entirely missing. An inherent fault in the rule of succession is that it gives implausibly precise results on the basis of very small samples.

The rule of succession is therefore at best applicable only where we are reasoning about a supposedly chance mechanism. And, even where the rule of succession is applied to such a supposedly chance mechanism, there must not be more than two possible outcomes for any one trial of the mechanism. Otherwise contradictions may result. For example, suppose that an urn contains only white, black, and yellow balls, and that we draw first a white ball from it, next a black one, and next a yellow one—replacing each ball after it has been drawn. The probability that the fourth ball to be drawn will be white is, according to the rule of succession,

$$\frac{1 + 1}{3 + 2} \quad \text{or} \quad \frac{2}{5}.$$

By parity of reasoning this is also the probability for the fourth drawing to be black, and the probability for the fourth drawing to be yellow. But such a set of probabilities contravenes the Pascalian principle of additivity. According to that principle the probabilities of the three possible outcomes should sum to 1, and in fact they sum to $\frac{6}{5}$.

Moreover, Laplace's rule of succession turns out not even to be a necessary consequence of Pascalian axioms. Rather the probability-function embodying it is just a special case of c^*, which itself is just one out of the infinitely many different c-functions—all conforming to Pascalian axioms—that can be based, as Carnap showed (§ 11), on a choice of measure for logical range.[15] Even where the rule of succession is applicable it carries no greater inherent authority than does any of the other

---

[15] See R. Carnap, *Logical Foundations of Probability*, pp. 227-8; A, Pap, *An Introduction to the Philosophy of Science* (London: Eyre and Spottiswoode, 1963), 201-2; and I. Niiniluoto, 'Inductive Logic as a Methodological Research Programme', in M.L.D. Chiara *et al.*, *Logic in the 20th Century* (special vol. of *Scientia*; Milan, 1983), 83.

functions that are co-ordinate with it as a priori measures of logical probability.

How are we to do better than this?

Let us assume that the evidence about the relative frequency in the sample grounds a corresponding judgement of probability for the whole population concerned. This judgement can be understood either in terms of a relative frequency analysis or in terms of a propensity one. The problem is then how we may determine our empirically based entitlement to infer from that judgement and any other relevant premisses to a probabilistic conclusion about a particular individual. If, for example, our premiss is that the general probability of a ship's returning safely is $\frac{19}{20}$, under what circumstances is it safe to infer that the probability of the next ship's returning safely is $\frac{19}{20}$? The key to the solution of the problem lies in distinguishing the assessment of this inference's credibility from the assessment of the premissed general probability—a distinction that is excluded by the way in which the straight rule and the rule of succession approach the problem.

Let us consider an example in detail. Suppose that, on the basis of a randomly selected sample, the estimated probability that a person will survive to the age of sixty-five, on the evidence that he is a lorry-driver, is 0.8. No doubt the worth of the estimate may be rated by some approved statistical parameter, such as a Neymanian coefficient of confidence, that depends on the size of the sample (pp. 118–19). But the judgement itself is an explicitly general judgement of conditional probability, in the sense that it does not assert anything about a particular person. From it we can derive its instantiation for a particular person, say, Smith, only in the form of an implicitly general judgement—that is, only on the assumption that our reference to Smith does not add to or subtract from the evidence on which the probability is conditional. Now, on the unconditional issue no such assumption is possible. If we want to infer Smith's *unconditional* survival prospects—that is, not the probability that he will survive to sixty-five on the evidence known about him, but just the probability that he will survive to sixty-five—we cannot avoid the need to allow for the fact that he, Smith, may be specially circumstanced in some relevant way: lorry-driving may be his work, but hang-gliding may be his hobby. The statement of the unconditional probability is implicitly singular, not implicitly general. Survival to the age of sixty-five may be quite common among lorry-drivers in general but much rarer among hang-gliding lorry-drivers. So inferability to the estimate that the unconditional probability of Smith's surviving to sixty-five is 0.8 must depend on how big a spread of the relevant facts about Smith is included in the premises along with the general judgement of probability that pertains to it. And this is true however large the size of the sample on which the estimate is based.

Schematically we can write the propositional function or predicate-schema Hx here for anyone's surviving to the age of sixty-five, Ex for anyone's being a lorry-driver and a hang-glider and . . ., Hs for Smith's surviving to the age of sixty-five, and Es for Smith's being a lorry-driver and a hang-glider and . . . Then we can say that, if the premises are the estimated evaluation $p(Hx|Ex) = n$ and the observed fact Es, the derivability of a correspondingly estimated evaluation $p(Hs) = n$ depends upon how big a spread of the relevant facts is predicated by E. Indeed, it is just because that derivability varies in this way that (as we have already seen—p. 20 and pp. 60–1) we cannot identify statements of conditional probability like $p(A|B) = n$ with conditionalized statements of probability like 'If B, then $p(A) = n$' that permit inferences of uniform strength, by *modus ponendo ponens*, from B to $p(A) = n$.

Note too, by the way, that $p(Hs)$ need not equal $p(Hx)$ here, since $p(Hx)$ is explicitly general and is just the general probability of a person's surviving to the age of sixty-five, while $p(Hs)$ is the implicitly singular probability that Smith, in all his special circumstances, will do this. So we cannot use Bayes's theorem about the relation between monadic and dyadic probabilities (see p. 23) to help the derivation. That theorem relates $p(Hx|Ex)$ to $p(Hx)$, not to $p(Hs)$. Similarly, the term 'statistical syllogism', which is sometimes used to describe such an inference from $p(Hx|Ex) = n$ and Es to $p(Hs) = n$, is peculiarly inappropriate for that purpose, because the kind of probability talked about in the major premiss differs from the kind of probability talked about in the conclusion (since the former is explicitly general and the latter is implicitly singular).

Philosophers sometimes invoke here Carnap's requirement of

total evidence. For a conditional probability-judgement to be applied as the major premiss of a prediction or explanation of an individual fact, they say, it must be based on all the available evidence that is relevant to the conclusion. Or, if they prefer a relative-frequency theory of probability to a logical-relation one, they may invoke Hempel's requirement of maximal specificity for the reference class or Salmon's requirement that the reference class be the broadest homogeneous class of which the individual concerned is a member.[16] But in practice such requirements can rarely, if ever, be satisfied. Even to know just the *available* evidence (physical, meteorological, geological, astrophysical, epidemiological, economic, socio–political, etc.) bearing on a person's survival to sixty-five one would have to work away indefinitely, since what is not learned today might, with sufficient effort, be learned tomorrow. And almost certainly, if one were thinking in terms of relative frequencies, one would soon be reduced to a reference-class of one member—the person himself—so that no statistical data could be compiled. Accordingly inferability here is normally a matter of degree, not of all or nothing. What is important in practice is for the evidence to have as big a spread as is permitted by the methodology of estimation, by pertinent economic constraints, by the current state of relevant scientific knowledge, by the nature of the subject-matter, and by any other limits to enquiry. It follows that at least comparative judgements of evidential spread have to be made, and it may be worth while investigating whether different quantities of evidential spread can also be ranked or measured. Even where some theory about economic rationality assumes perfectly informed agents and therefore treats all judgements of probability as being on the totality of possible evidence, we still need to be able to evaluate the less perfect states that exist in real life in order to make due allowances in applying the theory to actual situations. In the real world people are occupied with what is better and what is worse, not with what is perfect. But obviously important questions will arise about the structure of those judgements that assess

---

[16] Carnap, *Logical Foundations of Probability*, p. 211; C.G. Hempel, *Aspects of Scientific Explanation and Other Essays in the Philosophy of Science* (New York: The Free Press, 1965), 397; and W.C. Salmon, *The Foundations of Scientific Inference* (Pittsburgh: University of Pittsburgh Press, 1966), 91.

evidential spread. In particular we need to ask: how are those judgements evaluated and do they themselves have a Pascalian structure?

Keynes was the first to broach this issue seriously, but only in a rather tentative and guarded way.[17] He held a logical relation theory of probability (as remarked in § 11) and treated the probability of *A* on *B* as a property of the argument from *B* to *A*. The probability of the argument depends for its value, he thought, on the balance between the favourableness and unfavourableness of the evidence that *B* states in relation to *A*. But he considered that there may be another respect in which some kind of quantitative comparison between arguments is possible.

He wrote:

This comparison turns upon a balance, not between the favourable and the unfavourable evidence, but between the *absolute* amounts of relevant knowledge and relevant ignorance. As the relevant evidence at our disposal increases, the magnitude of the probability of the argument may either decrease or increase, according as the new knowledge strengthens the unfavourable or the favourable evidence; but *something* seems to have increased in either case,—we have a more substantial basis upon which to rest our conclusion.[18]

Keynes gave a name to this basis by saying that an accession of relevant evidence increases what he called the 'weight' of an argument. Thus the weight of an argument is independent of the correctness or incorrectness with which such-or-such a probability is assigned to the argument. And it is also not necessarily determined by the probable error of the argument's conclusion (where that conclusion assigns a value to a magnitude). So weight does not depend on mere numbers of evidential instances. Keynes remarked that, metaphorically, the weight of the argument from *B* to *A* measures the *sum* of the favourable and unfavourable evidence that *B* states for *A*, and the probability measures the *difference*. But he did not suggest any method by which weight might be measured and in fact admitted that often one cannot even compare the weights of different arguments. He thought that, 'in deciding on a course of action, it seems plausible to suppose that we ought to take

[17] J.M. Keynes, *A Treatise on Probability*, pp. 71–8.
[18] Ibid. 71.

account of the weight as well as the probability of different expectations'. But he found it difficult to think of any clear example of this, and he did not feel sure that the theory of evidential weight has much practical significance.

Because Keynes held that probability should be thought of as a logical relation (and because he apparently had no conception of argument, or deducibility, from zero premisses), he could hardly allow a place for judgements of unconditional probability other than as mere ellipses of 'ordinary speech'.[19] *A fortiori* he could hardly appreciate the existence of the problem of how to grade our entitlement to detach an unconditional probability from a conditional one. It is scarcely surprising, therefore, that Keynes admitted to doubting whether the theory of weight had any practical significance, since by his very treatment of probability as a function of ordered pairs of propositions he had cut himself off from the possibility of articulating the nature of this significance.

But Keynes was right to insist that the weight and the probability of an argument are independent of one another. Though both are properties of ordered pairs of propositions (if we adopt a logical-relation account of probability), we can have arguments where both weight and probability are high, arguments where both are low, and arguments in which one of the two is high and the other low. We can assess the weight of an argument without knowing the value of its probability, and we can assess its probability without knowing its weight. Moreover, we can assess the weight of an argument without knowing the size of the sample from which its probability has been estimated; and we can grade that estimate by some appropriate statistical criterion (such as a Neymanian coefficient of confidence: pp. 118–19) without knowing the argument's weight.

I have been assuming here that, when talking about weight, what we are interested in is the degree of derivability of an implicitly singular monadic probability judgement, such as the derivability of $p(Hs) = n$ from premisses $p(Hx|Ex) = n$ and Es. If, instead, what is to have its degree of acceptability evaluated on the evidence is the statement Hs itself, and if 'weight' is the name given to this degree of acceptability, weight will not then be

[19] Ibid. 7.

altogether independent of the probability stated in the explicitly general judgement $p(Hx|Ex) = n$. Indeed, under those conditions weight will not measure the absolute amount of relevant evidence stated by Es, but rather the extent to which the spread of evidence available is sufficient to justify accepting Hs on the ground that its probability on that evidence is sufficiently higher than that of any rival hypothesis. And Levi[20] accuses Keynes of begging the question because, according to Keynes, weight does measure the absolute amount of relevant evidence. But there is nothing question-begging in Keynes's discussion of the subject. He and Levi are just using the same term to talk about different parameters.

It is also worth nothing that judgements of weight have a different logical structure from judgements of Pascalian probability. This may be shown both in regard to negation and also in regard to conjunction.

Consider negation first. Because Pascalian probability is additive, $p(Hx|Ex) = n$ is necessarily equivalent to $p(\text{not-}Hx|Ex) = 1 - n$ and $p(Hs) = n$ is necessarily equivalent to $p(\text{not-}Hs) = 1 - n$. From this it follows that the derivability of $p(\text{not-}Hs) = 1 - n$ from premises $p(\text{not-}Hx|Ex) = 1 - n$ and Es must be just the same as the derivability of $p(Hs) = n$ from premises $p(Hx|Ex) = n$ and Es, even when both derivabilities are very low, or very high, and therefore not mutually complementary. Correspondingly the weights of the arguments from Es to Hs and from Es to not-Hs must be reckoned the same. Hence the additivity of Pascalian probability in effect ensures the non-additivity of weight. Weight is therefore a non-Pascalian parameter of evidential strength. Indeed, on Keynes's definition, though not on Levi's (see above), one can evaluate the weight of the argument from Es to Hs without coming to any implicit conclusion whether, on balance, Es favours Hs or not-Hs. Keynesian weight is logically independent of Pascalian probability.

Again, if the only evidence we have about Smith is that he is a twenty-five year-old lorry-driver, the number of relevant facts that we know about him is the same whether we are considering the probability that he will survive to the age of sixty-five or the

[20] I. Levi, *Gambling with Truth* (New York: Knopf, 1967), 142.

probability that he will marry before the age of thirty or the probability of the conjunctive prediction that he will do both. And, even if we also know that Smith is engaged (which is relevant to his date of marriage but scarcely relevant to his survival to the age of sixty-five), the weight of evidence for the conjunctive conclusion is just as strong as, but no stronger than, the weight of evidence for the less weightily supported conjunct. So the *weight* of an argument for a conjunctive conclusion need not normally be less than the weight of the least weighty argument for one of its conjuncts, even though the *probability* of the argument for the conjunction—because of the standard multiplicative principle for conjunction (§ 3)—is normally less than the probability of the argument for either conjunct.

Nor is the need to assess weight alongside Pascalian probability confined to those probabilities that are conceived of as logical relations. Keynes himself recognized that, if instead we think of a probability as the frequency with which members of one specified class are also members of another, the weight of such a relative frequency can be increased by a relevant partitioning of its reference class. The relative frequency of survivors to the age of sixty-five among those lorry-drivers who are also hang-gliders has a greater weight than their relative frequency among lorry-drivers in general, even though the relative frequency itself is lower. Of course, because the relative frequency analysis of probability cannot (see pp. 48–9) apply to implicitly or explicitly singular judgements, we must again envisage that the conception of probability used in the conclusion about Smith's survival prospects will differ from the conception of probability used in the major premiss on which the derivation of that conclusion is based. But the strength of our entitlement to make the derivation will still depend on the relevant weight, though here—in the context of a major premiss about a relative frequency—weight has to be regarded, like probability, as a property of an ordered pair of classes rather than as a property of an ordered pair of propositions.

Again, assessments of weight also have a function to perform in association with personalist conceptions of probability. Coherence alone is an insufficient condition for the rationality of a betting-system. Even if no one may make a Dutch book against you (see p. 60), your bets may still be irrational because you have taken too little of the available information into account. Perhaps you should have checked at least on how your favourite horse performed previously on a race-track as muddy as today's. And the Bayesian procedure of conditionalization (pp. 68–9) is a personalist's strategy for increasing weight. As the Bayesian takes into account more and more beliefs about relevant items of evidence, his probabilistically graded strength of belief in a certain hypothesis may fluctuate. It may go down when some items are taken into account and up when others are. But, whatever its level at the later of two successive stages, that level will be the result of more considerations than was the level at the earlier stage. So the weight of the belief, on the accumulated evidence, will be greater. Of course, if all relevant evidence could always be identified and exploited, every exercise of Bayesian method could be pushed through to completion. But in practice, as already remarked, the requirement of total evidence is a rather utopian ideal, and there is, therefore, undeniable room for comparisons of weight to be associated with declarations of personal probability.

Nor is there any difficulty in seeing how assessments of weight may also be associated with judgements of propensity-type Pascalian probabilities, since these may be either singular or general. But, where an indifference-type analysis is appropriate, assessments of weight have no role to play. Once the alternative outcomes in a supposed game of chance have been specified, any a priori calculations that ensue depend on just that specification alone. Weight of evidence comes into the picture only if we try to determine the probabilities of those outcomes empirically. And so, because writers about probability have so often derived their primary stimulus to reflection from a priori problems about aleatory models, it is scarcely surprising that many of those writers have found it easy to overlook the issues that arise about weight. Similarly, an excessive concentration on examples involving given, not derived, monadic probabilities has tended to blind decision-theorists to the fact that in deliberating under uncertainty we often need to assess weights as well as probabilities.[21]

But how exactly is weight to be assessed? As we have seen it is

[21] See e.g. R.C. Jeffrey, *The Logic of Decision* (New York: McGraw-Hill, 1965).

independent of the size of the sample from which a probability is estimated. So how can it be gauged?

It cannot be right to say, though it is often said, that, because a personalist analysis ties probability to strength of belief, such an analysis allows a probability judgement to reflect awareness of the weight of the evidence as well as awareness of the degree to which that evidence tends in a specified direction. For, as you learn more about a particular horse, say, your personal odds on its winning the race may either shorten or lengthen. Personal odds are a poor indicator of felt weight if, with the same increase of weight, they can become either shorter or longer.

It is sometimes suggested instead that, if the probability that a person assigns to his belief on given evidence may be quantified in terms of the lowest odds at which, given the evidence, he would accept a bet on the truth of his belief, then the weight of the given evidence in relation to that belief may be taken to be reflected in the amount that he is prepared to bet. A person might be expected to put a larger sum at risk when there is more evidence from which to estimate appropriate odds. But other considerations also may affect our attitude towards the size of a bet. Suppose that there is a great deal of evidence, and that this evidence suggests the appropriateness of very long odds. Would you really be willing to risk losing just as large a part of your fortune then as you would risk losing if the odds, on the same amount of evidence, were much shorter?

It is also sometimes suggested that the weight of a probability-judgement may be taken to vary inversely with the mathematical expectation of gain from the acquisition of further relevant evidence. But this suggestion is open to at least two cogent objections. First, one may well need to estimate the weight of already acquired evidence independently of the expectation of gain from the acquisition of further evidence, in order to be able to compare the greater utility of having an evidentially even weightier answer to one question than of having it to another. It may be much more important to have such an answer to the question 'What is the probability that Smith will survive to the age of seventy?' than to the question 'What is the probability that Smith's cat will survive to the age of fifteen?' Secondly, what are we to say when, for example, a vital eye-witness has died without ever disclosing what he saw, or when no eye-witness at all was present? The expectation of any kind of gain from further research in that direction may then be zero, but the weight of evidence about what actually happened would not normally be thought to have been increased because of the missing data. This is because the weight of the evidence already obtained is being assessed by comparison with some supposed list of relevant kinds of evidential fact, not of actually discoverable relevant fact. So, even if we had all the available evidence, our argument might still not have maximal weight. Sometimes, for example, the prosecution cannot find enough evidence to prove guilt beyond reasonable doubt, even though someone must undoubtedly have committed the crime in question.

Nor will it do to equate superiority in weight with superiority in Pascalian probabilistic relevance. If $p(A|B_1\&B_2)$ is not equal to $p(A|B_1)$, then B_2 is said to be relevant to A, given B_1; and, if the difference between $p(A|B_1\&B_2)$ and $p(A|B_1)$ is greater than that between $p(A|B_1\&B_3)$ and $p(A|B_1)$, then B_2 may be said to be more relevant than B_3 to A, given B_1. For example, in assessing the probability of a thirty-year-old's survival to the age of seventy, his previous medical history may be more relevant than his sex. But, when a relevant premiss is thus added to the evidence on which a probability is assessed, the extent of increase in weight does not depend for its size on the extent of the new premiss's relevance, as can easily be shown. Suppose a set of evidential items B_1, B_2, . . . B_{100} in regard to a hypothesized conclusion A. Suppose too that quite a lot of these items, taken on their own, ground low probabilities in favour of A, quite a lot ground high probabilities, and quite a lot ground intermediate probabilities at various levels. One way of ordering these items would be to begin with those highly in favour of A, then proceed with those slightly less in favour, and so on down, ending up with those highly in favour of not-A. In such a carefully graduated order the extent of the relevance of each new piece of evidence after the first, would normally tend to be small. So if the weight of the probability were to be affected by the extent of the relevance of each incremental piece of evidence, the additional effect on the overall weight would be minimal. But, if instead the evidential premisses were ordered so as to alternate as violently as possible between favourable and unfavourable items, the overall effect on the weight would be very different, if extent of relevance was allowed to affect the issue at each incremental step. Hence, if we allow the extent of an added premiss's relevance to affect the cumulative weight of an argument, we could end up with different weights for arguments to the same conclusion from logically equivalent conjunctions of premisses, just because we calculated these weights on the basis of different orderings for the conjoined premisses. Of course, the order in which different items of evidence are stated may have a different psychological effect on some people. But it ought not to affect the logical cogency of the evidential statement as a whole. So the weight added by a new piece of evidence is not to be measured by the magnitude of its relevance.

Indeed, it looks as though weight cannot be *measured* at all, but only compared or, at best, ranked within a fairly narrow field of comparison. Roughly, we need to identify, for a particular category of hypothesis, those families of mutually exclusive predicates that contain at least one predicate the ascription of which is relevant to at least one hypothesis within the category, in the way that, for example, the predicate 'has already had a coronary incident' is relevant to any hypothesis about thirty-year-old person's expectation of survival to the age of seventy. We need then to order those families of predicates, perhaps exploiting for the purpose any differences in extent of relevance,[22] And where we concern ourselves only with arguments from premisses that contain just predicates belonging to the first family, or just those predicates plus predicates belonging to the second family, or just predicates from each of the first three families, we shall be able to rank the weight of the argument in accordance with the number of different predicate-families instantiated in the premisses.

So it seems that the Keynesian weight (i.e. evidential spread) of an argument is a (sometimes rankable) characteristic that has an important function to perform in our reasonings about Pascalian probability but has a logical structure that defies any attempt to map it on to the Pascalian calculus.

§ 15 HOW ARE DIFFERENT CONCEPTIONS OF PROBABILITY POSSIBLE?

Both realist and idealist interpretations are possible for non-Pascalian principles of probability. Different types of pro-

---

[22] See L. Jonathan Cohen, 'Twelve Questions about Keynes's Concept of Weight', *British Journal for the Philosophy of Science*, 37 (1985), 263–78, for further details. For a claim that the weight of a probability may be equated with its degree of counterfactualizability see L. Jonathan Cohen, *The Dialogue of Reason* (Oxford: Clarendon Press, 1986), 182.

bability, whether Pascalian or non-Pascalian, are generated by differences within the gradation of inferability that are analogous to differences between different systems of deducibility, as when we compare the additivity issue in the theory of probability with the completeness issue in the theory of deductive systems.

In § 14 I showed how we need a certain type of non-Pascalian assessment of the strength of the evidence for or against a specified proposition in order to complement one use to which Pascalian conditional probabilities are often put—namely, use as premisses for the derivation of the corresponding singular and unconditional probabilities. We need this type of non-Pascalian assessment in order to deal with that dimension of credibility which rests on the weight of the evidence as distinct from that which rests on the extent to which the evidence is favourable or unfavourable. Note, however, that we have so far been considering evaluations of weight only in association with evaluations of Pascalian probability. For a weight-dependent evaluation of evidential support that was operative on its own we should need to regard the weight of one proposition, B, for another, A, as greater than zero only where B is on balance in favour of A: $p(A|B)$ would have to be greater than 0.5 but it would not matter by how much. We should thus be interested only in directed weight—weight that on balance pushes our conclusion in a specified direction—and such a weight vector would obviously have a different negation principle from pure weight. If B states any positive weight of evidence for A, it will now state none for not-A. But the conjunction principle for directed weight will be the same as that already determined for pure weight (§ 14).

Now, if either directed or undirected weight is a useful mode of non-Pascalian assessment, there is no reason to suppose that its underlying, non-Pascalian structure may not be shared by other modes of assessment also. That is to say, just as there are various probabilistically useful interpretations of the Pascalian calculus of chance, so too there may be various useful interpretations of at least one non-Pascalian calculus. Indeed, it is already clear (§ 9) that, by following a non-additive principle for negation, judgements of propensity can take on a non-Pascalian logic instead of a Pascalian one, so that we have here a realist version of non-additive probability alongside the idealist version that is constituted by judgements of directed Keynesian weight. Correspondingly, alongside the non-multiplicative conjunction principle for Keynesian weight (§ 14), we have standard systems of many-valued logic in which the truth-value of a conjunction is no lower than the lowest truth-value of a conjunct[23]—rather than being determined by a multiplicative principle as in Reichenbach's Pascalian system. Of course, I have not yet proposed axioms for a suitable non-Pascalian calculus (see § 21 below). And we should not expect that every useful interpretation of the Pascalian calculus is matched by a useful interpretation of such a non-Pascalian one. Neither the indifference analysis nor the relative frequency analysis are likely to have useful non-Pascalian counterparts, because they depend essentially on the existence of appropriate given ratios. But from what has already been said it is clear that we may legitimately expect such counterparts for Pascalian analyses in terms of propensities, logically characterizable relations, multiple truth-values, or belief-strengths.

Nor should anyone be surprised that there are so many different types of Pascalian probability-judgement, if he is prepared to think of probability as a gradation—whether by subjective or objective criteria—of inferability. For, if we consider the situation where inferability is not a matter of degree, but of all or nothing, a wide variety of differences is familiar. There are systems of deductive inferability that claim to depend on necessary truths, such as laws of logic, and systems that claim to depend on contingent truths such as supposed laws of nature. There are logics of terms and logics of propositions. There are systems that are open to the substitutivity of co-extensive predicates; and systems that are not. There are systems that allow no inferences about an individual that cannot be made also about any other individual, and systems that do not. There are systems that are counterfactualizable, in the sense that they license inferences irrespective of the premises' truth-values, and systems that are not counterfactualizable, in the sense that they license inferences only from true premises. Accordingly, on the assumption that judgements of probability grade inferability, we must expect that these judgements will exhibit a corresponding diversity. And we have, indeed, already

---

[23] See N. Rescher, *Many-valued Logic* (New York: McGraw-Hill, 1969), 131.

found (in § 12) that just such a diversity exists and forms the basis for the widely differing analyses of probability that philosophers have sometimes produced. Probability-judgements may be either necessary or contingent. Probability may be viewed as a function either of terms or of propositions. Statements of probability may be either extensional or non-extensional. They may be either general or singular, and either counterfactualizable or non-counterfactualizable. Differing analyses of probability are made possible by the variety of possible combinations of such options that they can exploit. So all this pluralism may be viewed as operating within the framework that is constituted by the unifying conception of probability as a gradation of inferability.

Moreover, that framework is capable of generating non-Pascalian options as well as Pascalian ones. Consider again the situation where inferability is not a matter of degree, but of all or nothing. Then, assuming that negation is always expressable in such a deductive system, one can distinguish between systems of inferability that are complete and systems that are incomplete. A system is complete, in the relevant sense, just so long as any sentence of the system is inferable from the postulates of the system if and only if its negation is not inferable. Now, if probability is to be conceived as degree of inferability, the deductive inferability of A from B is that limiting case of probability where $p(A|B) = 1$ and the non-inferability of not-A from B is stated correspondingly as $p(\text{not-}A|B) = 0$. So, if $p(A|B) = 1$ if and only if $p(\text{not-}A|B) = 0$, it looks as though we are dealing with a complete system and that we may expect that in general the probability or inferability of A, given B will vary inversely with the probability or inferability of not-A, given B. What emerges is thus the standard Pascalian principle for negation: $p(A|B) = 1 - p(\text{not-}A|B)$. Accordingly completeness as a property of certain deductive systems, may be viewed as a limiting case of probabilistic additivity (or complementationality), and probabilistic additivity (or complementationality) may be viewed as a generalization of completeness. And it is mathematically provable that if degrees of inferability are to be measured over a Boolean domain, with a complementational principle for negation, all the other principles of the Pascalian calculus must

also be obeyed.[24] In a consistent but incomplete deductive
system, however, there must be at least one sentence such that
neither it nor its negation is inferable. That is to say, when inferability is described in terms of probability, there must be an A
and B such that both $p(A|B) = 0$ and also $p(\text{not-}A|B) = 0$
because neither A nor not-A is inferable. It follows that any
generalization of inferability in an incomplete system will have
a non-Pascalian structure, in virtue of excluding an additive,
i.e. complementational, principle for negation. Indeed, the
additivity issue is about as important for differentiating between
Pascalian and non-Pascalian probabilities, as the parallel lines
issue is for differentiating between Euclidean and non-
Euclidean spaces.[25]

No doubt many other concepts of probability are also
possible. The aim of the present chapter has not been to
construct an exhaustive semantic and syntactic taxonomy for
such concepts, let alone an epistemological taxonomy for their
applications (empirical/a priori, idealist/realist, on balance of
evidence/on amount of evidence, etc.). The aim here has been
merely to illustrate the nature of the pluralism that seems to be
justified in our philosophy of probability, to argue that this
pluralism is quite compatible with accepting that there are
special roles for particular concepts of probability in particular
contexts, and to elucidate why the existence of such a rich
plurality of probability-concepts is only to be expected. So, if we
now revert to the earlier problem about the gradation of ampliative induction, we can approach it with a relatively open mind.
There is no single concept of probability that we can know in
advance must somehow be fundamental to the evaluation of
inductive reasoning. Rather, we shall have to investigate quite a
variety of concepts, both Pascalian and non-Pascalian, in regard
to their suitability for this particular purpose.

Note, however, that in investigating which Pascalian or
non-Pascalian concepts of probability are most suitable for this

---

[24] R. T. Cox, *The Algebra of Probable Inference* (Baltimore: Johns Hopkins Press, 1961),
4–5, and J. R. Lucas, *The Concept of Probability* (Oxford: Clarendon Press, 1970), 33 ff.

[25] For a study of some early work on non-additive probability see G. Shafer, 'Non-
Additive Probabilities in the Work of Bernoulli and Lambert', *Archive for the History of
Exact Sciences*, 19 (1978), 309–70.

or that purpose we leave on one side any psychological questions about which concepts are actually used by people in this or that context of reasoning. Philosophy here, as elsewhere, pursues a normative rather than a descriptive end. During the last twenty years experimental psychologists have conducted a lot of research into the ways in which people without any relevent training measure or compare probabilities. But unfortunately this research has sometimes been marred by an a priori assumption, on the part of the investigators, that use of the term 'probability' (and its equivalents in other languages) admits of only one syntax and only one semantics. By imputing their own favoured interpretation to every use of the term the investigators have then put themselves in a position to claim the existence of systematic, non-accidental errors in the judgements of probability that are made by the subjects of their experiments. But, when due regard is paid to the variety of available conceptions of probability that may be used in appropriate contexts, the case for supposing the existence of such errors seems much less well supported. Many of the subjects may have been trying to answer different questions from those that the investigators took themselves to be asking. If one quantity of apples is larger than another by weight, a person who says that it is smaller has not necessarily made a mistake if he is comparing the two quantities by number or by volume rather than by weight.[26] So too in regard to probabilities.

[26] Relevant references are given in n. 32 to ch. II.

IV

The Pascalian Gradation of Ampliative Induction

Though an indifferentist conception of probability may be used to grade some kinds of generalization, it is inapplicable to ampliative induction in science. Nor can we measure the latter in terms of the relative frequency with which a hypothesis that is supported by such-or-such evidence turns out to be true. And if we try to replace the generalization that all *A*s are *B*s by the assertion of a very high propensity-type probability of *A*, given *B* (where estimates of this probability can be graded by standard statistical procedures), we find that the applicability of the generalization to an individual case has to be underwritten by a judgement of Keynesian weight, which introduces a non-Pascalian element into the situation.

We have seen elsewhere (§ 13) how different conceptions of Pascalian probability may be appropriate for different kinds of task, and also (§ 14) how for at least one purpose a non-Pascalian conception is indispensable. Clearly we need some system of gradation for ampliative induction, so as to be able to assess the extent to which a proposed generalization about all members of a certain class is supported by this or that body of evidence about some of its members. But is that need best served by a Pascalian or a non-Pascalian system? The present chapter will explore various Pascalian options and evaluate their viability. And it will begin with what were earlier (§ 5) called 'realist' interpretations of the Pascalian calculus.

In certain circumstances an indifference-type conception of probability (see § 6) seems applicable to the task. Consider, for example, a game of chance where the colour of a playing card is to be predicted. The card in question is to be drawn at random from a well-shuffled standard pack of fifty-two cards and restored to the pack when its colour has been noted, and this is to be done five times, with the pack reshuffled on each occasion.

Then consider how Pascalian probability might be used to grade progressively the validity of the generalization 'Every card drawn will be a red one', on the basis of uniformly confirmatory evidence from each of its instances. When only one confirmatory instance is known and the outcomes of four card-drawings remain as yet unknown, the probability that each of the four remaining instances is red will be $\frac{1}{16}$ (that is, $\frac{1}{2} \times \frac{1}{2} \times \frac{1}{2} \times \frac{1}{2}$), since we can apply the indifference theory here, as in any game of pure chance, and also treat each outcome as being quite independent of every other. Similarly, after two favourable draws the probability will be $\frac{1}{8}$, after three favourable draw $\frac{1}{4}$, after four favourable draws $\frac{1}{2}$, and after five draws 1. In each case we just need to calculate the ratio of chances. So in this kind of situation the indifference theory provides us, in the absence of disconfirmatory instances, with a Pascalian measure of inductive support that has the property essential to enumerative induction: it increases as the number of confirmatory instances increases. Or, more exactly, and more generally, we can say that, if m is the number of alternative outcomes that are possible at each draw in such a game and i is the number of draws that are still to be carried out, then the probability that the generalization is true, given that all the evidence so far is favourable to it, is $1/m^i$. (This result is reached by the following step. Let 'A' be 'the outcome of draw 1 is red and the outcome of draw 2 is red and . . . and the outcome of draw n is red', where there are n drawings in all. Let 'B' be 'The outcome of draw 1 is red and the outcome of draw 2 is red and . . . and the outcome of draw $n - i$ is red'. Then in virtue of its being a priori given that there are just n drawings we replace 'A' in '$\mathrm{p}(A|B) = 1/m^i$' by 'The outcomes of all the drawings are red'.)

It follows that if human scientists could be supposed to play a system of analogous games of chance with natural processes (for example, predicting the outcome of a particular type of medication), the evidential support available for successful scientific hypotheses could be measured by a Pascalian probability-function that was interpreted in accordance with the indifference theory. But unfortunately the analogy breaks down at several points. The number of co-ordinate alternative outcomes that are possible in any one trial of the issue investigated may be infinite, indeterminate, or at least unknowable. The total number of possible trials may also be infinite, indeterminate, or at least unknowable. And, even more importantly, the trial outcomes may not be independent of one another: where causal laws are operative the same cause is, other things being equal, expected to produce the same effect. In short, science is not a game of chance with Nature, and we can grade enumerative induction by an indifference-type Pascalian probability only when we are generalizing about outcomes over a selected finite set of trials in a supposedly genuine game of chance.[1]

Turning next to the relative frequency conception of probability, we can see that it could be applied to the gradation of ampliative induction, with a cogency appropriate to the circumstances, if we could estimate the relative frequency with which a hypothesis that is supported by such-or-such a kind of evidence is true.[2] But where (as often in natural science) a hypothesis is a generalization about an infinitely, or indeterminately, large domain, we can never know for certain (see § 23 below) that it is true, though we can know the evidence supporting or opposing it at any one time. So the relative frequency at issue would instead have to concern the number of hypotheses that remained unfalsified after some canonical interval. For example, the probability of the particular hypothesis that all swans are white, on the evidence that all the thousand observed swans are white, would be, with a rather low weight (see § 14 above), the relative frequency with which generalizations about plumage-colour remain unfalsified for, say, a hundred years, after a thousand favourable, and no unfavourable, instances have been observed. And we might obtain a rather higher weight (see § 14 above) for the probability of our hypothesis if the evidential instances were suitably varied in regard to features that are sometimes relevant to plumage-colour (season, sex, climate, and so on).

Nevertheless, any such gradation of a particular exercise in ampliative induction depends inevitably on contingent historical facts about the collection of relevant evidence. If research funds have not been made available for thorough ethological

---

[1] See also A. J. Ayer, *Probability and Evidence* (London: Macmillan, 1972), 30–3.
[2] See e.g. H. Reichenbach, *Experience and Prediction* (Chicago: Chicago University Press, 1961), 397 ff.

and experimental enquiries into plumage-colour, for example, we cannot expect many generalizations on that topic to have been even proposed, let alone falsified. But, if there has been a lot of funding over a long period, we may expect not only that many such generalizations have been proposed, but also that enough research has been done in the area for many relevant generalizations, whether explicitly considered or not, to have been falsified. In short, other things being equal, the probability assignable in this way to a particular hypothesis, on the evidence available at the time, will tend to vary *inversely* with the size of past funding for research in that field. So this method of assigning probabilities to particular hypotheses introduces a quite paradoxical type of dependence on the direction of previous research. One might well have supposed instead that the more research goes into a subject, the more reliable become the hypotheses that eventually issue: they are supported, as it were, by piles of eliminated conjectures. But the method of assessment under consideration measures the reliability of a hypothesis by a probability that is equal to the relative frequency of *un*falsified hypotheses in the field of enquiry.

It may therefore seem plausible to suggest instead that enumerative induction involves establishing some very high propensity-type probability (see § 8) on the basis of a very large sample. Thus, if the generalization to be inductively supported is that all *B*s are *A*s, this generalization would be treated as being equivalent to the estimate $p(A|B) = 1 - \epsilon$ where ϵ is very small, and the evidence would be constituted by a large sample of *B*s, in which the observed relative frequency of *A*s was at least $1 - \epsilon$. The relation between the evidential sample and the estimated propensity would then be evaluated by some conventional statistical procedure which relies ultimately for its validity on Bernoulli's limit theorem (see pp. 21–2 above). For example, we might aim at having an estimate that could be said to be correct within 95 per cent confidence limits.[3] Roughly, the observed relative frequency (within a stated degree of approximation) would then be forthcoming in appropriately large samples on 95 per cent of occasions, given the correctness of the

[3] See J. Neyman, 'Outline of a Theory of Statistical Estimation Based on the Classical Theory of Probability', *Philosophical Transactions of the Royal Society of London*, Ser. 236 (1937), 333 ff., esp. 348.

estimate. And this would be fine if we were interested in the properties of such samples, as in industrial quality-control, where no more than a certain percentage of imperfect batches can be tolerated. Or Fisher's method of significance-levels[4] can be used, whereby we can seek to avoid both the error of rejecting the null-hypothesis—the hypothesis that, in respect of the relevant relative frequency, the evidential sample is non-representative of the population as a whole—when we should accept it, and also the error of preferring the null-hypothesis when we should reject it. In the present kind of context, by determining conventionally the level of improbability at which we shall regard an evidential sample of a certain size as significant we can characterize the type of composition that, if it occurs in the sample, should make us reject the null-hypothesis. That is, our sample should be treated as representative if its occurrence would otherwise be highly improbable (for example, occurring on only 5 per cent of occasions). And this again would be fine, within any community of scientists that shared the same conventions about significance-levels.

But in transforming the problem about inductive support for a generalization into a problem about evidential samples for estimating a very high propensity we must not lose anything important from the characterization of the problem.

We have in any case to accept that, when this transformation is made, contraposability will no longer be logically guaranteed. 'All not-A are not-B' is logically equivalent to 'All B are A' but 'p(not-B|not-A) = n' is not necessarily equivalent to 'p(A|B) = n'. Similarly, while 'All B are A' logically implies 'All BC are A', 'p(A|B) = n' does not necessarily imply 'p(A|BC) = n'. Sacrifice of these, and connected, implications is a price that has to be paid by anyone who wishes to replace the problem about generalizations by a problem about high Pascalian probability.[5] Perhaps the price is too high.

Moreover, there is another kind of implication that we certainly cannot afford to lose, because it is integral to one of the main purposes that the discovery of well-supported generaliza-

[4] R.A. Fisher, *Statistical Methods for Research Workers*, 7th edn. (Edinburgh: Oliver and Boyo, 1938), 120 ff.

[5] As is recognized by, for example, H. Reichenbach, *The Theory of Probability* 2nd edn. (Berkeley: University of California Press, 1971), 435–6.

tions can accomplish. From a reliable law we can draw reliable conclusions in particular cases. That is how safe bridges are built and ships are navigated successfully. And we can draw these reliable conclusions in particular cases because the uniformity stated by the generalization is known to hold good in the kinds of circumstances prevailing in those cases. So the generalization has to be well-supported by variative induction if it is to constitute a reliable premiss for a sufficiently wide range of predictions in particular cases. There might be many instances that would support it by enumerative induction, but they might all have occurred in other circumstances than those for which the particular conclusion is desired—in bridges not exposed to high winds, for example. Analogously, if a judgement of high probability is to constitute such a premiss, it must (as we saw in § 14) have high Keynesian weight. In other words its reliability for the purpose is not established just by enumerative induction from the size of the evidential sample but also by partitioning the reference class in a way that ensures the applicability of the generalized statement of probability to the circumstances of the particular case. It follows that if we treat generalizations as high propensity-type probabilities we cannot regard sample-size as the only evidential parameter that should affect our employment of the generalization. We have to look also at the range of other relevant circumstances present in the evidential instances and to use the non-Pascalian mode of appraisal that the assessment of weight requires (§ 14).

§ 17. INDUCTIVE PROBABILITY UNDER A RANGE-THEORETICAL CONSTRUAL

Carnap's range-based analysis of inductive support does not apply satisfactorily to support for open-ended generalizations. Hintikka's system avoids Carnap's difficulty here. But both systems tend not to differentiate adequately between enumerative and variative induction and fail to represent the type of reasoning which determines our choice of properties to control as a basis for variative induction. It looks as though such a system should refer ultimately to overlaps between ranges of physically possible worlds, not of logically possible worlds. But any attempt to define confirmation thus would be circular.

Carnap's range-based theory of logical probability seems at first sight to provide us with a more promising approach to the gradation of ampliative induction. His preferred confirmation-functions certainly guarantee that new predictions of a particular kind get more and more probable as more and more old ones of that same kind turn out to be true. For example, as we have already seen (in § 11 above), it is a feature of his 1950 system that $c^*(Hc,Ha\&Hb) > c^*(Hc,Ha)$. And in Carnap's final version of this system it was proved more generally by Humburg that the degree of confirmation of a singular statement h_1 is always increased when in addition to original evidence stated in e, which is consistent with h_1, we accept a new evidential statement h_2 which reports another instance of the same property as h_1 reports: that is $c(h_1,e\&h_2) > c(h_1,e)$.[6] This theorem is known as the principle of instantial relevance.

But induction is concerned with evidential support for generalizations, and unfortunately Carnap's system does not produce satisfactory confirmation values for that kind of statement. Even his favoured confirmation-function c^* assigns a very small degree of confirmation to such a statement, whatever the evidence, when the supposed number of individuals in the universe is very large, and assigns zero when this number is infinite. (That is because in Carnap's system a generalization that everything has a certain property is equivalent to a conjunction of singular statements which say, in turn, of each individual in the universe that it has that property, and the larger the number of singular statements thus conjoined the lower the measure of the conjunction's range—since there are bound to be fewer possible worlds in which it is true.) But in actual science the number of individuals in a given domain of investigation is normally unknown, so that it cannot enter into calculations of the extent to which the evidence supports a given generalization. Nor is it normally assumed that generalizations over an infinite-membered domain are incapable of acquiring any positive degree of evidential confirmation, and that any one such generalization is thus as worthless as any other.

[6] J. Humburg, 'The Principle of Instantial Relevance', in R. Carnap and R.C. Jeffrey (eds.), *Studies in Inductive Logic and Probability*, i (Berkeley: University of California Press, 1971), 225–33.

Carnap argued that in practice we do not need confirmation values for generalizations over large numbers of instances. This is because an engineer who is building a bridge, and wishes to apply certain physical laws to the task, is chiefly interested in that bridge's not being a counter-instance to any of the laws on which he is relying, or in there being no such counter-instance among all the bridges that he will construct during his lifetime. He is not so interested in the immense, perhaps infinite, number of other instances 'dispersed through all time and space'. So Carnap held that 'what is vaguely called the reliability of a law is measured not by the degree of confirmation of the law itself but by that of one or several instances'. And he therefore sought to capture this idea by defining a new concept of 'instance confirmation'. If g is a generalization over a certain domain of individuals, the instance confirmation of g on the evidence stated by e is defined as being equal to $c^*(h,e)$, where h states in effect that a specified individual not mentioned in e fulfils the generalization g.[7]

Instance confirmation, however, as defined by Carnap, is very far from measuring what is often understood to be the level of evidential support for a generalization. For example, there may be quite strong evidential confirmation for the prediction that the weather will be sunny in Oxford tomorrow, but strong evidential disconfirmation for the generalization that the weather is sunny in Oxford every day. Nor can we easily dispense with assessments of inductive support for at least some propositions that are genuine open-ended generalizations. It is quite true that engineers, navigators, physicians, and others employed in day-to-day technology can for the most part restrict their horizons of intellectual interest. But, important as such technological purposes are, they are not the only purposes served by the advancement of scientific knowledge. Intellectual understanding, and the explanation of why things happen as they do, are also a legitimate objective. And that purpose requires us to see individual phenomena or particular regularities in the light of much more widely pervasive laws. To explain the positions of the planets, for example, on the occasions on which these have been observed, we need to be able to cite laws of planetary motion like Kepler's or general laws of motion like Newton's—not just knowledge of where the planets will be tomorrow or next week or of where they were a minute before they were observed. So questions are bound to arise about the strength of evidential support that exists for hypotheses stating such laws. And these questions do not remain unanswered. Scientists frequently draw inductive comparisons between one law-stating hypothesis and another. Philosophers of induction are therefore obliged to try and elicit the principles of gradation that are implicit in those comparisons. They cannot legitimately escape this obligation by confining their attention to the needs of engineers and other technologists.

Carnap's theory of logical probability gets into difficulties about inductive support for generalizations because it makes the measures of a universal proposition's range depend in part on the number of individuals in the domain. Accordingly Hintikka proposed a type of range-measure that was, in the case of universal propositions, independent of this number.[8] Suppose that we are given k primitive monadic predicates. By means of these predicates and the usual propositional connectives we can partition our domain of individuals, whatever its size, into 2^k different kinds (empty or non-empty), distinguished by the various complex predicates that describe them. For example, with two primitive predicates F and G, we should have four kind-describing complex predicates, namely, $F\,\&\,G$, $F\,\&\,not\text{-}G$, $not\text{-}F\,\&\,G$, and $not\text{-}F\,\&\,not\text{-}G$. Then we can describe a possible world by a sentence describing all the non-empty kinds of individuals in it. Such a sentence, which Hintikka calls a 'constituent', will be a consistent conjunction of sentences each of which asserts the existence of at least one individual belonging to such-or-such a kind, conjoined with a sentence asserting that every individual belongs to one or other of those kinds. A constituent thus determines a species of possible world, namely, that species of possible world in which just such-and-such kinds are instantiated, and because it is formulated in general terms—by means of existential and universal quantification—a constituent may be made true by each of many different state-descriptions (in

[8] J. Hintikka, 'Towards a Theory of Inductive Generalisation', in Y. Bar Hillel (ed.), *Proceedings of the 1964 Congress for Logic, Methodology and Philosophy of Science* (Amsterdam: North-Holland, 1965), 274–88.

Carnap's sense of that term: § 11). Hintikka supposes that an equal value should be assigned to each constituent, just as Carnap's c* was based on assigning an equal value to each structure-description, and that the value of each constituent may be divided among all the state-descriptions that make it true. A sentence's range is then to be measured, as Carnap measured it, by the sum of the values of the various state-descriptions in which that sentence holds, and degree of confirmation analogous to c* is to be defined in terms of the same ratio of range-measures that Carnap used for the purpose:

$$c^*(h,e) = \frac{m^*(e\&h)}{m^*(e)}.$$

In this system the measure of a generalization's range will be quite independent of the number of state descriptions that make any particular constituent true, and therefore quite independent of the numbers of individuals of various kinds in the universe or of the total number of individuals, because every generalization has an equivalent that is just a disjunction of constituents with the same complex predicates.

Hintikka's system thus avoids Carnap's difficulties about inductive support for generalizations over large numbers of individuals. It provides a realistic basis for comparing different generalizations in relation to the degree of support available for them from evidential instances. But it seems to fit elementary generalizations like 'All swans are white' rather more easily than it fits serious scientific hypotheses, such as those asserting one physical parameter to be such-or-such a function of certain others, like $e = mc^2$. Indeed, though it can apparently be extended to languages containing polyadic predicates as well as monadic ones,[9] its extendability to languages containing higher-order predicates as well as first-order ones has not been demonstrated. Nevertheless, if the system provided a correct measure of inductive support even for first-order generalizations about monadic properties, it would be a substantial achievement. So it calls for a careful assessment.

---

[9] See I. Niiniluoto, 'Inductive Logic as a Methodological Research Programme', in M. L. D. Chiara *et al.*, *Logic in the 20th Century* (special vol. of *Scientia*; Milan, 1983), 93.

Philosophers sometimes object to theories like Carnap's or Hintikka's that, quite apart from questions about the number of individuals presupposed, they make a proposition's degree of confirmation, for given evidence, depend on choice of language in another respect also, namely in regard to the number of primitive predicates. To this objection there are three plausible answers. One is that, as we have already seen (p. 80), it is possible to construct systems in which degree of confirmation is invariant under changes in the choice of primitive predicates within a particular family of primitive predicates. The second is that the impact of introducing new predicates into range-theoretical systems can be studied systematically.[10] And the third is that even within a single language it is possible to draw useful comparisons on the assumption of the language's adequacy.

But the fact remains that, so far as degree of confirmation is to depend on choice of language, we need to know not only what consequences flow from a change of language but also what kind of considerations justify such changes. An adequate analysis of inductive support that is based on a measure of range must treat the choice of relevant terminology as a procedure implicit in any chain of inductive reasoning. Such a choice is just as much in need of analysis, or rational reconstruction, as are any subsequent inferences that are drawn from the structure of the terminology chosen. For example, we may suppose that the term 'pregnant' was absent from the relevant terminology of those who obtained the original experimental results on the toxicity of thalidomide, since they failed to control (p. 30) those experiments for pregnancy. So what would, rationally, compel the addition of this term to the relevant terminology? We need to suppose some discernible incoherence between newly observed empirical facts and the assessment of degree of confirmation relative to previously observed facts. And the point is not just that on the new evidence the degree of confirmation is different but that even on the old evidence it was wrongly assessed. The experimenters were too confident that, on the evidence they had, thalidomide was non-toxic. Hence supposedly true assessments of the form $c(h,e) = n$, ought to be regarded as empirically

---

[10] See I. Niiniluoto and R. Tuomela, *Theoretical Concepts and Hypothetico-Deductive Inference* (Dordrecht: Reidel, 1973), 165–95.

falsifiable and their method of possible falsification needs to be analysed by inductive logicians, whereas in fact they are represented by Carnap and Hintikka as a priori or true by convention. In short, an adequate confirmation-metric for natural science ought to be empirically self-correcting. And neither Carnap's nor Hintikka's system has this property.

There is another feature of their systems that also needs to be discussed. Carnap's emphasis on the importance of the principle of instantial relevance (see above) has sometimes misled his critics into complaining that his preferred confirmation-function c^* offers an analysis of enumerative, but not of variative, induction. But this is not quite the right complaint to make. Carnap in fact pointed out[11] that c^* takes on a higher value not only when the total number of new instances is greater and other features are the same, but also when, with equal numbers of new instances, the number of different kinds from which the new instances are taken is greater or the instances are distributed more evenly among the kinds. So, superficially at least, Carnap's preferred confirmation-function does seem to reflect the requirements of variative induction, and Hintikka's does also.[12] But there are two underlying faults in the way in which a range-theory achieves this.

First, it amalgamates enumerative and variative support under a single measure, whereas in practice these are normally held apart and may be cited for different purposes. Thus, if the same scientific experiment is carried out a second time and has the same outcome, that is taken as helping to establish the genuineness of the experimental result. The result is then better entitled to count as a datum that constitutes support, or refutation, for a proposed hypothesis. But, if on the second occasion the experimenter fails to replicate the previous outcome, suspicion naturally arises that the description of the first occasion's relevant circumstances may have been incomplete or inaccurate in one or more respects. Of course, the flaw might be in the description of the second occasion's relevant circumstances. But

[11] In R. Carnap, 'On Inductive Logic', *Philosophy of Science*, 12 (1945), 72–97.

[12] See J. Hintikka, 'Induction by Enumeration and Induction by Elimination', in I. Lakatos (ed.), *The Problem of Inductive Logic* (Amsterdam: North-Holland, 1968), 191–216.

one way or the other the relevant circumstances of the two experimental trials must have been different if substantially different outcomes were produced. And in this way enumerative induction seems to be at work in our reasoning about the validity or authority of experimental reports. On the other hand, variative induction seems to be at work in our reasoning about the thoroughness with which such experiments test hypotheses. The thoroughness mounts as a greater variety of supposedly relevant factors are controlled in the tests, and support mounts at the same time if the hypothesis that is being tested remains unfalsified by any authoritative experimental data. But this important difference between the roles of enumerative and variative induction in experimental reasoning is totally obscured if a single confirmation-function is made to amalgamate both parameters. What is thus ignored is that we may wish to characterize some experimental data as well replicated but as the outcome of a rather weak test on a particular hypothesis, and other data as the outcome of a test that is rather strong but poorly replicated. The replication of a given experimental outcome, and the complexity with which the experimental test is structured, are mutually independent issues.

The second underlying fault in both Carnap's and Hintikka's treatments of variative induction is that they assign equal importance to each kind of primitive predicate that may occur in the description of evidential instances. That equality stems in turn from the fact that in Carnap's preferred system each structure-description is assigned an equal measure, and in Hintikka's each constituent is assigned this. But in the world of real science different variations of experimental conditions may well be of very different value. For example, in an experiment to test the toxicity of a pharmaceutical product the previous medical history of a patient may be much more important than his or her normal diet. Moreover, even if two experimental conditions may be of equal value when occurring on their own, they may be of very unequal value when each is combined with another particular condition. A new drug may be equally safe when taken in combination with standard doses of aspirin or of barbiturate, but not when taken in combination with both aspirin and alcohol or with both barbiturate and alcohol. Ultimately indeed what these facts call into question is the whole strategy of making degree of confirmation depend on a measure of *logical* range, whereby c(*h,e*) is defined as

$$\frac{\mathrm{m}(h\&e)}{\mathrm{m}(e)}.$$

What this definition does, in effect, is to make the degree to which *e* confirms *h* depend on a measure of the logically possible worlds in which *h* and *e* are jointly or severally true. But, if different experimental conditions are to count differently in certain cases, what is at issue is the *physical* effects of different conditions in different circumstances. So in the end every kind of logically possible world that is described by a structure-description or a constituent would have to be evaluated for its potential of ocurrence. We should be measuring physical range, as it were, not logical range.

To take an extreme case, let us suppose that it is physiologically impossible for a man or a five-year-old girl to become pregnant. Then in a language that included terminology for sex and age differences and for pregnancy it seems just as wrong for degree of confirmation to take into account the physiologically impossible worlds in which such events occur as to take into account logically impossible ones. Why should it matter at all, in relation to a particular description of evidence, that it is logically possible for the description to hold good in certain physiologically impossible worlds? Again, the idea behind relating confirmation to the ratio of m(*h&e*) to m(*e*) is that *e*'s confirmation of *h* may be seen as a measure of the overlap between those possible worlds in which both *h* and *e* are true and those in which *e* is true. Degree of confirmation thus measures, as it were, the extent to which the evidence narrows down the logical possibilities to those in which *h* is true. But what scientists ought to be interested in instead is the extent to which the evidence narrows down the relevant physical possibilities. And here again, as when we considered problems about the introduction of new terminology, it looks as though any adequate assessments of degree of confirmation by a range-theoretical method must be empirical judgements based on what we think that we know about physical possibilities and impossibilities, rather than a priori judgements based on calculations from the structure of our language.

It may seem, therefore, that there is nothing irremediably unsound in the range-theoretical approach to the analysis of ampliative induction. In order to avoid Carnap's difficulties about inductive support for law-stating generalizations, we need to base our measurements on the assignment of values to constituents rather than to structure descriptions. And in order to do justice to the realities of variative induction we need to assign these values in the light of what is physically possible rather than of what is logically possible. But, unfortunately, to require such an assignment is to make the whole procedure circular. On the one hand we need to derive our preferred confirmation-function's assessments of inductive support from premises about the differing degrees of physical possibility that it is appropriate to assign to different combinations of natural conditions: on the other hand we need to base those assignments on our preferred confirmation-function's assessments, in each case, of the support that the presence of one such condition gives to the presence or absence of another. The difficulty here is of the same kind as that remarked earlier in the case of indifference theories (pp. 45–6). Just as an indifference theory is circular if it has to presuppose an appropriate set of comparative judgements of probability over all the possible outcomes, so too a range-theoretical definition of one's preferred confirmation-function is circular if the range of a proposition has to be made an empirical issue and based on assessments of degree of confirmation.

This does not mean that Carnap's type of confirmation system has no legitimate domain of application. He himself constructed an example[13]—his only fully worked-out example—in which the universe consists of players in a chess tournament and their properties are being local or non-local, being junior or senior, being male or female, and being the winner or a loser. The evidence states the numbers of males and females among local juniors, local seniors, non-local juniors, and non-local seniors, and it is *assumed* that each of the ten players has an equal chance of becoming the winner. It is then possible to calculate a priori the degree to which the evidence range-theoretically confirms a hypothesis like 'a man wins', without even having to exploit the consequences of choosing one

---

[13] *Logical Foundations of Probability*, pp. 382 ff.

confirmation-function rather than another.[14] But this is like calculating probabilities in a game of chance that has ten co-ordinate possible outcomes altogether, with each of these outcomes falling into one or more other categories. And indeed any more complex example, in which structure descriptions (as for Carnap's c^*) or constituents (as in Hintikka's system) are assigned equal values a priori, would also resemble a game of chance, where the basic equalities are stipulated a priori in the rules. But we know no such set of rules for Nature. So the process of Nature cannot be treated as one big game of chance, and we have to do a lot of empirical work to discover the extent to which it admits of this or that combination of circumstances.[15]

§ 18. PASCALIAN GRADATION FOR VARIATIVE INDUCTION

Variative induction is important enough for us to ask whether a distinctively variative mode of inductive reasoning can be given a Pascalian representation. Keynes's system of gradation for inductive support rests on a principle of limited independent variety. That principle establishes a non-zero probability for the hypothesis under investigation, and the probability increases with each evidential instance that differs in some respect from all previous ones. But there are at least four objections that may be made to this analysis of inductive support.

[14] Carnap, *Logical Foundations of Probability*, p. 347.
[15] Useful discussions of Carnap's inductive logic by J.G. Kemeny, A.W. Burks, H. Putnam, and E. Nagel, together with Carnap's replies to each of these, are to be found in P.A. Schilpp (ed.), *The Philosophy of R. Carnap* (La Salle: Open Court, 1963), 711–825, 966–95. Carnap's later ideas about inductive logic are to be found in 'Inductive Logic and Rational Decisions' and 'A Basic System of Inductive Logic', in R. Carnap and R.C. Jeffrey (eds.), *Studies in Inductive Logic and Probability*; i (Berkeley: University of California Press, 1971), 5–171, and R.C. Jeffrey (ed.), *Studies in Inductive Logic and Probability*, ii (Berkeley: University of California Press, 1980), 7–155. The shift in Carnap's ideas is discussed from a Popperian point of view by I. Lakatos; 'Changes in the Problem of Inductive Logic', in Lakatos (ed.), *The Problem of Inductive Logic*, pp. 315–417. For an attempt to show how Hintikka's kind of analysis can be applied under conditions of conceptual change, see I. Niiniluoto and R. Tuomela, *Theoretical Concepts*. A reformulation of Carnap–Hintikka inductive logic is to be found in T.A.F. Kuipers, *A Survey of Inductive Systems* (Dordrecht: Reidel, 1978). The variety of available confirmation-functions is discussed in R. Carnap, *The Continuum of Inductive Methods* (Chicago: Chicago University Press, 1952); and J. Hintikka, 'A Two-Dimensional Continuum of Inductive Methods', in J. Hintikka and P. Suppes (eds.), *Aspects of Inductive Logic* (Amsterdam: North-Holland, 1966), 113–32.

So far we have been considering Pascalian modes of gradation for those forms of ampliative induction in which a superior number of favourable instances (with no, or hardly any, unfavourable ones) establishes superior merit whether or not these instances are thought to vary in any relevant respects. But, if we distinguish effectively, as suggested in § 17, between questions about the strength with which certain test-results, if replicable, support a particular generalization and questions about the replicability of those test results, we can see that, at least in natural science, mere multiplicity of instances is significant only for the replicability of test-results and not for the strength of support that they give.

The traditional argument for the superiority of variative induction is that it avoids the possibility of biased sampling which is inherent in enumerative induction. You may have seen a large number of hares that were grey and none that were not grey, but your observations were all of common hares in summer so that you never saw a mountain hare in winter—which would have been white. Hence perhaps you mistakenly concluded, by enumerative induction, that all hares are grey, whereas variation of the species observed or of the season of observation would have generated a more correct conclusion.

But this argument for the superiority of variative induction is of somewhat limited scope. The more homogeneous the domain over which you generalize (and elements of which you observe), the less needful variative induction seems to be.

A more powerful argument rests on the assumption that the generalization at issue is conceived to state a causal connection, a law of nature, or a consequence of one or more of these, as distinct from some accidentally operative uniformity. Characteristically such a generalization would be supposed to apply to counterfactual (possible but non-actual) instances as well as to actual ones. If penicillin cures septicaemia, then an adequate dosage of penicillin would have cured your cat's septicaemia last year. Now enumerative induction seems incapable of supporting any implication about counterfactual instances. However many evidential instances are observed they seem to have no describable connection with non-actual instances. But variative induction does establish such a connection. The wider the variety of circumstances to which a generalization is seen to apply, the wider the variety of counterfactual as well as of actual instances that it may be said to cover. In variative induction the potential hazards against which generalizations are checked are properties, characteristics, or conditions, not individuals. So a generalization that is supported by variative induction may be conceived to embrace counterfactual instances within its domain, just so far as these too exemplify the relevant properties, characteristics, or conditions.

Whether or not these arguments for variative induction are acceptable, it is at least worth examining whether some Pascalian conception of probability can be applied to an exclusively variative form of ampliative induction, in which additional favourable instances have evidential value only if they differ from previous instances and from one another in some relevant respects. Mill's attempt to carry out such a project suffered from various defects that were noted in § 4 above. Other attempts need therefore to be examined.

Keynes tried to construct a solution of the problem in terms of his conception of probability as a logical relation. He postulated that in any domain of inductive investigation a principle of limited independent variety operates.[16] He believed that Bacon had explicitly recognized the importance of this principle and that Mill too had used it though without explicit acknowledgement. According to the principle all the properties or qualities of the domain's individual elements are bound together in a limited number of groups. Every characteristic belongs to at least one group, within which the characteristics are invariably connected with one another through the operation of a distinct generative mechanism. But the same characteristic may belong to more than one group, just so long as the generative mechanism that produces all the characteristics within any one group can operate independently of each generative mechanism that produces the characteristics in another group. For example, there can be a plurality of causes for any one type of thing, as Mill also held (see p. 32). Moreover, there is some definite finite number of distinct groups, although there need be no such number of distinct individuals. And Keynes thought that events in Nature could be treated as constituting one such domain of

---

[16] J.M. Keynes, *A Treatise on Probability* (London: Macmillan, 1957), 258-61.

inductive investigation, and numbers another. Like Bacon (p. 8), but unlike Mill or Carnap, he conceived of ampliative induction as a logical procedure that was by no means confined to the investigation of Nature.

Keynes then builds up his analysis of inductive support on the basis of his assumption about limited independent variety.

His first step is to establish a non-zero prior probability for a typical hypothesis. Suppose, for example, that we are investigating in some domain whether everything that has the characteristic B also has the characteristic A. Since independent variety is limited A has to belong to at least one out of a finite number of groups of characteristics, though in advance of any specific information A has an equal probability of belonging to any one of them. And the same is true of B. Hence, if there are n distinct groups, and each is of antecedently unknown composition, the probability that A belongs to a particular group G is at least $1/n$, the probability that B belongs to group G is also at least $1/n$, and accordingly the probability that they both belong to G is at least $1/n^2$. It follows that there is antecedently some finite probability that A belongs to all the groups to which B belongs and thus that everything which has B has A. So Keynes's theory is at any rate not hit by the difficulty that Carnap encountered, whereby any generalization over an infinite domain had zero prior probability.

Keynes next points out that each evidential instance of B that differs in some respect from any previously noted instance of B can help to eliminate the possibility of B's belonging to any group to which A does not belong. Hence, as each such possibility is eliminated we may treat the probability that everything which has B has A as being correspondingly increased, since each step reduces the number of distinct groups about which it is not known whether B and A are both members.

Of course, Keynes recognized that by this method a numerically definite probability could be obtained for an induction only if we are able to make definite assumptions about the number of independent equiprobable causal mechanisms at work. But he pointed out that common-sense judgements of inductive probability were normally qualitative or comparative rather than numerical. People remark that certain inductive arguments are stronger than others, or that some are very strong. So Keynes was content that within his system inductive evaluations would normally just bear relations of greater or lesser to numerical probabilities according to the approximate limits within which our assumptions place the number of independent generative mechanisms. That is, his assessments of inductive support were, as we should now say, interval-valued.

Another notable feature of Keynes's system was that enumerative induction plays no part in it whatever. An additional evidential instance is of no inductive value unless, by exhibiting some hitherto unremarked combination of characteristics, it furthers the eliminative process. Nor does a particular location in space or time count as an inductively relevant characteristic in the investigation of natural processes. So, if an additional evidential instance is to have any value there, it must differ from previously noted instances in respect of some characteristic other than spatial or temporal location. Indeed in this connection Keynes invokes what he calls 'the Uniformity of Nature', according to which (as most investigators of Nature are prepared to assume) *mere* position in time and space cannot possibly affect, as a determining cause, any other characteristic. It is therefore no objection to his system that at any one time of investigation all the evidential instances are past or present, none future. Pastness, presentness, and futurity must also be inductively irrelevant if spatio-temporal location is. (A similar result was achieved in Carnap's system, by his preference for *symmetrical* c-functions—pp. 77–8).

Keynes acknowledged that the principle of limited independent variety was crucial to his system. But he argued that this principle did not have to be proved true, in relation to any particular domain for inductive investigation. It was sufficient, in his view, for the principle to have a finite probability a priori, which our experience has considerably increased. Indeed, he says, 'it is because there has been so much repetition and uniformity in our experience that we place great confidence in it'. But there are at least four points that can be made against Keynes here, and the approval that one accords to his theory must vary inversely with the strength that one attributes to these points.

First, it is by no means obvious that actual human experience has tended to increase the probability that the principle of limited independent variety is valid for Nature. As natural science progresses to new levels of understanding new properties of matter tend to be discovered and perhaps this is because Nature's independent variety is unlimited.

Secondly, even if the principle's probability has undergone some increase, this is quite compatible with its still being more probably false than true. But, if the principle on which our inductive reasonings rely is more probably false than true, then on the balance of probability our inductive reasonings are without any rational foundation. So Keynes has given us insufficient reason to suppose that our inductive reasonings do have a rational foundation rather than that they do not.

Thirdly, as well as these difficulties about the epistemology of the principle, there are problems about its implications. Keynes did not explain how exactly his method of inductive appraisal assigns antecedent probabilities to hypotheses about dyadic or relational characteristics as distinct from monadic ones, or to hypotheses about quantitative characteristics as distinct from qualitative ones. For example, if there is a non-denumerable infinity of points on a scale of physical magnitude—a scale of heat, say, or velocity—must there not be a corresponding infinity of generative mechanisms? And if you prefer to identify a single generative mechanism, such as molecular motion, as the cause of heat, you will be grouping parameters (of temperature, velocity, etc.), rather than single characteristics, into your supposedly finite number of groups, and this will interfere with the assignment of antecedent probabilities to hypotheses about monadic, qualitative characteristics.

Fourthly, Keynes assumes that within any domain of inductive investigation all mutually independent generative mechanisms are of equal inductive importance in relation to any one hypothesis, just as J. S. Mill (see pp. 36–7 above) assumed that in analogical reasoning every feature of similarity or difference between the two entities concerned is equally important. Yet (as already remarked in connection with Mill's account) the fact that two patients resemble one another in literary interests, for example, would normally be much less important for medical prognosis than that they have the same viral infection in their bloodstreams.[17]

---

[17] Keynes's views on induction are criticized from a different point of view in J. Nicod, *Geometry and Induction*, trans. M. Woods (London: Routledge and Kegan Paul, 1969), 173–242, where the importance of enumerative induction is defended.

§ 19. INDUCTIVE PROBABILITY UNDER A PERSONALIST
CONSTRUAL

The treatment of inductive support as a Pascalian probability
under a personalist interpretation has both advantages and disadvantages connected with its consignment of the calculations
that underlie the assessment of probability-values to a black-box
mechanism. A personalist analysis in terms of positive relevance
is more revealing. But while the former analysis presupposes the
Special Consequence Condition, the latter presupposes the
Converse Entailment Condition. These two conditions are not
co-tenable, and the positive relevance analysis has to be given
up. Moreover no Pascalian analysis can allow a theory to be well
supported when the evidence includes minor anomalies.

If we examine the applicability of a personalist conception of
Pascalian probability to the assessment of ampliative induction,
we can see that it has some advantages for this purpose over a
logical relation theory, while retaining whatever merit goes
along with treating degree of confirmation as having a Pascalian
structure.

It is clear that there is some such merit. For example, if the
results of testing our hypothesis turn out favourable to it but
were not otherwise to be expected, we normally think that our
hypothesis is better confirmed than if those favourable results
were in any case predictable from previously established
theories. A novel but successful prediction is always a feather in
the cap for a new theory. And this is reflected in *any* Pascalian
analysis of ampliative induction because of Bayes's law (p. 23).
For, according to that law, if the values of $p(H)$ and $p(E|H)$
remain unaltered (but non-zero), the value of $p(H|E)$ gets
bigger as that of $p(E)$ gets smaller without reaching zero. The
lower the prior probability of the evidence (provided it is non-
zero), the greater the probability of the hypothesis upon that
evidence (other things being equal). Moreover, because of this
Bayesian relationship, a hypothesis that predicts or explains two
mutually independent items of evidence will have a higher
probability on that combined evidence than on either evidential
item alone, since $p(E_1 \& E_2)$ will normally be less than $p(E_1)$.

But a personalist analysis does have some special advantages
also. It escapes several of the difficulties that beset a logical

relation analysis when applied to the task of assessing ampliative inductions. In particular, a personalist analysis says nothing about how a person does or should determine his lowest acceptable betting odds on a particular proposition. It treats the mind of an inductive reasoner as containing a black box that takes in all kinds of information and outputs acceptances or rejections of wagers for the purpose of Bayesian conditionalization (pp. 67–9). Consequently the strength of a person's belief in the truth of a hypothesis is not necessarily tied either to enumerative or to variative evidence, but his mind may be supposed to be fed with either type of information or both. Correspondingly a personalist analysis avoids having to face up to any special problems about calculating Pascalian probabilities for generalizations that are not restricted to the use of monadic first-order predicates. Carnap and Hintikka had to wrestle with those problems (see §§ 11 and 17) and Keynes's analysis suffered from ignoring them. But the personalist's black box takes care of all such difficulties for him. At the same time a personalist analysis does allow judgements of inductive probability to be sensitive to the different degrees of importance that are felt to characterize different kinds of evidential variation. No a priori principles of equality between different structure-descriptions, or between different constituents, are written into the personalist's black-box mechanism. Again, Keynes's relatively unobjectionable principle of the uniformity of Nature, whereby differences of time or place do not count as inductively relevant characteristics (p. 134) has a counterpart in de Finetti's principle of exchangeability (pp. 69–70). But the more controversial principle of limited independent variety has no counterpart in an application of a personalist analysis, or Bayesian methodology, to the assessment of ampliative induction. It is true that a rational man can hardly wager seriously on the truth of a generalization over an infinite or indeterminately large domain, since it would be possible to settle the bet only if the generalization were falsified and the bet was lost. But the generalization could, in principle, be over a domain that is as large as you please, just so long as its size is finite and determinate. So perhaps such a generalization could be adequate for most, if not all, of the explanatory purposes that Carnap's concept of instance confirmation (pp. 122–3) failed to serve.

A personalist analysis of ampliative induction does, however, have an important weakness which follows necessarily from its consigning the calculations that underlie the assessment of probability-values to a black-box mechanism. It tells us nothing about how a person does or should determine his lowest acceptable betting-odds other than that a rational person does so coherently on the basis of whatever evidence is available to him. So the analysis offers us no guidance on how to resolve controversies between those rational people who disagree with one another about the probability of a particular hypothesis. There may be detectable flaws in the analyses offered by logical relation theorists like Keynes, Carnap, or Hintikka. But at least they addressed this problem, whereas the personalist analysis seems just to duck the real difficulty. It does not take us behind the scenes, as it were, and provide us with a breakdown on how degree of confirmation is, or ought, actually to be determined. Carnap even came to think that personalism articulates the rational framework within which any choice of axioms for inductive logic has to be made. But he could not accept it as a satisfactory *substitute* for a range-theoretical approach to the analysis of induction.[18]

The situation is not quite so bad in this respect if the personalist analysis for degree of confirmation is supposed not to be the one that treats degree of confirmation as degree of probability *simpliciter*, but the more sophisticated one that treats degree of confirmation as the difference between prior and posterior probabilities, as in Hesse's account.[19] Thus on the former view E is said to give some positive confirmation to H if and only if $p(H|E)$ is greater than some chosen constant, such as $\frac{1}{2}$. But on the latter view E is said to give some positive confirmation to H if and only if E is positively relevant to H—that is, if and only if $p(H|E)$ is greater than $p(H)$. And this thesis does purport to provide at least a minimal insight into the calculations determining degree of confirmation. It does not tell us how the values of $p(H)$ and $p(H|E)$ are, or ought to be, established. But it does at least tell us to measure the difference between the one and the

---

[18] See R. Carnap, 'Inductive Logic and Rational Decisions', in Carnap and R. Jeffrey (eds.), *Studies in Inductive Logic* i. 25–7.

[19] M. Hesse, *The Structure of Scientific Inference* (London: Macmillan, 1974), 133–4.

other, while retaining the feature (referred to above) that, other things being equal, degree of confirmation is greater as p(E) gets smaller.

Another important difference between the implications of the simple probability analysis and the implications of the more sophisticated probabilistic relevance analysis has to be noted.

Consider a case where H logically implies H', and E gives some positive confirmation or inductive support to H. One intuitively plausible claim here is made by what is commonly called the 'Special Consequence Condition'. According to this principle E must give at least as much support to H' as it gives to H. And that allows us to exploit whatever support exists for a scientific theory whenever we apply a generalization which is derivative from that theory. Another intuitively plausible claim is made by what is called the 'Converse Entailment Condition'. According to this principle, if H logically implies H', H' supports H. And this fits well with the commonly held belief that a theory acquires some support from each independently established generalization that it entails.

But the Special Consequence Condition and the Converse Entailment Condition do not belong well together. The simple probability analysis implies the validity of the Special Consequence Condition and does not imply that of the Converse Entailment Condition. This is because the Pascalian calculus gives us $p(H'|E) \geqslant p(H|E)$ where $p(H'|H) = 1$, but it does not ensure $p(H|H') \geqslant \frac{1}{2}$ where $p(H'|H) = 1$. On the other hand the positive relevance analysis implies the Converse Entailment Condition and not the Special Consequence Condition. That is because the Pascalian calculus gives us $p(H|H') > p(H)$, where $p(H'|H) = 1$ and neither $p(H)$ nor $p(H')$ is zero or one, but it does not ensure $p(H'|E) > p(H')$ where $p(H'|H) = 1$ and $p(H|E) > p(H)$.

Indeed, not only do the simple probability analysis and the positive relevance analysis have these importantly different implications for the logical structure of inductive support. It is also impossible to conceive of any serious analysis that could accept both the Special Consequence Condition and the Converse Entailment Condition. That is because, if both principles are accepted, any proposition B may be shown to support any other proposition A, as follows. Consider the hypothesis $A\&B$.

By the Converse Entailment Condition B supports this hypothesis. But if B supports the hypothesis $A\&B$, then, by the Special Consequence Condition, B supports A.

It follows that, whatever our actual analysis of ampliative induction, we have to give up one or both of these two principles. Nor should that be surprising if we notice that the two principles reflect inherently different conception of support. According to the Special Consequence Condition the degree of support that the evidence gives to a hypothesis as a whole flows down to all the logical consequenes of the hypothesis. So this degree of support is conceived as permeating throughout the content of the hypothesis. Such a conception of support is typical of ampliative induction, where the observation of certain evidential instances is supposed to give a corresponding degree of support to a generalization as a whole. Thus the existing evidence comes to support predictions about new cases that are derivable from the generalization. But no such permeation of support is implicit in the Converse Entailment Condition. The support that H' gives H, when H entails H', may apply just to that part of the content of H which enables it to entail H'. Indeed, the greater the additional content that H possesses, the less the support that H' gives to H as a whole. And, in any case, in ampliative induction the typical relationship between generalization and the reports of evidential instances that support it is certainly not a relation of entailment. 'All swans are white' does not entail 's is a swan and white'. So the Converse Entailment Condition does not get a grip there.

Accordingly, in any analysis of inductive support we need to ensure conformity with the Special Consequence Condition, not the Converse Entailment Condition. It does not follow from this that the simple probability analysis has to be accepted, since an analysis in terms of Pascalian probability may not be the only one that allows deduction of the Special Consequence Condition. But the positive relevance account has certainly to be discarded, as an analysis for ampliative induction, since it implies the validity of the Converse Entailment Condition, which we have seen to be inappropriate for ampliative induction.

Moreover, there are two other good reasons why the positive relevance analysis can be questioned.

The first is that the positive relevance analysis allows evidence which disconfirms or undermines a hypothesis to support a conjunction of that hypothesis with any other hypothesis you please. For example, imagine a situation where H and H' are independent of one another and $p(H|E) = 0.9$, $p(H'|E) = 0.2$, and $p(H) = p(H') = 0.3$. We shall then have $p(H|E) > p(H)$, $p(H'|E) < p(H')$, and $p(H\&H'|E) > p(H\&H')$. So that in such a case, according to the positive relevance analysis, E disconfirms or undermines H' and yet still supports the conjunction $H\&H'$. Maybe this might be acceptable if H' made only a small and insignificant claim about the world, when compared with H. We might then feel inclined to concede that E on balance supported the conjunction $H\&H'$, just because it supported the major conjunct H. But unfortunately we could just as well be faced with the opposite situation, in which E came to support the whole conjunction just because it supported the minor conjunct.

The second additional argument against the positive relevance analysis is that, as Popper and Miller have shown,[20] it seems not to account for the ampliative element in ampliative induction. Let us suppose a (logically contingent) scientific hypothesis H, a statement of evidence E, and background knowledge B. Then, according to the positive relevance analysis, if the conjunction $H\&B$ entails E, we shall have $p(H|E\&B) > p(H|B)$ where $1 > p(E|B) > 0$. But H can be factored into two elements $H \lor - E$ and $H \lor E$, such that, though $E\&B$ supports $H \lor E$ (since $p(H \lor E|E\&B) = 1$ while $p(H \lor E) < 1$), E undermines or disconfirms $H \lor - E$ (since $p(H \lor - E|E\&B) < p(H \lor - E|B)$). And yet $H \lor - E$, though thus undermined by E, seems to be the ampliative element within the factorization of H into the two elements $H \lor - E$ and $H \lor E$, since $H \lor - E$ is equivalent to the (truth-functional) conditional $E \to H$. It is this conditional which represents the inferential move from the evidence E to the hypothesis H that goes beyond the evidence. So it ought not to be *dis*confirmed by E.

Thus, considerable difficulties confront the positive relevance analysis of ampliative induction. It certainly offers a somewhat

[20] K.R. Popper and D. Miller, 'A Proof of the Impossibility of Inductive Probability', *Nature*, 302 (1983), 687–8, and ibid. 310 (1984), 434. But see A.R. Rodriguez, 'On Popper–Miller's proof of the Impossibility of Inductive Probability', *Erkenntnis*, 27 (1987), 353–7, and E. Eells, 'On the Alleged Impossibility of Inductive Probability', *Brit. J. Phil. Sci.*, 39 (1988), 111–16.

more structured account of the situation than does the simple probability analysis. So, if ampliative induction is to be analysed in terms of a personalist concept of probability, the positive relevance analysis is potentially more illuminating than the simple probability analysis. But unfortunately the positive relevance analysis also generates undesirable paradoxes.

Is it possible to construct some less paradoxical analysis of ampliative induction in terms of a personalist conception of probability? Such an analysis would have to avoid assessing degree of inductive support by a pure posterior probability or by the difference between a posterior probability and a prior one. It would need to exploit some more complex function of the relevant probabilities. But there is at least one task that no such function could accomplish. It could not represent the attitude normal among scientists towards important generalizations, or systems of theory, that have been confronted by minor anomalies.

As an example of this attitude, consider how Newton's theory of gravitation was thought at first, even by Newton himself, to give a markedly incorrect value for the forward movement of the apse of the moon. It was not till 1752 that Clairaut showed how the theory could be made to produce results that agreed with the observed movements. Yet no serious thinker in the meantime either qualified or rejected Newton's theory because of its apparent failure to accord with known facts.[21] Similarly no serious thinker rejected Newton's theory because it failed to explain the movement of the perihelion of Mercury, although this movement was in the end explained only by Einstein's general relativity theory. So the history of science makes it clear that a theory may remain widely acceptable even when there is evidence that falsifies it, just so long as the theory has sufficient explanatory power elsewhere. It follows that, so far as a theory's level of inductive support is to constitute the overriding ground for its acceptability, a theory must be capable of being attributed

---

[21] See the remarks by Florian Cajori in the appendix to his edition of Newton's *Principia Mathematica* (Berkeley: University of California Press, 1962), 648 ff. Other examples are given by R.G. Swinburne, 'Falsifiability of Scientific Theories', *Mind*, 73 (1964), 434 ff., and I. Lakatos, 'Falsificationism and the Methodology of Scientific Research Programmes', in I. Lakatos and A.E. Musgrave (eds.), *Criticism and the Growth of Knowlege* (Cambridge: Cambridge University Press, 1970), 138 ff.

a substantial level of inductive support on the basis of evidence that includes minor anomalies, just so long as the favourable evidence is sufficiently strong. Schematically, therefore, we can say that the existence of an inconsistency between E and H should be compatible with E's giving a higher level of inductive support to H than to some comparable theory with which E is also inconsistent.

It is evident, however, that any such compatibility is ruled out not only if E's degree of inductive support for H is to be a simple probability but also if it is to be any function of Pascalian probabilities involving E and/or H. Because Pascalian probability functions are functions of the elements of a Boolean algebra, it can easily be shown[22]—as a consequence of Bayes's theorem —that, in assessing how much inductive support E gives to H, the only probabilities that we could need to take into account are those that are functions of $p(E|H)$, $P(H)$, and $p(E)$. And whatever the function we construct in terms of those probabilities we shall be unable to distinguish between the level of inductive support that E gives H, and the level that E gives H', in any case in which H and H' have the same prior probabilities and E contains anomalies for both H and H' but much stronger positive support for H than for H'. That will be because in such a case the values of $p(E|H)$ and $p(E|H')$ will both be 0 and therefore equal to one another, $p(H)$ and $p(H')$ will also be equal to one another, and there will be just one statement of evidence, E. Accordingly, on a Pascalian analysis of inductive support, if we want to regard some counter-instances to a particular hypothesis as unimportant anomalies that do not serve to give the hypothesis zero value, we have no alternative but either to revise this hypothesis so that it is no longer falsified or to claim that it is not intended to apply the domain of entities within which the counter- instances are found.

The overall position then is not that ampliative induction altogether resists gradation in terms of Pascalian probability, but that each method of securing such a gradation encounters problems that restrict the range of its validity or is forced into trade-offs that restrict its analytical value. Some methods are suited only to enumerative induction, some sacrifice the

[22] L. Jonathan Cohen, *The Probable and the Provable* (Oxford: Clarendon Press, 1977), 189–90.

connection between support for a generalization and support for particular predictions that derive from it, some cannot represent the existence of inductive support for generalizations over indeterminately or infinitely large domains, some rely on calculations from the structure of language where calculations from the structure of reality would be more appropriate, some stand or fall with the truth of some questionable metaphysical principle, some resist objections by sacrificing informativeness, and some can only be sustained if one is prepared to turn a blind eye to the paradoxes that they entail. It is obviously worth considering, therefore, whether any adequate analysis can be achieved in non-Pascalian terms. The next chapter will be concerned to explore the possibility of such an analysis and to evaluate what gains and losses result from adopting it.[23]

---

[23] For personalist analyses of induction see also J. Dorling, 'A Personalist's Analysis of Statistical Hypotheses and Some Other Rejoinders to Giere's Anti-Positivist Metaphysics', in L.J. Cohen and M. Hesse (eds.), *Applications of Inductive Logic* (Oxford: Clarendon Press, 1980), 271–81; P. Horwich, *Probability and Evidence* (Cambridge: Cambridge University Press, 1982); and R.D. Rosenkrantz, *Inference, Method and Decision: Towards a Bayesian Philosophy of Science* (Dordrecht: Reidel, 1977). For a critique of the personalist approach to induction see C. Glymour, *Theory and Evidence* (Princeton: Princeton University Press, 1980), 63–93. Further arguments against any Pascalian analysis of induction are to be found in R. Harré, *The Principles of Scientific Thinking* (London: Macmillan, 1970), 157–77 and K.R. Popper, *The Logic of Scientific Discovery* (London: Hutchinson, 1959), 251–81.

V

The Baconian Gradation of Ampliative Induction

§ 20. INDUCTIVE SUPPORT BY THE METHOD OF RELEVANT VARIABLES

In order to grade inductive support on the basis of evidential variety, we need to set up a list of relevant variables. By manipulating cumulatively increasing combinations of these variables we can, ideally, devise a series of canonical tests, such that the more complex the text a hypothesis has passed, the higher its inductive support. This Method of Relevant Variables elucidates 'consilience' and other ideas in the Baconian tradition. But it is always logically possible for newly discovered data to refute any assumptions about the list of relevant variables by reference to which we assess how much certain experimental results support a given hypothesis.

Let us look more closely into the structure and implications of respect for evidential variety in inductive reasoning.

It has already (§ § 17–18) become apparent that instantial variety is valueless unless it is potentially relevant to the kind of hypothesis under consideration. For example, von Frisch's hypothesis that bees discriminate between blue and other colours received more support from bees returning to a blue-coloured source of food that was moved around several different locations than it would have received from the same number of bees returning to a blue-coloured source of food that remained in the same place on an equal number of different occasions.[1] That was because relative location was known to be a potentially relevant factor in studies of bees' recognition-capacities: bees

[1] See K. von Frisch, *Bees, their Vision, Chemical Sense and Language* (Ithaca: Cornell University Press, 1950). This experiment is analysed in greater detail in L. Jonathan Cohen, *The Probable and the Provable*; (Oxford: Clarendon Press, 1977) 130–3.

have a good memory for places. And in the experiments on colour-recognition variation of the food's position served to eliminate the not wholly implausible hypothesis that memory of place, rather than of colour, was operative. So we have here a clear example of a case in which instantial variety is evidentially superior to instantial multiplicity. But take away relevance from the variety and the situation would be quite different. Suppose, for example, the blue-coloured source of food had been placed the same number of times in the same position but on different days of the week. That kind of variety in the evidence would have had no greater value than mere instantial multiplicity, since there has never been any reason to suppose that bees are influenced in their behaviour by the day of the week.

What is potentially relevant for hypotheses of one category, however, may be quite irrelevant for hypotheses of another and vice versa. Assessments of potential relevance can at best have only a local, not global, validity. Day of the week may be relevant to how certain kinds of people—especially religious people—behave under certain conditions, though quite irrelevant to how bees do. It follows that, where we conceive degree of inductive support to depend on evidential variety, we presuppose some division of hypotheses into distinct categories of enquiry that are defined by reference to their terminology and logical structure. This division may be adjusted from time to time as different lines of enquiry begin to diverge or coalesce. But cross-category comparisons of evidential support are inherently difficult. A hypothesis that has a great deal of variative support within its own category is obviously superior to one that has no support at all, or only a slight amount, in another category. But exact comparisons at intermediate levels are scarcely possible, because they would depend on the possibility of exact comparisons between the degree of potential relevance attributable to a certain characteristic or circumstance in one category of enquiry and the degree attributable to some other characteristic or circumstance in the other category. Indeed, comparisons of potential relevance are difficult enough even within a particular category. How can one tell whether a hypothesis about bees' response to colour should be judged to be better supported if it is apparently instantiated under change of location for a distinctively coloured source of food than if it is apparently instantiated under change of shape for this? And does greater inductive support come from instantiation under two changes of location—one vertical, say, and the other horizontal—than from instantiation under one change of location and one change of shape?

It is easy enough to see how a characteristic or circumstance qualifies for potential relevance within a given category of hypotheses: at least one such hypothesis must be falsified by the presence of this feature. Of course, in practice, the belief that it has been so falsified is itself open to falsification. The original result may not be replicated and another factor may turn out to have been operative instead. But, if we are entitled to presume the efficacy of the original feature in causing the falsification, we are entitled to treat that feature as potentially relevant. What is rather more speculative is to assume a *measure* of relevance, so as to permit comparisons between the inductive values of different kinds of instantial variety. One might go a little way towards achieving such a measure at any one time for a particular feature by counting the number of importantly distinct hypotheses, within the given category, that are currently believed to be falsified by the presence of the feature. But appropriate criteria of distinctness may be hard to establish here, and distinctness may itself be a matter of degree. The hypothesis that bees recognize red seems closer to the hypothesis that they recognize blue than to the hypothesis that they discriminate square shapes from circular ones.

The best way to sidestep all these problems is to give up any attempt to measure inductive support from evidential variety and to aim at ranking or comparing it. This aim can be achieved, within a particular category of hypotheses, by supposing a single idealized sequence of cumulatively more and more thorough tests, any one—or more—of which each hypothesis may in principle undergo. Any hypothesis may then be ranked in accordance with the thoroughness of the test that it is known to have passed, and any two hypotheses may be compared in terms of their rankings.

No doubt there are various ways of constructing such a sequence of tests. But the way that best reflects normal patterns of reasoning in experimental science requires us to introduce the concept of a relevant variable. A relevant variable, within a particular category of hypotheses, is a set of one or more features that are potentially relevant within that category and which are (if more than one) mutually inconsistent with one another. An example, for hypotheses about insects' recognition capacities, might be features of location-change, like being vertical or horizontal, or features of shape-change, like being rounded off or squared off, in the circumstances of the experiment. In each case these features are different from some non-relevant circumstances or characteristic, such as remaining in the same place, or retaining the same shape, respectively. We can think of these non-relevant circumstances or characteristics as being the relatively normal ones, divergences from which are introduced by the manipulation of relevant variables. If under some such manipulation a counter-instance to the hypothesis occurs, this is presumably caused by the presence of that relevant feature just in so far as no counter-instance occurred in the corresponding relatively normal situation. The relatively normal situation is commonly said then to function as a 'control'.

In practice, within a particular field of enquiry, experimental scientists generally have a rough scale of importance for relevant variables, depending partly on the accepted falsificatory efficacy of their variants and partly on convention. When time or money is in short supply, only the most important relevant variables are manipulated in a test. But, given an ordering for the list of relevant variables, it is possible to conceive of a canonical sequence of more and more thorough tests. Suppose that our hypothesis is of the form 'Anything that is A is B'. Then a favourable result for canonical test t_1, in an ideal case, would be constituted by an instance of A that is also B, in circumstances that are normal in relation to all relevant variables: the bees' food-source would be unmoved, and its shape unchanged, when their ability to recognize it is tested. What has been eliminated thus is the possibility that normal circumstances suffice to falsify the hypothesis that is being tested. The evidence furnished by the test-result gives the hypothesis 1st-grade support, whereas an unfavourable test-result here, or evidence that is not the outcome of any canonical test, gives 0th grade support. A favourable result for test t_2, in an ideal case, would be constituted by a favourable result for test t_1, together with instances of A that are also B under each variant of the first relevant variable (for example, change of location) in circumstances that are normal in relation to all the other relevant variables (such as shape of the food-source). What has been eliminated thus is the possibility that, in normal circumstances, manipulation of the first relevant variable suffices to falsify the hypothesis that is being tested: the bees' recognition-capacity is not defeated by vertical or horizontal shifts in the location of their food-source, and the evidence now gives the hypothesis 2nd-grade support. A favourable result for test t_3, in an ideal case, would then be constituted by a favourable result for test t_1, together with instances of A that are also B under each possible combination of a variant of the first or second relevant variables with zero or more variants of the second or first relevant variable, respectively, in circumstances that are normal in relation to all the other relevant variables. That is, alterations of location are now tried out in the various possible combinations with alterations of shape. This test would have an analogous eliminative power giving 3rd-grade support, and subsequently numbered tests would be correspondingly more and more thorough in virtue of their cumulative complexity, with favourable results providing higher and higher levels of inductive support for the hypothesis in question in virtue of their superior eliminative power.

A hypothesis that fails a particular test would also fail any more complex test, because of the cumulative complexity built into the canonical sequence of tests: where $j > i > 0$, each test t_j always includes each test t_i. But the converse would not hold. A hypothesis might fail a more thorough test, t_j, but pass a cruder one, t_i, so that the evidence's support for the hypothesis is at least ith-grade but less than jth-grade. Consequently it is possible for a hypothesis to have greater-than-zero inductive support even on the basis of evidence that includes counter-instances. The Method of Relevant Variables, as we may call the system of assessment that has just been described, is therefore not hit by the problem about anomalies that confronts a Pascalian analysis (p. 142), as when Newton's theory of universal gravitation was agreed to have strong evidential support even though it was known not to explain the movement of the perihelion of Mercury.

Where a hypothesis has instead the form 'Anything that is A is thereby caused to be B', a similar sequence of tests would apply, except that in each trial a successful result would require not just an instance of *A* that is also *B* but, in addition, as what is called a 'control', an instance of not-*A* (some normal situation upon which *A* has not intervened) that is also not-*B*. And correspondingly appropriate adjustments serve to adapt this method of comparing or ranking inductive support to the task of evaluating scientific generalizations that correlate different qualitative or quantitative variables with one another or to the task of evaluating more comprehensive theories.[2] Thus Newton found the connection between spectral colours and different degrees of refrangibility of light rays to be unaffected by the position of the glass, by unevenness of the glass's thickness, by the size of the aperture through which the sun's rays enter, by the angle of these rays' incidence, and so on.[3]

But it is obviously not an essential feature of a canonical test on a hypothesis, at any level of complexity or thoroughness, that the circumstances of the test have to be artificially created. If the hypothesis can be observed in operation over an appropriate variety of naturally occurring circumstances, there is no need for experimental contrivance. What shows the grade of inductive support that exists for the hypothesis is the failure of the hypothesis to be falsified in such-or-such circumstances, irrespective of how those circumstances came into being. The Method of Relevant Variables is in principle applicable in non-experimental sciences (astronomy, ethology, etc.), as well as in experimental ones, even though there may be many practical problems about finding or constructing just the right combinations of circumstances for a particular type of test. Equally it does not matter to the Method of Relevant Variables whether facts constituting a canonical test-result are observed before or after the appropriate hypothesis has been thought up: inductive support is a timeless, quasi-logical relation (see pp. 11–13). Nor does it matter if the variations supporting one theory are described in the language of another. The assessment of inductive support is not tied to any dichotomy between theoretical and observational terminology.

---

[2] Details are given in Cohen, *The Probable and the Provable*, pp. 144–57.
[3] See I. B. Cohen (ed.), *Isaac Newton's Papers and Letters on Natural Philosophy* (Cambridge: Cambridge University Press, 1958), 47–52.

One point of special interest arises in regard to the application of the Method of Relevant Variables to inductive reasoning about wide-ranging explanatory theories. If the explanatory range of one such theory not only embraces, but also extends beyond, the range of another, it is normally considered induct-ively superior to the latter. But in assenting to this intuitively cogent principle we must exclude those cases in which superior explanatory power is achieved trivially, as happens when two mutually independent explanatory theories are tacked into one by conjunction. So, as a sign that no such trivial extension lies at the root of a particular theory's superior explanatory power, we normally welcome the ability of a theory to lead us to some new kind of knowledge. That is, we look to the possibility of deriving novel kinds of prediction that are then experimentally confirmed, as Bacon, Leibniz, Lakatos, and many others have emphasized.[4] Alternatively, it may be that two surprisingly separate sets of phenomena have each independently led us to propose the same theory as an explanation for them. As already remarked (in § 3) Whewell pointed out the importance of such a 'consilience' of inductions, and cited as an example the way in which Newton's theory of universal gravitation 'which had been inferred from the *Perturbations* of the moon and planets by the sun and by each other, also accounted for the fact, apparently altogether dissimilar and remote, of the *Precession of the equinoxes*'.[5]

How does the Method of Relevant Variables represent these facts? First, the different kinds of phenomena that a relatively comprehensive theory ought to explain, in a particular area of enquiry, may be regarded as the relevant variables for that theory, even if no variants of these different variables are in practice ever combinable.[6] So the greater, and therefore the more surprising, the variety of phenomena that a theory

---

[4] F. Bacon, *Novum Organum*, bk. I, aphorisms ciii, cvi, cxvii, in *The Works of Francis Bacon*, ed. J. Spedding, R. Ellis and D.N. Heath (London: Longmans, 1859), i. 204, 206, and 212; G.W. Leibniz, *Die philosophischen Schriften von G.W. Leibniz*, ed. C.J. Gerhardt (1865), i. 196; I. Lakatos, 'Falsificationism and the Methodology of Scientific Research Programmes', in I. Lakatos and A.E. Musgrave (eds.), *Criticism and the Growth of Knowledge* (Cambridge: Cambridge University Press, 1970), 124.

[5] W. Whewell, *The Philosophy of The Inductive Sciences*, 2nd edn. (London: J.W. Parker, 1847), ii. 66 (Whewell's italics).

[6] See Cohen *The Probable and the Provable*, pp. 152-7.

explains, the more thorough the test that it passes and therefore the greater its inductive support from the evidence. Secondly, trivial increases in support are in any case barred by the conjunction principle that is shown below (p. 158) to follow from the Method of Relevant Variables: no conjunction of two propositions can have higher inductive support on given evidence than the less-well-supported conjunct. Thirdly, a theory that generates novel and successful kinds of prediction is in effect expanding our knowledge of relevant variables and is correspondingly more valuable, other things being equal, than a theory that just satisfies our existing expectations.

There is an interesting difference here between the implications of a Pascalian mode of assessment for inductive support and the implications of the Method of Relevant Variables. Any Pascalian mode of assessment implies, as we have seen (pp. 136–7), that the greater the improbability of the evidence, the greater the probability of the hypothesis upon that evidence (other things being equal). And, of course, a high Pascalian improbability that a statement is true is equivalent to a high probability that it is false. So, on a Pascalian analysis of inductive reasoning, a theory gains support from the sheer novelty of a piece of evidence in its favour only if there is a prior reason or tendency to regard the statement of that evidence as false. But according to the Method of Relevant Variables what is required in such cases is not necessarily the presence of a prior reason or tendency to regard that statement as false: it suffices to note the absence of a prior reason or tendency to regard the statement as true. Thus the Method of Relevant Variables admits a wider spread of cases in which the novelty consideration operates. Indeed, while the Method of Relevant Variables treats the *novelty* of awareness of the fact as sufficient to enhance its confirmatory value, the Pascalian analysis requires that fact also to be a *paradoxical* one. But it is doubtful whether the actual history of science reflects so strong a requirement in the matter, nor are there any obvious reasons why it ought to do so.

This point also affects the analysis of what Whewell called 'consilience' (see above). As was remarked in an earlier section (p. 137), a hypothesis that predicts or explains two mutually independent items of evidence will, other things being equal, have a higher Pascalian probability on the combined evidence than on either evidential item alone. So a Pascalian analysis does appear to represent the value of consilience. But it achieves this only at the cost of treating the pertinent evidential items as paradoxical rather than just novel.

The Method of Relevant Variables is an idealization or rational reconstruction, not a description, of what actually goes on. It generalizes and systematizes the intuitions underlying Bacon's tables of presence and absence and Mill's Methods of Agreement and Difference (§ 4). The manipulation of a relevant variable, so as to diverge from a relatively normal situation, echoes Mill's Method of Difference, as does the treatment of causal generalizations. The canonical proliferation of trials, in each of which a different combination of variants of relevant variables is present, echoes Mill's Method of Agreement. But, in order to give explicit recognition to the various ways in which Mill's statement of his Methods represents a somewhat crude and oversimplified system of gradation for inductive reasoning from instantial variety, it is necessary to show what a system of gradation for this would ideally be like. Actual scientific reasoning no doubt falls somewhere intermediate between what Mill's Methods license and what the Method of Relevant Variables does. And for the most part we can live with such an intermediate position, given the constraints on research that are imposed by shortage of available resources, by social pressures for useful results, and so on. Nevertheless it is useful here to set up cognitive ideals as canonical standards, even if only to be able to tell, when reviewing any working judgement of inductive support, how far intellectual values have been subordinated to practical ones.[7] Moreover arguments based on the Method of Relevant Variables are also available for use by scientists in retrospective assessments of what they or their colleagues are justified in claiming to have achieved. Nor is the Method of Relevant Variables the only philosophical idealization that has been proposed in this area. As Ramsey himself was prepared to concede, for example, the personalist theory of probability rests on an underlying idealization about human decision-making (p. 59). Idealization is often

---

[7] A fuller account of the Method of Relevant Variables is given in Cohen, *The Probable and the Provable*, pp. 135–44.

as useful for theory construction in philosophy as it is in natural science.

The Method of Relevant Variables also echoes Keynes's principle of limited independent variety (pp. 133–6), in so far as the *assumed* list of relevant variables at any one time is a finite one and each variant of any one variable is logically independent of any variant of another variable. The Method of Relevant Variables licenses the construction of a plurality of higher-level empirically corrigible theories that state which variables are relevant, in what order of importance, to which categories of ordinary-level hypotheses.

In the progress of human knowledge we always enter into some pre-existing state of the art: if a solitary infant survives to a solitary maturity he will not contribute to the development of science. So there is always some empirical information already available to suggest how we might begin to formulate an ordered list of relevant variables for a given category of hypotheses. And, while we use the list as an (often highly tentative) basis for our inductive evaluations, experience will show, from time to time, how the list should be corrected, extended, or pruned, or how our hypotheses should be recategorized. For example, when pre-clinical tests did not disclose the toxicity of thalidomide, the tragic discovery of its teratogenic properties revealed later that the pregnancy issue should be included in the list of relevant variables for testing hypotheses about the non-toxicity of such drugs. That is, the results of the tests were ˙not replicated in actual practice, with the result that the operation of a hidden variable was diagnosed: some critical factor was absent in the tests and present on some real-life occasions. But at any one time we can test a hypothesis only up to the limit of what we then believe we know about relevant variables. Accordingly, if a hypothesis survives even the most thorough canonical test that we then think to be appropriate, it is reasonable for us then to believe that we know it to be true. Correspondingly scientists often claim to know such-and-such a law or to have proved such-or-such a hypothesis.[8] But others may later nevertheless discover

[8] For example, G. Thomson, 'Matter and Radiation', in R. Harré (ed.), *Scientific Thought 1900–1960: A Selective Survey* (Oxford: Clarendon Press, 1969), 52 ('proof' of the nature of radioactivity), and N.W. Pirie, 'The Viruses', ibid. 237 ('knowledge' of effects of virus infection). Compare A. Einstein and L. Infeld, *The Evolution of Physics* (Cambridge: Cambridge University Press, 1938), 156 ('proof' of the existence of electromagnetic waves).

that hidden and uncontrolled variables were at work in producing the results of earlier tests and that their predecessors were wrong to believe that they knew the truth of their hypotheses. Equally, someone may discover later that his predecessors were wrong to believe that they did not have fully adequate evidence for the truth of a particular hypothesis (which they nevertheless believed to be true) just because at the time they thought their list of relevant variables was incomplete: they knew the truth of the hypothesis but did not know that they knew it. And it follows from this latter point that, in regard to knowledge that is based on ampliative induction in accordance with the Method of Relevant Variables, we cannot accept the so called *KK* thesis,[9] whereby a person's knowing that *p* entails that he knows that he knows that *p*.

This incompatibility with the *KK* thesis is due ultimately to the fact that any judgement of inductive support—that is, any judgement that a particular hypothesis has such-or-such a level of support on given evidence—must, if it is made in accordance with the Method of Relevant Variables, be itself an empirically corrigible judgement, just because, as we have seen, our list of relevant variables for that category of hypotheses is always open to revision on the basis of new experiences. Any claim to inductive knowledge is then indefinitely defeasible. On the other hand, where evaluations of inductive support on given evidence are demonstrable a priori, as on Carnap's theory (§ 17), it will follow that, if the evidential support for a hypothesis were so strong that its truth could be said to be known, then that too could be said to be known. Where judgements of inductive support are a priori, the *KK* thesis applies.

Nor is it only the principle of limited independent variety that fragments, in the Method of Relevant Variables, into a plurality of empirically corrigible theses. The same holds for the principle that Mill called 'the law of causation' (§ 4) and Keynes 'the Uniformity of Nature' (§ 18). To assume that only such-and-such characteristics or circumstances are potentially relevant within a particular category of generalizations is to assume that only the presence of one or more of those features ever falsifies a generalization which holds good in at least one instance when none of those features are present. Moreover, a feature that is

---

[9] See e.g. J. Hintikka, *Knowledge and Belief* (Ithaca: Cornell University Press, 1962), 28–9, 103–25.

assumed to be potentially relevant because it falsifies a generalization on one occasion must also be supposed to falsify it on every other occasion that is similar in relevant respects. Otherwise there would have to be some additional reason why it falsified the generalization on that one occasion. And, if a generalization holds good on at least one occasion despite the presence of this or that combination of relevant variants, it must also be supposed to hold good on any other occasion when the only potentially relevant variants present are the same ones. Otherwise one is not assuming that only the presence of one or more features out of the appropriate list of potentially relevant variants is capable of falsifying the generalization. In short, the thesis that certain variables are all and only those that are potentially relevant within a given category of generalizations implies that (for any such generalization) the results of any test constructed in the canonical way, on the basis of those variables, should always be replicable. Failure to replicate a test-result is always a ground for supposing that there is some mistake in current assumptions about what variables are potentially relevant or about how the various different categories of generalizations are constituted. So it is not a global and apparently unfalsifiable law of causation that is involved in every attempt to replicate a test-result in a particular field of enquiry, as Keynes (though not Mill—see pp. 31–2) seems to have supposed, but rather an empirically corrigible thesis which is only about the kinds of uniformities that exist within that field of enquiry. Such a localized thesis[10] has itself a certain degree of higher-level inductive support, which at any one time we may, or may not, judge accurately from the evidence of previous research.[11]

[10] Localization is a strategy that has been pursued by quite a number of writers in the philosophy of induction: see the papers and bibliography in R.J. Bogdan (ed.), *Local Induction* (Dordrecht: Reidel, 1976).

[11] Some discussions of the Method of Relevant Variables (by I. Levi, A.W. Burks, S. Blackburn, R. Hilpinen, A. Margalit, J.L. Mackie, and M. Hesse, with replies by L.J. Cohen) are to be found in L.J. Cohen and M. Hesse (eds.), *Applications of Inductive Logic* (Oxford: Clarendon Press, 1980), 26–7, 64–7, 172–201, 207–14, 245–50. See also I. Levi, 'Support and Surprise: L.J. Cohen's view of Inductive Probability', *British Journal for the Philosophy of Science*, 30 (1979), 279–92.

§ 21. THE LOGICAL SYNTAX OF THE METHOD OF RELEVANT
VARIABLES

Baconian gradations of inductive support have a logical syntax
(for conjunction, etc.) that cannot be mapped on to the Pascalian
calculus. This system can instead be systematized within a
generalized modal logic. The Carnapian and Baconian systems
of inductive reasoning can then be compared with one another
on a common basis.

In § 20 we sketched how inductive support may be graded by
the Method of Relevant Variables. This method of gradation
incorporates and develops certain key ideas of those philosophers (in particular Bacon, Mill, and Keynes) who thought
that evidential variety, rather than instantial multiplicity,
deserves paramount respect in ampliative induction. But Mill
and Keynes thought also (as we saw earlier in § 4 and § 19) that
the gradation of inductive support from evidential variety has a
logical syntax that is Pascalian. On their view, any function that
measures one proposition's support for another on this basis
must conform to the familiar principles of the classical calculus
of chance: the complementational law for negation, the
multiplicative law for conjunction, and so on. So the question
that arises now is whether the Method of Relevant Variables
generates evaluations of inductive support that are also subject
to these familiar principles. Are those evaluations related to one
another by a Pascalian logical syntax? And it will be convenient
henceforth to refer to those evaluations as 'Baconian', because
they are a systematic development of Bacon's seminal ideas, just
as the modern mathematics of probability is a systematic
development of Pascal's seminal ideas.

Of course, as we saw in § 20, the Method of Relevant
Variables supplies at best a locally valid method for ranking, not
measuring, inductive support. If the number of relevant
variables is finite, that method maps pairs of propositions (typically a generalization and a description of test-results) on to the
first $n + 1$ integers ≥ 0, where n is the number of cumulatively
more and more complex tests that are constructable for the given
category of generalizations. But this restriction to a ranking

function does not suffice to exclude the possibility of an underlying, though unknown, measure-function. One can at least conceive of a field of intellectual judgement in which only rankings and comparisons are practically possible though what are ranked are Pascalian probabilities of which the absolute values are unknown. In such a field of study the ranking for a conjunction of two hypotheses, for example, would always be lower than that for either conjunct, given that neither ranking for a conjunct was maximal or minimal, because of the underlying operation of the multiplicative principle for the Pascalian probability of a conjunction. The product of two numbers m and n, where $1 > m > 0$ and $1 > n > 0$, must always be less than either m or n itself.

However, though the mere fact of restriction to ordinal values does not exclude an underlying Pascalian syntax, the specific pattern of rankings that is generated by the Method of Relevant Variables does indeed suffice to exclude this. Consider what happens in the case of conjunction, as in the case of von Hess's hypothesis that both fishes and invertebrates are colour-blind.[12] Let E state evidence that a generalization H passes test t_i, in the appropriate series of more and more thorough canonical tests, and also that another hypothesis H' passes test t_j, where j is greater than, or equal to, i. Then E must state evidence that the conjunctive hypothesis $H\&H'$ passes at least test t_i, since that hypothesis must resist falsification under all possible combinations of variants of relevant variables manipulated in test t_i. In other words, if the support that E gives H' by Baconian methods is greater than, or equal to, that which it gives H, the support that it gives the conjunction $H\&H'$ is equal to, *not* less than, that which it gives H. So the Pascalian, multiplicative principle for conjunction is not operative here.

Perhaps someone will object that the proposed non-Pascalian principle cannot be correct because it seems to allow the possibility of a positive level of support for a proposition that conjoins two conflicting hypotheses. E might give some support to H and some to H', we shall be told, but if H and H' conflict they cannot possibly both be true and consequently their conjunction cannot deserve to be attributed any positive support. If the Method of Relevant Variables entails this attribution in certain cases, it must obviously be rejected.

---

12 K. von Frisch, *Bees*, p. 4.

But the Method of Relevant Variables entails no such thing. Suppose the conflicting hypotheses are 'All A are B' and 'All A are not-B', respectively. Then any test that the one passes will be failed by the other, so that, by the Method of Relevant Variables, it is impossible for both hypotheses to have a positive level of support: at least one of the two hypotheses must fail test t_1. And, if therefore at least one of the two must have a zero level of support, so too must the conjunction. That is, a proposition that conjoins two conflicting hypotheses cannot have a positive level of support from any evidence.

Someone may object: 'What about a case in which two hypotheses are not logically incompatible, but are highly unlikely, on the basis of other evidence, to be both true?' Well, what this other evidence then shows, if we rely on it, is the presence of a serious flaw in any series of tests by which the conjunction of the two hypotheses is reckoned to have greater than zero support. Though the conjunction principle for the Method of Relevant Variables is a priori, the appropriateness of a particular series of tests is an empirical issue.

Moreover, this conjunction principle for the Method of Relevant Variables not only excludes any underlying conception of inductive support as a Pascalian probability. It can also be shown to exclude inductive support from being thought of as some complex function of any of the related Pascalian probabilities.[13] Indeed, a similar conclusion results from the fact that the Method of Relevant Variables allows the possibility of situations in which a hypothesis has some level of positive support from a statement of evidence that also falsifies it. The statement could report evidence to the effect that the hypothesis passes a less thorough test and fails a more thorough one. Such a hypothesis would cope adequately with the more highly relevant variables, but fail to cope when some less important ones are introduced into the tests. And we have already seen (pp. 142-3) that no simple, or complex, Pascalian analysis of inductive support can accommodate treatment of minor anomalies in this way.

How then can we systematize the logical syntax of Baconian support-gradings? Attention to that question is vital. For, if a philosopher (like Mill, Keynes, or Carnap) succeeds in

---

[13] The proof is given in Cohen, *The Probable and the Provable*, pp. 190-9.

demonstrating that his analysis of inductive support-gradings has a *Pascalian* structure, what the demonstration achieves is not merely a clarification of that analysis but also—to some extent—a confirmation of it. Inductive support, so analysed, has been shown to instantiate a pattern of logical syntax that has several familiar and established manifestations in other kinds of gradation of certainty. A somewhat controversial thesis has been strengthened, it may be hoped, by the acquisition of respectable associations, much as Pascal and the Port-Royal *Logic* originally (§ 3) brought intuitive beliefs about certain non-aleatory issues within the scope of the familiar mathematics of chance, in order that they should be consolidated thereby. So, if the logical syntax of inductive support-gradings generated by the Method of Relevant Variables were wholly idiosyncratic, an analysis in terms of that method would be at a corresponding disadvantage in comparison with any Pascalian analysis.

As it turns out, however, though Baconian evaluations of inductive support do not conform to Pascalian principles, they do conform to the principles of a generalized modal logic, and this modal-logical connection serves in turn to corroborate the legitimacy of such an analysis. The key idea here is that a generalization which holds good (or would hold good) under all manipulations of relevant variables must state a law of nature or a consequence of one, while generalizations that hold good (or would hold good) only under less thorough tests have a status analogous to, but falling suitably short from being, that of such a statement. So a generalization of the latter kind may be said to have a certain degree of legisimilitude, or similarity to law, depending on the thoroughness of the test that it is thought capable of passing. If the evidence is, in effect, that a generalization has been instantiated in all the various combinations of circumstances that constitute test t_i, then background assumptions, conventions or beliefs about relevant variables constitute laws that authorize us to infer from this evidence that the generalization has ith degree legisimilitude. And that is what it means, according to the Method of Relevant Variables, to say that the generalization has ith grade inductive support on the evidence. An inductive support-grading on this view is typically a law-like conditional statement (supported by background evidence) of which the antecedent is a statement of the current evidence and the consequent is a statement that a certain generalization has a specified degree of legisimilitude.

It follows that there is an important difference here from the position on a Pascalian analysis, like Keynes's or Carnap's. A judgement of inductive support here has the structure of a law-like conditional statement, not of a conditional probability, so that the grading of the generalization itself is detachable. Symbolically, where E is the statement of evidence and G the generalization, what the judgement in effect normally asserts is 'It is in accordance with an accepted law that if E is true then G has such-or-such a level of legisimilitude'. So, given E, we can normally detach the specified level of legisimilitude for G, whereas from the Pascalian probability $p(G|E) = n$, we cannot given E, detach $p(G) = n$ except in special circumstances (see also §§ 3, 14, and 26).

In an ordinary modal logic there is either an operator to express 'necessarily', in terms of which 'possibly' is defined as 'not necessarily not', or an operator to express 'possibly', in terms of which 'necessarily' is defined as 'not possibly not'. If we generalize on the former type of logic appropriately there will be a sequence of such operators, which we may symbolize (in relation to a category of generalizations for which there are n relevant variables and therefore a series of n canonical tests[14] as nec_1, nec_2, etc. up to and including an operator nec_{n+2}. The operator nec_{n+2} is to express logical necessity. Just below the latter operator is one that expresses the possession of at least natural necessity—the quality of being a law of nature (capable of withstanding all canonical tests) or a consequence of one. So the top two operators are to imply truth. That is to say, 'If $nec_{n+2}A$, then A' is to be a principle of the system, and so is 'If $nec_{n+2}A$, then A'. Modal operators numbered less than or equal to n are not to imply truth, and thus can be used to imply levels of legisimilitude at which there is still a risk that a more thorough test may reveal falsity. But a higher-numbered modal operator will always imply a lower one: that is 'If $nec_j A$, then $nec_i A$, where $j > i$' is a principle. So '$nec_i A$' expresses the fact that A has *at least* ith degree legisimilitude, while 'not-$(nec_{i+1}A)$' expresses the

---

[14] A more complex system of numbering modal operators is needed where the number of relevant variables is assumed to be denumerably infinite. Such a system is described in Cohen, *The Probable and the Provable*, pp. 222–33.

fact that A has *at most* ith degree legisimilitude. Familiar modal principles from the Lewis–Barcan calculus S4[15] may then be generalized, so that we have, for example, 'If nec_i (if A, then B), then, if nec_iA, then nec_iB' as another principle.

This kind of generalized modal logic can be rigorously formalized and a large number of theorems derived.[16] Some of the theorems are analogous to those derivable within the Pascalian calculus. Thus a theorem is derivable which corresponds to the Special Consequence Condition for inductive support (see pp. 139–40). Such a theorem echoes the fact that any logical consequence of what is unfalsified by certain potentially relevant circumstances will certainly also fail to be falsified by them. But other theorems are radically different from those derivable within the Pascalian calculus. Thus we obtain 'If nec_iA and nec_jB, then $nec_i(A\&B)$' where $j \geqslant i$. This accurately reflects the way in which the Method of Relevant Variables treats conjunction, as we have already seen (§ 21). But it is radically different from the multiplicative principle for conjunction that is integral to the Pascalian calculus.

The 'possible worlds' metaphor, which has been used to provide a systematic formal semantics for ordinary modal logic,[17] may also be used not only to do this for generalized modal logic but also to elucidate the way in which generalized modal logic provides a logical syntax that fits the Method of Relevant Variables. Roughly,[18] a logically possible world is said to be physically possible in relation to a particular category of generalizations if it contains nothing to falsify any such generalization that holds good in the actual world. A physically possible world W is said to be a t_i world for a particular category of generalizations, if every physically possible combination of characteristics and circumstances that can occur in test t_i for that category, is instantiated in W, and no other features are instan-

---

[15] See C. I. Lewis and C. H. Langford, *Symbolic Logic* (New York: Dover, 1932), and R. C. Barcan, 'A Functional Calculus of First Order Based on Strict Implication', *Journal of Symbolic Logic*, 11 (1946), 1–16.

[16] Cohen, *The Probable and the Provable*, pp. 229–40.

[17] See G. E. Hughes and M. J. Cresswell, *An Introduction to Modal Logic* (London: Methuen, 1968), 75 ff.

[18] A fuller account is given in Cohen *The Probable and the Provable*, pp. 240–2, where it is also shown why the appropriate system generalizes the Lewis–Barcan calculus S4, and not S5.

tiated in it. So the actual world, and physically possible worlds that are as rich in instantiated features as it is, each contain a plenitude of relevantly different events. Moreover, each t_i world is said to contain nothing that falsifies any generalization that holds good in a t_j world, where $j \geqslant i$. And a generalization may be said to have at least ith degree legisimilitude if it holds good in any (and therefore in every) t_i world. The execution of an experimental test t_i can thus be thought of as being ideally a simulation of a minimal t_i world, though in practice it is often very difficult to ensure that no hidden variable is operative (no relevant impurities in the materials, no extraneous forces affecting the apparatus, no unregistered alterations of procedure between trials, and so on).

We are also now in a position to epitomize the difference between a Carnapian system of inductive reasoning and a Baconian one. The former is based on measuring the logical range of a proposition by reference to the sum of the values severally assigned to each logically possible world in which the proposition holds good. The latter is based on ranking the legisimilitude of a generalization by reference to the richest kind of physically possible world—highest grade of relevantly eventful world—in which the generalization always holds good. In the former case we calculate a priori from a quantitative summation of possible worlds: in the latter we base ourselves empirically on a qualitatively determined ordering of them. The Carnapian system, mapping pairs of propositions on to real numbers, can give us a single, globally applicable, mathematically convenient measure. But unfortunately it is a measure for which there is no mode of empirical validation. The Baconian system, mapping pairs of propositions on to ordinal numbers, can give us only a plurality of locally applicable and mathematically unsophisticated criteria. But the moulding or remoulding of these criteria is inherently sensitive to the changing state of empirical knowledge about their subject-matter.[19]

---

[19] That is why the Method of Relevant Variables escapes the anti-inductivist threat of historically oriented philosophers of science like Hanson, Toulmin, etc.: see L. Jonathan Cohen, *The Dialogue of Reason* (Oxford: Clarendon Press, 1986), 118–28. A more extensive overview of the situation is afforded by J. E. Adler, 'Criteria for Good Inductive Logic', in L. J. Cohen and M. Hesse (eds.), *Applications of Inductive Logic*, pp. 379–405.

§ 22. SOME NON-STANDARD INTERPRETATIONS OF BACONIAN LOGICAL SYNTAX

The level of a generalization's inductive support from available evidence may be affected by introducing appropriate modifications into its antecedent or into the characterisation of its domain. When the implications of this are explored it becomes clear that Keynesian weight is closely interconnected with Baconian legisimilitude. Light is also shed thus on the relationship between scientific idealizations and the evidence that supports them. And the same underlying structure is found in other types of reasoning, such as in the jurisprudence of common law.

The Pascalian calculus is open, as we have seen (§§ 5–13), to a variety of different interpretations or applications for the gradation of certainty. So too, it turns out, is the generalized modal logic that articulates the syntax of Baconian judgements. Indeed, because of these two facts, if a logical syntax that is suggested for the gradation of certainty is *not* open to a variety of fruitful uses for the purpose, it can hardly have a strong claim on our interest or attention.

Consider first Keynes's concept of weight, which was discussed above in § 14. Roughly, the weight to be associated with the Pascalian probability $p(A|B)$ is the *spread* of relevant evidence that B affords in regard to A. More exactly, we can say that, for any n, the weight of an ordered pair of characteristics or circumstances A and B, where $p(A|B) = n$, is to be understood as the reliability with which $p(As) = n$ may be inferred from Bs (where As and Bs attribute A and B, respectively, to a particular entity s). And this reliability is to be graded by the extent to which B embraces all the characteristics or circumstances that are potentially relevant to A. Smith's probability of survival to the age of seventy is more reliably inferred from premises about his present age *and* his present state of health than from just a premiss about his present age. Thus we can imagine B to be a sequence of appropriately selected characteristics or circum-

---

For philosophies of induction that are neither Pascalian nor Baconian see S. F. Barker, *Induction and Hypothesis* (Ithaca: Cornell University Press, 1957) and G. Schlesinger, *Confirmation and Confirmability* (Oxford: Clarendon Press, 1974).

stances C_1, C_2 . . . that are conjunctively attributed to s; and, as the sequence gets longer, so the conditional 'If C_1s&C_2s& . . ., then p(As) = n' is less exposed to falsification. Moreover, this is true whatever the particular entity s may be. So we are dealing here implicitly with a generalized conditional proposition that is supposed to become less and less exposed to falsification as its antecedent gets more and more heavily qualified in relevant respects.

A close connection with the Method of Relevant Variables now begins to emerge. In the Method of Relevant Variables, we standardly hold the content of a generalization constant and grade its legisimilitude. But, if at some level of test-thoroughness, the hypothesis fails an appropriate test, an alternative, non-standard procedure is available. Instead of grading the legisimilitude of the generalization at less than maximal because of this test-result, it is possible to qualify its antecedent in such a way as to avoid the kind of falsification that produces the unfavourable test-result. Whatever the variants of relevant variables that are responsible for such falsifications, the hypothesis can be modified in a way that will exclude it from purporting to cover situations in which those variants are present. But, in order for the legisimilitude of a hypothesis to be thus increased by the insertion of qualifications into its antecedent, those qualifications have to be necessary for the avoidance of falsification. That is, the hypothesis in its unmodified form needs to be one that would be falsified by the presence of some characteristics or circumstances that are excluded by the modification. For example, if bees fail to re-identify a food-container where the container is red, perhaps the hypothesis about their ability to re-identify food-containers should be restricted to those food-containers that are yellow, blue-green, blue, and ultra-violet. In this way any desired level of legisimilitude can be obtained for a hypothesis in the face of adverse evidence, though at the cost of introducing a corresponding level of reduction in the scope of the claim that it makes. And, when we increase legisimilitude by this means in the case of generalizations that evaluate a monadic probability in their consequent, we are implicitly increasing what Keynes called the weight of the corresponding dyadic probability. That is, when we increase the legisimilitude of a generalization that has the form 'For any x, if C_1x&C_2x& . . .

$\&C_i x$, then $p(Ax) = n'$, by qualifying its antecedent in further favourably relevant ways, we thereby change the underlying conditional probability into one that has greater weight. This probability is now $p(Ax|C_1x\&C_2x\& \ldots \&C_{i+1}x)$, say, not $p(Ax|C_1\&C_2x\& \ldots \&C_ix)$. So, because of this correspondence in value, gradings of weight must have, *mutatis mutandis*,[20] the same logical syntax as statements about legisimilitude. For example, the conjunction principle, as we have already seen (§§ 14 and 21), is the same.

Admittedly the concept of relevance that is employed in determining whether the presence of a certain condition or circumstance increases weight is different from the concept of relevance that is employed in determining whether it increases legisimilitude. The former depends on an inequality between Pascalian probabilities (§ 14), the latter on avoiding the falsification of some generalization within the category (§ 20). But in any area of enquiry in which it is assumed that, whether or not they are ever actually discovered, uniformities rather than probabilities lie at the roots of the data, the two concepts of relevance must be co-extensive in regard to any particular grading of weight or legisimilitude.

Moreover, our ability to increase the legisimilitude of a generalization by qualifying its antecedent is not limited to generalizations that have evaluations of Pascalian probabilities in their consequents. We can do this also, as shown above, for ordinary generalizations that have the form 'For any x, if $C_1x\&C_2x\& \ldots \&C_ix$, then Ax'. Hence, so far as the reliability of any inference authorized by such a generalization—an inference from premises $C_1s, C_2s, \ldots C_is$ to conclusion As—is graded by the legisimilitude of the generalization, this reliability will increase with the number of appropriately chosen premises. We thus have a way of grading the credibility of a singular proposition, on favourable evidence, which depends on the extent of that evidence. The credibility of As given $C_1s\&C_2s\& \ldots \&C_is$ is equal to the legisimilitude of the generalization that the conditional statement 'If $C_1s\&C_2s\& \ldots C_is$, then As' instantiates. And such a way of grading credibility may conveniently

[20] The Special Consequence Condition, in particular, requires some modification: Cohen, *The Probable and the Provable*, 186–7.

be called 'Baconian probability', because it obviously contrasts with the use of Pascalian probability for this purpose. The Pascalian probability of a proposition on stated evidence grades the extent to which that evidence favours rather than disfavours the proposition. The Baconian probability grades instead the extent of the relevant evidence that is stated, when that evidence in any case favours the proposition rather than disfavours it.

Note how this contrast corresponds with the difference that was remarked earlier (pp. 17–8, p. 57, p. 104) between the intuitive concept of probability that is complementational—because it treats the credibility of a proposition as being equal to the incredibility of its negation—and the intuitive concept that is non-complementational—because under appropriate conditions it allows the credibility of a specified proposition and the credibility of its negation to be both rather low. Correspondingly the Pascalian calculus affords us the theorem $p(A|B = 1 - p(\text{not-}A|B)$, whereas the generalized modal logic, within which the logical syntax of Baconian probability may be developed, supplies instead the theorem 'If $p(A|B) \geq i$ and $p(\text{not-}A|B) \geq i$, then $p(\text{not-}B) \geq i$'.[21] That is, the negation principle for Baconian probability represents a kind of generalization of the idea of proof by *reductio ad absurdum*. If on a stated evidential premiss B both A and its negation have some degree of credibility, and so the conjunction of A and its negation is implied to have some degree of credibility, then a corresponding degree of credibility must attach to the denial of that premiss. So in the logic of Baconian probability a relative limit is imposed on the extent to which a proposition and its negation may both be equally credible on the evidence stated, since as the level of this credibility mounts, so too must credibility of the proposition that there is something false in the statement of evidence. There is thus a relative limit on the height to which the Baconian probabilities, on given evidence, of two contradictory propositions can rise, when these probabilities are equal to one another, though there is no limit short of zero to which they can fall. The ultimate reason why both can fall to zero is that they both stem from the legisimilitude-levels of appropriate covering generalizations, and it is quite possible for two conflicting

[21] Ibid. pp. 217–44, esp. p. 223.

generalizations, like 'Anything if *B* is *A*' 'Anything if *B* is not *A*', both to have 0th grade legisimilitude, if neither has passed even the simplest canonical test. But the principle of complementationality limits the depth to which the Pascalian probabilities of two contradictory, and equiprobable, propositions can fall at the same time as it limits the height to which those probabilities can rise: specifically, they can neither both fall lower than 0.5 nor both rise higher than that same point.

Similarly, Baconian probability (like legisimilitude) conforms to a non-multiplicative principle for conjunction. We have already remarked (pp. 19–20) on the suitability of such a principle for judgements of credibility in certain contexts. And it is arguably needed in any court of law that requires proofs of fact to be established on the balance of probability, as for civil cases in the Anglo-American system.[22] The point is that two or more independent issues may be at stake in a case and then a multiplicative principle for conjunction generates paradox. For, even if a plaintiff proved each of two such issues with a satisfactory Pascalian probability of 0.6, say, he would have established only a 0.36 Pascalian probability of being in the right overall, whereas separate proofs of each issue are normally taken by the courts to prove the case as a whole.

Again, we remarked earlier (pp. 20–1), on the need, in certain forensic contexts, for judgements of probability to be necessarily contraposable. We may want our logic or mathematics to ensure an equality between the probability that a particular accused is guilty, given that such-and-such evidence is before the court, and the improbability of that evidence's being before the court, given that the accused is not guilty. And, whereas Pascalian conditional probabilities are not necessarily contraposable and so cannot capture this intuition, a dyadic judgement of Baconian probability is necessarily contraposable in the required way because it stems from the legisimilitude of its covering generalization.

Moreover, when we develop the logical syntax of Baconian probability we come across yet other features that, in certain

[22] Cohen, *The Probable and the Provable*, pp. 58–67, 265–7. An analogous problem arises about the standard of proof in criminal cases. For another point of view see Sir R. Eggleston, *Evidence, Proof and Probability*, 2nd edn. (London: Weidenfeld and Nicolson, 1983), 34–49.

contexts, may be preferable to the syntactic principles of Pascalian probability. Thus it may sometimes seem paradoxical that, though a very minute value for the monadic Pascalian probability $p(A)$ is in principle compatible with a very high value for the dyadic Pascalian probability of the same proposition $p(A|B)$, a zero value for the Pascalian $p(A)$ requires a zero value for $p(A|B)$. Cannot belief in a particular outcome sometimes seem quite groundless on prior reflection, until evidence favouring it begins to come in? We obviously need to distinguish here the non-inferability of A on prior grounds from the inferability of not-A (see pp. 112–13). The Baconian $p(A) = 0$ expresses the former, while the Pascalian $p(A) = 0$ expresses the latter. Correspondingly, a zero value for the monadic Baconian probability $p(A)$ is in principle compatible with any value whatever for the dyadic Baconian probability $p(A|B)$.

Another pattern of reasoning that has an important isomorphism with the Method of Relevant Variables is the establishment of idealizations, as when Boyle's law is argued to be true of perfect gases though not of actual ones, or the velocity of a falling body is correlated with its period of fall on the assumption that it is falling in a frictionless medium. Some philosophers[23] suppose that this pattern of reasoning is inherently different from induction, on the ground that it does not aim to register and systematize observed phenomena but rather to establish models that oversimplify reality. However, to look at the matter thus you have to conceive induction as a rather crude and unstructured procedure in which people build solely on what they have passively observed. Once the importance of experimental interference with Nature is accepted and the Method of Relevant Variables is properly understood, it is apparent instead that idealization is a form of variative induction. It is a way of ensuring maximal legisimilitude if the generalization in question would be falsified not only where any variant of a particular relevant variable is present but also in the normal situation (see pp. 148–50 above) where no such variant is present. For example, the standard equation for the velocity of a falling body fails to hold not only in the special case of a stone falling in water

---

[23] For example, L. Nowak, 'Idealization and Rationalization: An Analysis of the Anti-Naturalist Programme', *Epistemologia*, 2 (1979), 287–8.

or treacle—on which many substances float—but also in the normal case of a stone falling in the earth's atmosphere. So idealization has some similarity to the procedure of qualifying a generalization that underlies judgements of weight or of Baconian probability. Like that procedure idealization aims at the modification of a hypothesis, rather than its rejection, in the face of falsifying factors. But in the case of weight or Baconian probability the modification is achieved by complicating the antecedent of the hypothesized generalization, whereas in the case of idealization it is achieved by simplifying the domain to which the generalization applies. The particles of a perfect gas, for example, have positions but no dimensions or interactions.

Perhaps someone will object that if an idealized generalization does not have to be true of the actual world, but only of some much more jejunely furnished non-actual world, there can be no inductive grounds for choosing between one such idealization and another. No observable fact, he may say, is predictable from, or explainable by,[24] any idealization, and therefore no inductive confirmation or disconfirmation of it is possible. So the Method of Relevant Variables tolerates any idealization whatever, because no experience in the actual world could ever falsify a generalization that purports to apply only under conditions that do not occur in the actual world.

But the objection misses a crucial feature of the procedure whereby the appropriate modification of a generalization can raise its legisimilitude. The point is that the modification has to be one that is necessary if falsification by the evidential facts is to be avoided: if the modification is not made, those facts suffice to falsify the generalization. This requirement operates, as we saw, when such a modification takes the form of introducing an appropriate qualification into the generalization's antecedent. And it operates also when the modification changes instead the generalization's domain of application. When we want such a generalization to have high legisimilitude, we seek a generalization that has no other modifications than those forced on it by the evidential facts. So every difference between the values of a

---

[24] For the claim that idealized generalizations cannot generate explanations in accordance with the covering law model see N. Cartwright, *How the Laws of Physics Lie* (Oxford: Clarendon Press, 1983), 44–53.

particular physical variable that are predicted to hold in certain circumstances under ideal conditions, and the values that are observed to hold in those circumstances under conditions occurring in the actual world, has to result from features of the actual world that are excluded by the idealization: if it were not for the idealization, the value predicted would be the one that is actually found. Correspondingly, any idealization implying unexplainable differences from values in the actual world has to be rejected or treated with reserve. Of course, the processes of approximation, by which observable evidence from the actual world is matched to generalizations applying only to an ideally simplified world, are in practice often delicate and difficult, allowing room for considerations of theoretical elegance to enter into the precisification of the ultimate solution. But in principle idealizations are to be graded inductively, by the Method of Relevant Variables, in terms of those criteria of legisimilitude that are appropriate to their category of subject-matter.

So far, in the present section, we have discussed various non-standard ways in which the Method of Relevant Variables impinges on the gradation of legisimilitude. The situations envisaged were those where, in place of assuming a fixed formulation for a hypothesis about some factual issue and examining the conditions under which this or that grade of legisimilitude would be assignable to it, we instead assume a desired degree of legisimilitude for the hypothesis and examine the conditions under which this or that reformulation would be appropriate to it. Indeed, if we consider only the appropriate types of modification in the antecedents of our hypothesis, the underlying modal calculus can actually be interpreted as a logical syntax for gradings of evidentially permissible simplification. That is, if H is an unmodified hypothesis in a particular category, then, for every support assessment stating that on the evidence of E, H has ith grade support, there is an equivalent statement of evidentially permissible simplification stating that, on the evidence of E, the simplest fully supported version, or versions, of H has, or have, ith grade simplicity, according to appropriate criteria of simplicity.[25] But in all this the

---

[25] See L. Jonathan Cohen, *The Implications of Induction* (London: Methuen, 1970), 142–55, for the details of this.

subject-matter of the hypotheses considered is standard enough: namely, the properties of observable objects, causal relations between observable events, correlations between physical parameters, and so on. What is non-standard is the mode of inductive reasoning.

It is also possible, however, to reason inductively about non-factual issues. For example, as we saw earlier (§ 2) Bacon thought that when people extract general legal maxims from judicial decisions in particular cases they use the same patterns of reasoning as are used in experimental science. Jurists opposing an inductivist analysis of common law reasoning, like Bacon's, have sometimes pointed out that a great deal of this reasoning is concerned to establish the correct meanings of legal rules rather than their truth or validity. They have argued thence that the determination of vagueness is a function of legal reasoning which sharply differentiates it from any kind of deduction or induction.[26] But we have already seen how the appropriate reformulation of a hypothesis in the light of relevant evidence may be seen as an exercise in ampliative induction. And the Method of Relevant Variables can be shown to constitute a systematic basis for the analysis of reasoning in common law jurisprudence.[27] To regard a hitherto ignored type of circumstance as material to a decision in a particular trial is comparable with discovering the operation of a hidden variable in a particular natural-scientific experiment. Again, Keynes and Polya, developing the hints of some older mathematicians, such as Euler and Laplace, thought that ampliative induction was a mode of justification for mathematical conjectures that is useful where a demonstration is not available.[28] (This inductive procedure is essentially *non*-demonstrative and so is not to be confused with what is often called 'recursive induction', whereby what is mathematically demonstrable about the first member of a series, and also about the successor of any member about which it is demonstrable, is held to be demonstrable about

[26] For example, O.C. Jensen *The Nature of Legal Argument* (Oxford: Blackwell, 1957), 28, and E.H. Levi, 'An Introduction to Legal Reasoning', *University of Chicago Law Review*, 15 (1948), 502.

[27] See Cohen, *The Implications of Induction* 155–71.

[28] J.M. Keynes, *A Treatise on Probability* (London: Macmillan, 1921), 242–3, and G. Polya, *Patterns of Plausible Inference* (Princeton: Princeton University Press, 1954), 109 ff.

every member of the series.) And, though Keynes and Polya thought that any ampliative inductive justification of a mathematical conjecture should be assessable by an appropriate Pascalian credibility-function, Lakatos developed some of Polya's ideas in a way that, in effect, exhibited a non-standard use of the Method of Relevant Variables. He was particularly concerned to explore the various ways in which a mathematical conjecture might be revised, rather than rejected, in the face of counter-examples.[29] Moreover, several other kinds of non-factual issues are open to inductive reasoning in accordance with the Method of Relevant Variables. For example, we can grade the acceptability of ethical, grammatical, or philosophical principles, or of computer-implementable expert systems programs, in this way.[30]

In general a subject-matter is implied to admit of such inductive reasoning if non-accidental uniformities are thought capable of existing in it. But it is important to be careful about what exactly are to count as the evidential data in each case. Harman has argued, for example, that scientific theories have an explanatory role in relation to particular observings that ethical theories do not have in relation to particular exercises of our moral sense. He points out that neither the relevant moral principles nor the wrongness of the act contribute anything towards explaining why you have the moral feelings that you do when you see some children setting fire to a cat.[31] But what kind of explanation is at issue here? If the explanation in question is of some matter of fact—that is, if it is an explanation that a causal or statistical hypothesis or a scientific theory might provide—then of course one should not expect any normative judgement to provide that type of explanation. Indeed, when it is claimed that norms can constitute a topic for inductively supported generalization as well as facts can, then an intrinsic part of the claim is that explanatory inductive generalization

---

[29] I. Lakatos, 'Proofs and Refutations', *British Journal for the Philosophy of Science*, 14 (1963-4), 1-25, 120-39, 221-45, 296-342.

[30] See Cohen, *The Implications of Induction*, 172-82 and, for inductive reasoning in philosophy, L. Jonathan Cohen, *The Dialogue of Reason* (Oxford: Clarendon Press, 1986), 63-148.

[31] G. Harman, *The Nature of Morality* (New York: Oxford University Press, 1977), 1-9.

need not be tied up exclusively with factual explanation in terms of causes, probabilities, and so on. More specifically, if the explanation sought is not of why you have the moral feelings that you do but rather of why the moral feelings that you have are the right ones to have—that is, if the explanation sought is not an explanation of your attitude's *de facto* psychological properties but of its *de jure* normative status—then the relevant moral principle may provide a perfectly good explanation. You are right to be outraged by what the children are doing to the act, people might say, because it is an act of wanton cruelty. And the relevant datum in such a case is the wrongness of the act, which normal people feel, rather than the fact that they feel this wrongness.

We need to note here, however, that the general theories, principles, and so on that are cited in our explanations serve this explanatory purpose best if they also have inductive support that is independent of the items currently requiring explanation. Moreover, it is by no means the case that every inductively supported generalization provides the best explanation of its own evidential support. The blackness of the birds that we now see on the summer fields is perhaps best explained by the operation of their genes, or by the operation of certain environmental factors in the evolution of their species, but not at all well explained by the fact that they are crows and the generalization that all crows are black. Yet they constitute inductive evidence for that generalization. So it is certainly not safe to suppose that induction is always an inference to the best explanation.[32]

Finally, it should be noted that, while the Method of Relevant Variables imposes a realist interpretation on the underlying Baconian syntax, an idealist interpretation is also possible. That is, we can discern this generalized modal structure not only in judgements of legisimilitude—that is, in judgements about the objective falsificatory powers of relevant factors—but also in certain kinds of judgement about the subjective acceptability of hypotheses. Levi's logic of acceptability, for example, which was developed on the basis of earlier work by G.L.S. Shackle, has a non-multiplicative principle for conjunction that is isomorphic with the principle implicit in the Method of Relevant Variables.[33]

---

[32] *Pace* G. Harman, *Thought* (Princeton: Princeton University Press, 1973), 130–41.

[33] See I. Levi, *Gambling with Truth* (New York: Knopf, 1967), and 'Potential Surprise: its Role in Inference and Decision-Making', in Cohen and Hesse (eds.), *Applications of Inductive Logic*, pp. 1–27.

In sum, then, what has been shown in the present chapter is that the Method of Relevant Variables presents us with a mode of ampliative induction which is based on relevant evidential variety. It systematizes some key intuitions in the Baconian tradition, but has a non-Pascalian structure which may be articulated in a generalized modal logic. This logic is applicable over a wide field of reasoning-patterns, and we must therefore now pass on to examine some further considerations that bear on the relative merits of Pascalian and Baconian analyses of ampliative induction.

VI

Four Paradoxes about Induction

---

§ 23. THE CLASSICAL PROBLEM OF INDUCTION

Hume's problem about induction cannot be resolved by reference to the ideas of Bernoulli, of Kant, or of Harré and Madden. Nor is it satisfactory to accept Hume's own resolution of the paradox by reference to the operation of our natural inclination. Popper's earlier treatment of the issue tended to cut science off from any rationally defensible utilization, while any serious exploitation of the concept of verisimilitude, as in his later writings on the subject, tends to topple over into unacknowledged inductivism. Since Hume attacked the rationality of induction by stressing those features in which it apparently differs from deduction, we may answer his attack by stressing those features in virtue of which it resembles deduction. Deducibility must be seen as a limiting-case of inducibility, whether the latter be conceived in Pascalian or in Baconian terms. But we can never have conclusive certainty about any fact that is as yet unobserved.

Paradoxes have always been a stimulus to philosophical analysis. Where irresistible considerations seem to lead to opposed conclusions, philosophical intervention is needed. But the guiding motivation of such intervention is to maintain the consistency of the whole intellectual framework within which we reason, not just to solve a particular puzzle in its own terms. So in examining various paradoxes about induction we should treat them as providing a battery of tests that any adequate account of induction should pass, rather than as constituting a set of unrelated problems that admit of mutually independent solutions.

The classical paradox about induction arose as a by-product of empiricist epistemology in the late seventeenth and early eighteenth centuries. It was hinted at in Locke's *Essay* and else-where[1] and explicitly formulated for the first time in Hume's *Treatise*[2] though neither Locke nor Hume used the term 'induc-tion' at all in this context.[3] The paradox was generated by the fact that, according to an empiricist, the premisses of our factual knowledge were all particular, distinct perceptual experiences, not general principles of any kind, whereas the content of our factual knowledge seemed to include many causal laws and other generalizations about natural processes. A rationalist could claim that such general conclusions were deducible, in accord-ance with standard logical rules, from even more general premisses that Providence had kindly made self-evident. But there was no way that these general conclusions, with their implications about the as yet unperceived, could be so deduced from premisses about particular past events. Indeed, there was nothing logically impossible, nothing self-contradictory, in supposing such a commonly accepted conclusion to be false even though the premisses were true.

So just at the very period at which the scientific revolution seemed to have produced its greatest theoretical achieve-ment—Newtonian mechanics—the triumph of empiricist over rationalist epistemology seemed to imply, if Hume was right, that this achievement had no rational foundation. No valid inference was possible from the past to the future, or from what is in sight to what is out of sight. Nor was it any use trying to rescue the situation by an appeal to some overarching principle about the uniformity of nature, whereby, in relevant respects, the future might be guaranteed to be like the past and unseen instances of a property like seen ones. With such a principle as a major premiss, Hume thought, the requisite deductions would be forthcoming. But, he pointed out, the truth of that major

---

[1] See J. Locke, *Essay Concerning Human Understanding* (London; T. Basset, 1690), bk. IV, ch. 3, § 14 *ad fin.*, and ch. 6 § 16; and J. R. Milton, 'Induction before Hume', *British Journal for the Philosophy of Science*, 38 (1987), 49–74.

[2] *A Treatise of Human Nature*, (1739), ed. L. A. Selby-Bigge (Oxford: Clarendon Press, 1888) bk. I, pt 3, Sect. 14.

[3] Neither Locke's *Essay* nor Hume's *Treatise* pays any attention, whether critical or commendatory, to Francis Bacon's inductive methodology, though Bacon's writings were well known and widely read in the century after his death.

premiss would itself be at least as impossible to substantiate by formallogically sanctioned deduction from the ultimate premisses of experience.

Of course, where induction is not about factual matters, but about a system of ethical principles, say, or of common law maxims (see p. 172), no such paradox need arise, since a general rule authorizing inductive inference may be supposed to be implicitly stipulated with the imposition of the system. Justice requires that like cases be treated alike, and legislators can decide to impose justice on a human community. But we humans cannot decide to impose uniformity on the processes of Nature.

One tempting line of approach to Hume's problem is via Bernoulli's limit theorem (see pp. 118–19). If under appropriate assumptions the examination of a sufficiently large sample can let us learn something, with a corresponding degree of confidence, about the probability with which a certain characteristic exists in a specified population, then it looks as though a confidence-function can operate here as a measure of predictability by enumerative induction. But the value of such a function for this purpose is restricted by our having to assume that the sample is not biased by some lack of homogeneity in the population. If we want to calculate the survival prospects of a twenty-year-old student, we should be wary of drawing our sample solely from the members of our university's rock-climbing club. Of course, as the weight of the evidence (see § 16) goes up, it would be normal to discount this kind of worry. But assessments of weight rely on the assumption that existing judgements of evidential relevance will remain true for the future. So there is no escape here from the jaws of Hume's problem: we are merely shifting the point at which the bite is felt.

Some philosophers have tried to resolve Hume's problem by proposing a different view of the typical premisses from which reasoning about causal connections proceeds. Thus Kant argued that the objects of our perceptual judgements must themselves be structured by the category of cause and effect, if we are to have the kind of experience that we do have. And every particular cause must presuppose a uniformity of causal connection. So the uniformity of nature pervades the whole of the perceivable world. But the details of Kant's intricate argument are notoriously open to criticism.[4] Nor is it at all clear from Kant's text why the actual procedures of enumerative or variative induction should have any rational cogency. His theory does not elucidate why superiority in the number or variety of evidential instances can justify grading the support for one hypothesis higher than that for another. There is, for example, no attempt at a transcendental argument for a principle of limited independent variety (see § 18).[5]

Harré and Madden[6] have claimed that Hume was wrong to regard the objects of our perception as distinct existences. Instead, Harré and Madden argue, objects intrinsically possess causal powers which they exercise on one another, and the rationality of inductive inferences is founded on these links of natural necessity. But unfortunately all the old difficulties about proving the uniformity of nature arise again about proving the reality of causal powers. One can hardly rely on arguing that such powers are to be seen all round us, since so many philosophers, over so many centuries, have evidently failed to see them anywhere. And one can hardly argue that their underlying reality is established by the observable uniformities that they produce, since it is just those observable uniformities about which, according to Hume, we have no justifiable certainty.

Hume's own way of handling the problem was to accept the sceptical conclusion. On his view human beings, like animals, have a natural inclination to believe in the existence of a causal connection between one kind of event and another, whenever they have observed events of the one kind uniformly followed in their experience by events of the other. And the inclination becomes proportionately stronger, according as the events in question resemble the hitherto observed ones more closely. This natural inclination suffices for all the practical purposes of life.

---

[4] I. Kant, *Critique of Pure Reason* (1781), trans. N. Kemp Smith (London: Macmillan, 1929), 218–27. For an example of the criticism see S. Körner, *Kant* (Harmondsworth: Pelican Books, 1955), 87.

[5] Indeed, Kant had at one time held that natural variety is *un*limited: W. R. Shea, 'Filled with Wonder: Kant's Cosmological Essay, *The Universal Natural History and Theory of the Heavens*', in R. E. Butts (ed.), *Kant's Philosophy of Science* (Dordrecht: Reidel, 1986), 110–14.

[6] R. Harré and E. H. Madden, *Causal Powers: A Theory of Natural Necessity* (Oxford: Blackwell, 1975).

So the absence of any rational justification for the belief is a matter of concern only to philosophers, and the latter can dispel their worries at any moment by leaving their studies and indulging their natural inclinations.

Such a resolution of the paradox has at least three weaknesses. In increasing order of importance they are as follows.

First, it is in any case an inaccurate psychological observation that when people believe in a causal connection they have previously perceived a constant conjunction, since the causal connections that we discover in everyday life are not to be identified with the underlying uniformities that scientists aim at discovering. We all believe that a fire emits sensible heat although we also know that heat insulation often prevents this emission. The causal connections that we talk about in everyday life are sequences of events that hold good only in normal circumstances, not universally. But Hume could easily have corrected himself on this point, without sacrificing anything integral to his sceptical thesis.

Secondly, and more importantly, Hume seems to be arguing with his readers and trying to persuade them of the existence of a psychological law. This law is to the effect that people develop the natural inclination which Hume describes whenever they have observed the corresponding conjunction of events to be uniformly present in their experience. But belief in the existence of such a psychological law can itself have no rational foundation, if Hume is right, since *no* causal law then has a rational foundation. So, like many other sceptics, Hume can be hoisted on his own petard. If what he says is true, we should already believe it before reading what he says, and if somehow we do not already believe it he can certainly give us no reason for doing so. Either way his remarks are pointless.

Thirdly, just as Hume's resolution of the paradox makes no allowance for his own apparent ability to argue about psychological laws and the strength of evidence for their existence, so too it makes no allowance for the many ways in which scientists reason with one another about what the laws of nature are and what the strength of evidence is for their existence. Since these scientists apparently think that they are appealing to rationally cogent considerations, some account of those considerations is needed along with a brief explanation of their plausibility.

Indeed Hume himself does give an account of them in another section of his *Treatise* where he speaks of 'rules by which to judge of causes and effects', of 'the LOGIC that I think proper to employ in my reasoning' on the subject, and of a constant conjunction that 'proves' a causal connection.[7] But this way of speaking is not consistent with the sceptical thesis that is Hume's dominant doctrine, since it concedes the existence of an inductive logic, however jejune, as distinct from the deductive logic which is all that Hume's sceptical thesis admits. Nor does Hume ever offer any explanation of why it is that scientists and others come to believe that they are appealing to rational considerations, which could stand beside his explanation of why they come to believe in the existence of this or that natural uniformity.

Popper's way of handling the problem[8] is to accept Hume's conception of logical reasoning as being purely deductive, but to reject any inference from this that certain characteristic patterns of scientific thinking are inherently non-rational. On Popper's view, though ampliative induction has no logical validity, that does not detract from the rationality of science since valid scientific thought is always deductive, never inductive. And valid scientific thought is deductive because scientists properly seek to falsify their conjectures, not to verify them. For falsification the standard logical procedure of *modus tollendo tollens* suffices, in that, if a prediction deducible from a generalization is falsified, so too is the generalization itself. Admittedly scientists require any conclusive falsification of a hypothesis to be replicable in order to guarantee inter-personal objectivity. So that it might seem as though Popper has to let inductive reasoning come in again by the back door in order to establish the replicability of any test-result that is supposed to falsify a hypothesis conclusively. But Popper treats the claim that such-or-such a test-result is replicable as being subject in its turn to the falsificatory procedures of deductive logic. There is thus on his view an inevitable regress by which systems of theory are tested by deducing from them statements of a lesser level of universality, which are then in turn themselves testable, and so on. At any one time the

---

[7] Bk. I, pt 3, Sect. 15.

[8] K.R. Popper, *The Logic of Scientific Discovery* (London: Hutchinson, 1959), 29–30. The main text of this book was originally published in German as *Logik der Forschung* (Vienna: Julius Springer, 1934).

regress is just interrupted in practice at some point by scientists' decision or convention to accept a testable proposition without (as yet) actually testing it further.

Of course, falsification will not do the whole job, because at any one time, in a particular field of enquiry, more than one hypothesis may survive the toughest tests currently available. How, then, does one choose between one unfalsified hypothesis and another? In such a situation, Popper said,[9] scientists prefer the hypothesis that has most content, as measured by its prior improbability (which is to be judged in Pascalian terms). And Popper's philosophy of science thus faces in a direction starkly opposite to the philosophy of those who, like Carnap (see § 17 above), consider that the proper aim of scientists is to maximize the Pascalian probability of their hypotheses on the available evidence, since, other things being equal, the probability on the evidence will, according to Bayes's Law (p. 23), be lower if the prior probability is lower.

Later Popper came to think that his conception of scientific reasoning needed supplementation, for two main reasons.[10] First, it did not do justice, he thought, to the fact that theories which are known to be false may nevertheless be very highly regarded by reputable scientists. Minor anomalies are not treated as grounds for rejecting a powerful theory that has no serious competitor in its field (see pp. 142–3 above). So one needs to find a way of distinguishing between false theories that are more valuable and false theories that are less valuable. Secondly, there is a deeply engrained idea among scientists that they are engaged in a search for truth, albeit for relevant and interesting truth, and this idea is not at first sight compatible with the doctrine that they characteristically seek to falsify their hypotheses rather than to verify them.

Popper therefore developed a measure of verisimilitude whereby even false hypotheses might be compared with one another in respect of their truth-content. In terms of such a measure an appropriate value was to be attached to powerful theories that encountered minor anomalies, and at the same time due regard could be paid to the intuitive idea that scientists are engaged in a search for truth. As it turned out there were

[9] K. R. Popper, *The Logic of Scientific Discovery*, pp. 113–19.
[10] K. R. Popper, *Conjectures and Refutations: The Growth of Scientific Knowledge* (London: Routledge and Kegan Paul, 1963), 215–48.

serious flaws in Popper's own measure for verisimilitude,[11] and other measures have been proposed to take its place, sometimes directed towards assessing the quantity of true content and sometimes towards assessing closeness to truth.[12] But any admission of the importance of verisimilitude tends to jeopardize the integrity of Popper's anti-inductivist stance. This becomes clear when we consider whether verisimilitude can be measured.

If there is never any effective way even of estimating, let alone of accurately measuring, the relative verisimilitude of two falsified theories in the light of the available evidence, then the concept of verisimilitude is idle. Under those conditions it would have no discoverable application and nobody could be said to be aiming at superior verisimilitude because nobody could hope to recognize when or where this had been achieved. But, if the concept of verisimilitude is not idle and there is sometimes an effective way of estimating relative verisimilitude in the light of the available evidence, then it looks as though induction is being allowed back under another name. It is just that instead of trying in such cases to establish the absolute and unqualified truth of his hypothesis, a scientist is said to be trying, more modestly, to establish its superior share of, or closeness to, the truth. And Popper himself suggests that, where two theories have both been falsified but one has withstood some tests that the other has failed, this would count as evidence that the former has greater verisimilitude than the latter. We should then 'accept' the former theory, he says, 'because of experiments which were crucial between' the two theories.[13] But there is little essential difference between this procedure and what the Method of Relevant Variables entails in a similar context (see § 20). What is really being sought is legisimilitude, not just verisimilitude.[14]

[11] P. Tichy, 'On Popper's Definition of Verisimilitude', *British Journal for the Philosophy of Science*, 25 (1974), 155–60, and D. Miller, 'Popper's Qualitative Theory of Verisimilitude', ibid. 166–77.

[12] See e.g. G. Oddie, *Likeness to Truth* (Dordrecht: Reidel, 1986); I. Niiniluoto, *Truthlikeness* (Dordrecht: Reidel, 1987); and the collection of papers by various authors: T.A.F. Kuipers (ed.), *What is Closer-to-the-Truth?* (Amsterdam: Rodopi, 1987).

[13] Popper, *Conjectures and Refutations*, p. 235.

[14] On resemblances between Popper's philosophy of science and Bacon's see P. Urbach, 'Francis Bacon as a Precursor to Popper', *British Journal for the Philosophy of Science*, 33 (1982), 113–32. On resemblances between Popper's philosophy of science and the philosophies of Whewell and of Peirce see I. Niiniluoto, 'Notes on Popper as Follower of Whewell and Peirce', *Ajatus*, 37(1978), 272–327.

Nor should this be surprising, since only legisimilitude, not verisimilitude, can guarantee the applicability to counterfactual
instances that is often needed when knowledge of general laws or
causal connections is exploited (see pp. 131–2).

Indeed, it seems a general weakness in Popper's position that
when attempts are made to buttress it against obvious implaus-
ibilities it tends to topple over into some kind of unacknowledged inductivism. Lakatos, for example, wanted to emend it
in a different direction. Instead of considering the rationality
issue in relation to single hypotheses, Lakatos thought rather
about research programmes, in which a series of hypotheses
replaced one another as the programme either succeeded or
petered out.[15] But (though his objections to the qualification of
hypotheses in the light of new evidence were too sweeping[16]) the
criteria that Lakatos proposed for telling a 'progressive' from a
'degenerating' research programme were largely the same as
those familiar in the inductivist tradition for choosing between
better and worse theories. What makes the move from theory to
theory a progressive research programme is that it achieves
some kind of consilience and also leads to novel predictions that
are subsequently confirmed (compare pp. 151–3 above). Moreover, even a Popperian emphasis on falsification is quite compatible with the Baconian conception of induction by elimination. Bacon himself wrote that 'the foundations of true induction
are laid in elimination'.[17]

On the other hand, if we stay with the hard core of Popperian
anti-inductivism we are left with a conception of pure science as
a mode of enquiry that reacts excessively to minor anomalies
and is totally cut off from any rationally defensible utilization for
technological purposes. In Popperian science, unfortified by the
doctrine of verisimilitude, we aim at maximizing the boldness of
the theories that we entertain and at rejecting all falsified
theories if a competing theory survives available tests. But what

---

[15] I. Lakatos, 'Falsification and the Methodology of Scientific Research Programmes', in I. Lakatos and A. Musgrave (eds.), *Criticism and the Growth of Knowledge*
(Cambridge: Cambridge University Press, 1970), 91–195.

[16] For a relevant example (Mendelian genetics) see R.D. Rosenkrantz, *Inference,
Method and Decision* (Dordrecht: Reidel, 1977), 127–8.

[17] *Novum Organum*, bk. II, aphorism xix: *The Works of Francis Bacon*, ed. J. Spelding, R.
Ellis, and D.N. Health (London: Longman, 1859) i. 260 see also bk. I, aphorism xlvi
(*Works*, i. 166).

reason has an engineer or physician to believe that such surviving claims are also *true*? According to anti-inductivist
Popperianism he can have none. The alleged justification for
building an aircraft in a certain way or for prescribing a certain
pill is not the evidential support that exists for saying that the
theory endorsing such action is true but rather the fact that this
theory is the boldest to escape falsification from available
evidence. In other words Popperian technology encourages
engineers and physicians to take as big a risk as the circumstances allow, since it does not burden them with the duty to
possess even a partial justification for the truth of any predictions that they make. But fortunately our engineers and physicians have so far failed to respond to this encouragement: many
of us would not be still alive if they had done so.[18]

Accordingly it looks altogether too paradoxical to suppose, as
Hume and Popper do, that only deductive inferences are
rational. Not surprisingly, therefore, some philosophers, like
Strawson,[19] come to assume, in one way or another, that the
whole problem is resolved just by rejecting this supposition.
Some inferences, they say, are *inductively* valid, in that it is
rational, or reasonable, to proportion one's convictions in such
cases to the multiplicity or variety of the evidential data. That is
exactly what such a term as 'rational' means there. So it is wrong
to suppose, we are told, that any further justification of induction is either necessary or possible. To ask whether inductive
procedures are rational is like asking whether the law is legal.

But this is no answer to Hume. It begs the question, since the
rationality of induction was just what Hume was attacking by
stressing the differences between induction and deduction. The

---

[18] For an attempt to develop a form of Popperianism that is not open to this criticism
see J. Watkins, *Science and Scepticism* (London: Hutchinson, 1984), 337–48.

[19] For this see P. F. Strawson, *Introduction to Logical Theory* (London: Methuen, 1952),
248–50. See also A. J. Ayer, *The Problem of Knowledge* (Harmondsworth: Penguin Books,
1956), 74–5, and P. Edwards, 'Bertrand Russell's Doubts about Induction', in A. Flew
(ed.), *Logic and Language* (Oxford: Blackwell, 1951), 68–70. Further recent analyses of the
problem are to be found in G. H. von Wright, *The Logical Problem of Induction* (Oxford:
Basil Blackwell, 1957); N. Rescher, *Induction* (Oxford: Basil Blackwell, 1980); D. C.
Stove, *The Rationality of Induction* (Oxford: Clarendon Press, 1986); and in a useful collection of papers by various authors, R. Swinburne (ed.), *The Justification of Induction*
(Oxford: Oxford University Press, 1974).

issue that has to be settled may be put in these terms: what entitles us to use the same evaluative term 'rational', or 'reasonable', in both contexts? Hume pointed out a pervasive lack of analogy between, on the one hand, reasoning from premisses to logically implied conclusions, and, on the other, reasoning—vulgarly so called—from premisses about the already observed to conclusions that embrace the as yet unobserved. The former is a product of thought, he argued, the latter of custom; the former justifies certainty, the latter not; the former cannot be rejected without self-contradiction, the latter can; and so on. It does not matter here whether we speak of 'reasoning' or of 'rationality' or of 'validity'. The question that arises is the same: how can we establish the existence of a sufficiently strong analogy between deduction and induction so as to undermine Hume's scepticism?

The clue to an answer for this important question lies in the fact that inductive reasoning is a matter of degree, not of all or nothing. So deducibility must come to be seen as a limiting case to which inductively based inferability may be seen to exhibit gradable degrees of approximation, whether we analyse such gradations in terms of Pascalian probability, Baconian legisimilitude, or some other kind of parameter. We are not then left with two different kinds of inferential rationality, a deductive kind and an inductive kind, but rather with one or more scales of rationality or reasonableness, on each of which deductive inferability figures as a limiting case. Indeed, we have already seen (§ 15) that in order to understand why there is such a variety of different conceptions of Pascalian probability we can usefully regard probability as a gradation of inferability. The diversity of available interpretations for the Pascalian calculus can then be seen to correspond with the familiar diversity of systems for deductive inferability. Similarly, the Method of Relevant Variables, in each of its varied applications, was seen (§ 21) to conform to the rules of a generalized modal logic, with degrees of legisimilitude mounting towards necessity. There is, therefore, no case now for supposing, as Hume supposed, that deductive and inductive thinking are so different from one another that the former possesses some honorific status to which the latter does not even approximate. Rather there is an obvious analogy between judgements of the form 'The inference to A

from *B* is logically certain' and judgements of the form 'The inference to *A* from *B* has this-or-that level of probability', since both kinds of judgement conform to the same Pascalian axioms. And there is also an obvious analogy between judgements of the form 'The proposition that if *A*, then *B*, is necessary' and 'The proposition that if *A*, then *B*, has this-or-that level of legisimilitude' since both kinds of judgement conform to the same modal-logical axioms.

Of course, there is another aspect of Hume's problem which these logico-syntactic *rapprochements* between deduction and induction can do nothing to resolve. Hume insisted that no conviction about the future, or the unseen, could ever be justified on the basis of the evidence that we at present have. And, if we read 'justified' here as meaning 'conclusively justified', we must surely agree with him. The validity of the inductive inferences that we make from available evidence must depend on the reliability of the assumptions that we adopt about such inferences in each recognized category of factual enquiry. However various the evidence that we at present have, there must always remain the possibility, as we saw (§ 20), that our assumed list of relevant variables, or our assumed categorization of hypotheses, will at some time be held to be faulty. Our evaluation of the evidence may then have been incorrect either because the results of some past experiment were affected by the undetected operation of an unlisted variable or because a new experiment can be designed in which such a variable is deliberately manipulated. In other words any inductive judgement is itself empirically corrigible. Conclusive certainty is never inductively justifiable.

But that is a deprivation that we can live with. To keep our minds open to the possibility of new evidence is all that it requires of us, and while we do this we are still entitled to claim an appropriate degree of justification for the theories that have survived the most thorough tests which we at present believe ourselves capable of devising. Human rationality requires us at any one time to do the best we then can, not to do the best that could ever be possible.

§ 24. THE PARADOX OF THE RAVENS

Hempel's paradox of the ravens arises from the fact that three propositions about inductive confirmation that are each independently plausible are not co-tenable. Scheffler sought, unsatisfactorily, to resolve the paradox by defining confirmation in such a way that logically equivalent hypotheses may not be equally confirmed by given evidence. Hempel's kind of solution is more satisfactory. It requires a Pascalian measure for confirmation and relies on our already knowing that black ravens are much rarer than non-black non-ravens. Alternatively, if we grade confirmation by the Method of Relevant Variables, our resolution of the paradox must point out that known relevant variables operate causally on plumage-colour rather than on species-membership.

Hume's argument against the rationality of induction rested on his assumption of a deductivist paradigm. He looked at induction from the outside, as it were, and could see in it only a varying strength of mental process, not a gradable pattern of evidential justification. But, even when we look at induction from the standpoint of its own apparent rules and principles and acknowledge the analogies that rebut Hume's scepticism, we may still find ourselves confronted with antinomy and paradox.

One such antinomy is commonly called 'the paradox of the ravens', and is best known from Hempel's publication of it in 1945.[20] Here we may formulate the core of the problem in terms of three propositions that are not co-tenable despite the fact that each has considerable intuitive appeal:

(1) Any object that is both an A and a B confirms the hypothesis that everything which is an A is a B.

(2) Any object that confirms a hypothesis confirms also any proposition that is logically equivalent to that hypothesis.

(3) A white handkerchief does not confirm the hypothesis that all ravens are black.

[20] C.G. Hempel, 'Studies in the Logic of Confirmation', *Mind*, 54 (1945), 1–26, 97–121, repr. with some changes, in C.G. Hempel, *Aspects of Scientific Explanation and Other Essays in the Philosophy of Science* (New York: Free Press, 1965), 1–51. The germ of the problem originally appeared in C.G. Hempel, 'Le Problème de la vérité', *Theoria*, 3 (1937), 206–46.

These three propositions can easily be seen to generate an antinomy. A white handkerchief is a non-black thing that is a non-raven. So, according to (1), it confirms the hypothesis that everything which is non-black is a non-raven. And therefore, according to (2), it confirms the logically equivalent hypothesis that all ravens are black. But that is inconsistent with (3) which asserts, plausibly enough, that a white handkerchief does not confirm the hypothesis that all ravens are black. It follows that, if a coherent account of inductive reasoning is to be presented, one or more of the premises on which this antinomy rests has to be rejected as false or inapplicable.

Thus some philosophers have held, in effect, that (2) is the source of the trouble. For example, Scheffler has argued[21] for the importance of the notion of 'selective confirmation' as distinct from the notion of 'confirmation' defined in (1). He stipulates that for a piece of evidence to be said to confirm a hypothesized generalization *selectively* it must not only satisfy that generalization but also refute its contrary. So, on the one hand, an object that is both an A and a B selectively confirms the hypothesis that everything which is an A is a B, as in (1), because it not only satisfies that generalization but also refutes its contrary, namely the hypothesis that everything which is an A is not a B. On the other hand, selective confirmation is not automatically transmitted to equivalent propositions, as in (2) because not every object that selectively confirms 'All As are Bs' will also selectively confirm 'All non-Bs are non-As'. The contrary of 'All non-Bs are non-As' is 'All non-Bs are As.' and the latter generalization is not refuted by an object that is both an A and a B, even though such an object does satisfy the former generalization. In other words, if we interpret 'confirms' in (1) and (2) as 'selectively confirms', we have to accept that (2) is false: the confirmation attributable to a specified hypothesis may not be attributable to a logically equivalent hypothesis. And the paradox then dissolves because the confirmation that a white handkerchief gives to the hypothesis 'All non-black things are non-ravens' is not now automatically passed on to its equivalent 'All ravens are black' and thus no conclusion is generated that is incompatible with (3).

[21] I. Scheffler, *The Anatomy of Inquiry: Philosophical Studies in the Theory of Science* (New York: Knopf, 1963), 283–9.

Scheffler's solution of the paradox is clearly inconsistent with any analysis of confirmation in terms either of simple Pascalian probability or of positive Pascalian relevance. That is because such an analysis is compelled by the logical syntax of Pascalian judgements to accept (2): logically equivalent propositions are interchangeable with one another within any judgement of Pascalian probability, since they give each other the probability 1 (see pp. 85–7). So it may seem that, if Scheffler's preferred criterion of confirmation is to be provided with a rationale, this is best found in the Baconian idea of eliminative induction, whereby support for one hypothesis is built up by excluding its rivals. Because Scheffler's solution assumes that every object or event that confirms a hypothesis must eliminate a contrary hypothesis, it seems to go along with the Baconian method that was described in §§ 20 to 21. But in fact there is an important difference, because, so far as 'confirms' means the same as 'inductively supports', the Method of Relevant Variables is just as much committed to the truth of (2)—which Scheffler rejects—as is any Pascalian analysis. As we saw (pp. 139–40) any judgements of inductive support that are based on the Method of Relevant Variables must accord with the Special Consequence Condition. And it is easy to see that the Special Consequence Condition entails (2). For that principle gives us both that, if H logically implies H', then E's support for H' is greater than or equal to its support for H, and also that if H' logically implies H, then E's support for H is greater than or equal to its support for H'; and when these two corollaries of the Special Consequence Condition are conjoined the conjunction is equivalent to (2).

But, even apart from considerations germane to the Method of Relevant Variables, it is arguable that a solution which is bought at the price of rejecting (2) is too costly to be satisfactory. If it is logically necessary for H to be true if and only if H' is true, it hardly seems conceivable that there should be evidential support for H which is not also evidential support for H'. Accordingly it may seem tempting to argue not that (2) is false but just that it does not apply in the context in which the paradox is supposed to be generated. The reason why (2) does not apply here would be that the hypothesized generalizations with which principles of inductive logic, like (1), (2), and (3), are concerned, carry an existential implication. On this view a hypothesis of the form 'Everything which is an *A* is a *B*' or 'All *A*s are *B*s', asserts not only that if there is anything that is an *A* it is also a *B*, but also that there is something which is an *A*. Consequently 'All ravens are black' is not to be regarded as logically equivalent to 'All non-black things are non-ravens', since the former generalization logically implies that there is something which is a raven but does not imply that there is something which is a non-black thing, while the latter generalization has the opposite sense. Hence the white handkerchief that, because it is a non-black non-raven, confirms 'All non-black things are non-ravens', does not confirm 'All ravens are black' and so (3) is not contradicted.

But, as Hempel himself pointed out, such an argument rests on a rather shaky foundation. The representation of every general hypothesis by a conjunction of a universal conditional and an existential sentence would invalidate many deductive inferences that are generally accepted as logically permissible in scientific reasoning. Thus, for example, the assertions that all sodium salts burn yellow, and that whatever does not burn yellow is no sodium salt, are customarily treated as logically equivalent formulations. Moreover, there are many kinds of generalization in natural science for which it would be very difficult to determine the exact location of an existential implication. Consider the hypothesis that, if a person after receiving an injection of a certain test substance has a positive skin reaction, he has diphtheria. Should we construe the existential clause here as referring to persons, to persons receiving the injection, or to persons who, upon receiving the injection, show a positive skin reaction? To the extent that the decision seems arbitrary, the alleged existential implication seems unattached. One could add, too,[22] that so far as the assertion of 'All *A*s are *B*s' commits a speaker to the existence of *A*s, it also normally commits him to the existence of non-*A*s (else he would have said 'Everything is a *B*'), to the existence of *B*s (since he is committed both to the existence of *A*s and to the view that all *A*s are *B*s), and to the existence of non-*B*s (since if everything were a *B* there would be

---

[22] M. Fisch, 'The Paradoxes of Confirmation and their Solutions' (M.A. Dissertation at the University of Tel Aviv: May, 1981).

no point in asserting that all *A*s are *B*s). So the assertion of 'All non-*A*s are non-*B*s' has just the same existential commitment as has the assertion of 'All *A*s are *B*s'. And in any case there are many uses in science for generalizations that definitely lack any existential implications, because they relate to ideal or extreme conditions which are either not known to exist or even known not to exist. These generalizations are certainly a target for inductive reasoning (as we saw in § 22), and the paradox will still arise about them even if it fails to arise in more homely fields of enquiry, like ornithology.

Accordingly Hempel was ready to accept the applicability of (2) and, with it, the argument that any white object confirms the hypothesis that all ravens are black. He thus treated (1) as stating a sufficient, but not a necessary, condition for confirmation. But he gave two reasons for rejecting proposition (3).

The first reason was that any generalization of the form 'Everything which is an *A* is a *B*' or 'All *A*s are *B*s' asserts something about, and imposes a corresponding restriction on, all entities of the appropriate category (for example, on all physical objects). It is not just about all *A*s, and so, specifically, 'All ravens are black' is not just about all ravens. Hence there is no entity of the appropriate category that is not caught up in the generalization, and any such entity, even a non-raven, is therefore in a position to constitute confirmatory or disconfirmatory evidence.

But Hempel's argument here is not very persuasive. If there is a concept of confirmatory evidence such that any entity within the domain of a generalization constitutes either confirmatory or disconfirmatory evidence for that generalization, then that unlocalized (see p. 156) concept of confirmatory evidence is not a very interesting or important one. It excludes any such entities from being regarded as irrelevant to the confirmation or disconfirmation of the generalization. If the generalization that all ravens are black is supposed to be 'about' physical objects, then the colours of shoes and ships and sealing-wax are all to be regarded as relevant to its truth. Thus the field of relevant investigation is made unacceptably large, and recognition of this provides a motive for taking the scope or domain of the generalization to be co-extensive with the category of entities denoted by its antecedent term. But, if we therefore fall back on taking the domain of 'All ravens are black' to be just ravens, we have done nothing to eliminate the paradox.

Hempel's other reason for rejecting proposition (3) was that when we judge the extent to which some object confirms a stated hypothesis we tend tacitly to introduce a comparison of the hypothesis with a body of evidence which includes not only that particular object but also other items of information with which we happen to be acquainted. For example, suppose that in support of the hypothesis 'All sodium salts burn yellow' somebody was to adduce an experiment in which a piece of pure ice was held into a colourless flame and did not turn the flame yellow. That result might be held to support the hypothesis in question because it confirms the generalization 'Whatever does not burn yellow is no sodium salt'. And yet at the same time this appears paradoxical, because we happen to know anyhow that ice contains no sodium salt and thus our experiment seems irrelevant to the hypothesis that it was designed to test. Disregard the background knowledge, argues Hempel, and the paradox disappears.

But this argument is not very persuasive either. The sodium salt example introduces a special feature that is not present in the way in which the original paradox of the ravens may be presented. It involves a piece of chemical knowledge that had at one time to be discovered by empirical scientific enquiry, namely the knowledge that ice contains no sodium salt. But the knowledge that handkerchiefs are not ravens is part of the a priori linguistic competence with which we approach any intellectual problem. It cannot so easily be disregarded in order to resolve a particular paradox.

The spirit of Hempel's solution (though not of his arguments for it) is better maintained if confirmation is treated quantitatively rather than qualitatively and degrees of confirmation are measured in Pascalian terms. This approach to the problem was originally taken by Hosiasson-Lindenbaum[23] and was followed by Mackie[24] among others. We are still to reject (3) but to hold that the degree to which a white handkerchief confirms 'All

---

[23] J. Hosiasson-Lindenbaum, 'On Confirmation', *Journal of Symbolic Logic*, 5 (1940), 133–48.

[24] J.L. Mackie, 'The Paradox of Confirmation', *British Journal for the Philosophy of Science*, 13 (1963), 265–77.

ravens are black' is very small—so small, indeed, that we can easily understand why we might suppose it to be altogether non-existent. Mackie claims that to develop such a solution we have to appeal to what he calls the 'Inverse Principle', which states that a hypothesis H is confirmed by an observation-report E in relation to background knowledge K if and only if the observation-report is made more probable by adding the hypothesis to the background knowledge. That is, $p(E|H\&K)$ must be greater than $p(E|K)$, and E confirms H better the more the adding of H to K raises the probability of E. He then argues that, if we assume this principle and assign probabilities according to the relative sizes of the several classes constituted by all ravens, all non-ravens and so on, observation-reports of the form 'This is a black raven' will confirm the hypothesis 'All ravens are black' far more than do observation-reports of the form 'This is a non-black non-raven'.

Much the same result is achieved if instead of Mackie's Inverse Principle we adopt either the simple probability analysis of ampliative induction or the positive relevance analysis (§ 19). This is because of the relationship between $p(E|H\&K)$ and $p(H|E\&K)$ that is determined by Bayes's law, in the form

$$p(H|E\&K) = \frac{p(E|H\&K) \times p(H|K)}{p(E|K)}.$$

Indeed one can easily see from this law that, other things being equal, $p(H|E\&K)$ will get larger as $P(E|K)$ gets smaller, and vice versa. So that because non-black non-ravens are common objects, with a relatively high probability of occurrence, they can do little to raise the probability of the hypothesis 'All ravens are black', whereas black ravens are relatively rare objects and will raise that probability much more (see pp. 136–7).

This way of resolving Hempel's paradox will not satisfy anyone who is intuitively convinced that any observations of non-black non-ravens are totally irrelevant to any judgement of the evidential support or confirmation that exists for the hypothesis 'All ravens are black'. All that such a resolution of the paradox can do to explain away those intuitions is to suggest that they arise from mistaking a very, very low degree of relevance for no relevance at all.

Philosophers who find this explanation implausible, and also wish to retain (2), have no alternative but to reject (1), and the

Method of Relevant Variables provides a rationale for so doing. According to that method there are just two ways in which a hypothesis may be shown to possess inductive support. Either an appropriately structured test on the hypothesis turns out to have satisfactory results, or the hypothesis is shown to be the logical consequence of one or more propositions that have been satisfactorily so tested. It follows that the evidence which supports a hypothesis, according to the Method of Relevant Variables, is constituted by the results of canonical tests on that hypothesis or on logically entailing ones, and not by objects that just happen to satisfy the antecedent and consequent of the hypothesized generalization. Observation of a black raven, *tout court*, does not provide any inductive support for the hypothesis that all ravens are black, nor does a non-black non-raven provide any inductive support for the hypothesis that all non-black things are non-ravens. Thus (1) is rejected and the paradox cannot be generated in Hempel's terms.

But that is not enough to dispose of the underlying problem, if the paradox can be restated in terms of a concept of confirmation that conforms to the Method of Relevant Variables. And indeed it might seem that the paradox reappears if (1) is replaced by

(1′) Any set of objects that are both *A*s and *B*s in each of an appropriately selected variety of circumstances, confirms the hypothesis that everything which is an *A* is a *B*

and (3) is replaced by

(3′) A set of white handkerchiefs in each of the circumstances referred to in (1′) does not confirm the hypothesis that all ravens are black.

For in the light of (1′) and (2) it might seem that a set of white objects that have been observed in an appropriately wide variety of circumstances confirms the hypothesis that all ravens are black, whereas (3′) denies that such a set of objects does confirm the hypothesis.

However, when we use the Method of Relevant Variables we are always in the position of having to exploit background knowledge or belief or assumptions about what variables are indeed relevant to the hypothesis under examination. If we have no such knowledge or belief or assumptions, we are not in a position to test the hypothesis appropriately. Now, we may well know of circumstances that are relevant to hypotheses of the category to which 'All ravens are black' belongs. There are circumstances like season, climate, diet, and so on, that may cause a bird to change its plumage colour. But how could we have the requisite kind of knowledge or belief about the hypothesis 'All non-black things are non-ravens'? In order to have it we should need a list of variables relevant to hypotheses of this category—that is, a list of types of circumstances that have sometimes falsified such hypotheses by causing objects or events that satisfy their subject-terms to fail to satisfy their predicate-terms. But in fact we have no information about circumstances that can thus turn a non-raven into a raven or a non-swan into a swan. Such metamorphoses, or changes of species-membership, do not occur within our experience and are contrary to what is thought genetically possible. Consequently, even if a set of white objects were observed in a wide variety of circumstances, it would give no support thereby to the hypothesis that all non-black things are non-ravens, if we are to judge support by the Method of Relevant Variables. And unless there is some support for that hypothesis the paradox cannot get off the ground. Or, in other words, though 'All non-black things are non-ravens' must have the same grade of inductive support, on given evidence, as 'All ravens are black', such evidence must be the outcome of tests on the latter proposition, not the former, if we adopt the Method of Relevant Variables.

In sum, so far from its being the case that the paradox arises because we take background knowledge into account inappropriately, as Hempel held, we actually have to take background knowledge into account, quite properly, in order to dissolve the paradox. While a Pascalian analysis of inductive reasoning requires us to invoke contingent beliefs about the numbers of the objects concerned so as to reject (3), a Baconian analysis in terms of the Method of Relevant Variables requires us to reject (1) and then to invoke contingent beliefs about the direction in which the relevant variables operate in canonical tests.[25]

[25] Many other discussions of Hempel's paradox are to be found, such as M. Black, 'Notes on the "Paradoxes of Confirmation" ', in J. Hintikka and P. Suppes (eds.), *Aspects of Inductive Logic* (Amsterdam: North-Holland, 1966), 175–97; P. Suppes, 'A Bayesian Approach to the Paradoxes of Confirmation', ibid. 198–207; G.H. von Wright, 'The Paradoxes of Confirmation', ibid. 208–18; R. Swinburne, *An Introduction to Confirmation Theory* (London: Methuen, 1972), 152–73, which includes a useful

§ 25. THE 'GRUE' PARADOX

Goodman's 'grue' paradox cannot be resolved by restricting the terminology of our hypotheses to purely qualitative terms that imply nothing about a particular time or place. And Goodman's own solution, in terms of a preference for what he calls 'entrenched' predicates, would force science into an excessively conservative posture. Instead we need to invoke either Bayes's theorem or the Method of Relevant Variables.

The definition of confirmation that is invoked in the paradox of the ravens is also involved in another paradox, propounded by Goodman.[26] Suppose that all emeralds examined before a certain time t are green. At time t, then, all our relevant observations confirm the hypothesis that all emeralds are green. But consider the predicate 'grue' which applies to all things examined before t just in case they are green and to other things just in case they are blue. Obviously at time t, for each statement of evidence asserting that a given emerald is green, we have a parallel evidence-statement asserting that that emerald is grue. And each evidence-statement that a given emerald is grue will confirm the general hypothesis that all emeralds are grue. Hence a hypothesis implying that all emeralds subsequently examined will be green and a hypothesis implying that they will all be blue are both confirmed at t by evidence statements describing the same observations. Two mutually conflicting hypotheses are equally well confirmed by the same evidence. Moreover, since t may be whenever you please, the evidence collected prior to t may contain very, very many green emeralds but the incompatible predictions will still be equally well confirmed at t. And by choosing an appropriate predicate instead of 'grue' we can clearly obtain equal confirmation for any prediction whatever about other emeralds, or indeed for any prediction whatever about any other kind of thing. For example, suppose 'grue' applies to all things examined before t if and only if they are

pre-1972 bibliography; H. Gaifman, 'Subjective Probability, Natural Predicates and Hempel's Ravens', *Erkenntnis*, 14 (1979), 105–47; and M. Fisch, 'Hempel's Ravens, the Natural Classification of Hypotheses and the Growth of Knowledge', *Erkenntnis*, 21 (1984), 45–62.

[26] N. Goodman, *Fact, Fiction and Forecast* (London: Athlone Press, 1954), 73–120.

green and to other things if and only if they exist in a world in which pigs have wings. Then, if emeralds examined before *t* are green, we can predict that after *t* pigs will have wings. Nor is this type of paradox confined to temporal extrapolations from observable evidence. If 'grue' is redefined so as to apply to all things examined in the observer's own laboratory if and only if they have one characteristic, and to other things if and only if they have a different one, then an analogous argument seems to lead to the absurd conclusion that no experimenter is ever entitled to draw universal conclusions about the world outside his laboratory from what goes on inside it.

There are essentially two assumptions that combine to generate this paradox. One is that a report of an *A* which is *B* confirms a hypothesis of the form 'All *A*s are *B*'. The other is that a term like 'grue' can occur as the predicate of a well-confirmed hypothesis. And in so far as the latter assumption carries little intuitive conviction, because 'grue' is such a bizarre term, it obviously needs to be discussed first. To reject that assumption we apparently need to impose some terminological constraint on the confirmation of our hypotheses, so that the occurrence of a predicate like 'grue' within a hypothesis comes to count against the well-confirmedness of that hypothesis. But what are the crucial features that a predicate has to have in order to be like 'grue' in relevant respects?

The most obvious suggestion to make is that the predicates which are likely to be troublesome are those that imply some spatial or temporal restriction or a reference to some particular individual. Such predicates occur typically in statements of what is accidentally true, while hypotheses that state natural laws characteristically concern all ravens, say, or all emeralds, or all pieces of copper. If, as we commonly suppose, Nature is uniform throughout space and time, a description of its laws need make no reference to particular places or times. Now to predicate 'grue' of emeralds, it may be said, is not to say the same thing about all emeralds, but to say one thing about all those examined before a particular point in time and another thing about the remainder. So 'grue' does not belong in the terminology of confirmable hypotheses about natural laws.

But there is no guarantee that we could not replace 'grue' by an equivalent disjunction of complex descriptions, built up from purely qualitative terms that imply nothing about particular times or places. Each group of emeralds examined before *t* would then consist of the only emeralds to satisfy such-or-such a description (about size, shape, dents, scratches, flaws, etc.) and the disjunction of those descriptions would pick out all and only the emeralds examined before *t*. So the paradox could then be stated without the introduction of any bizarre terms like 'grue' into our vocabulary.

Goodman's own defence of the paradox here is rather different. He argues that the concept of what is to count as a purely qualitative term is unclear. The temptation is just to take it for granted that 'green' and 'blue' are purely qualitative because they are basic colour-terms and involve no reference to a particular time or place, while 'grue' is not purely qualitative because it does involve such a reference: similarly 'bleen' is not purely qualitative if it applies to emeralds examined before time *t* just in case they are blue and to other emeralds just in case they are green. But, as Goodman points out, if we treat 'grue' and 'bleen' as basic and define 'green' and 'blue' appropriately, we shall find that 'green' and 'blue' come to involve a reference to a particular time or place. For example 'green' will apply to emeralds examined before time *t* just in case they are grue and to other emeralds just in case they are bleen. And similar redefinitions are available for any other supposedly qualitative terms.

Perhaps it will be suggested instead that comparative simplicity, not qualitativeness, is the distinguishing mark of the predicate that will be acceptable in such a context. An analogous problem arises, it may be said, where the values of some quantitative physical variable have been plotted on a graph, against certain values of some apparently correlated variable (such as the velocity of a falling body against the time for which it has been falling). Any number of different curves can be drawn through the whole set of plotted positions, and no finite number of additional plottable positions will determine one curve uniquely. Which of these curves is to be preferred? Presumably the one described by the simplest mathematical equation. So is not comparative simplicity also the reason why, in the situation described, we prefer 'All emeralds are green' to 'All emeralds are grue'? Wherever our choice of hypothesis is under-determined by the evidential data, it may be said, we have to supplement our criterion of confirmation by an appropriate principle of terminological selectivity.

No doubt some accepted set of criteria for comparative simplicity have to be invoked when fitting a description to a set of data, especially when those data are quantitative. Fewer arithmetical operations, lower numerical exponents, shorter symbolic expressions, etc. are all prima facie desirable features in any mathematical formula involved. But any such set of criteria have to be considered as relative to an assumed list of primitive, undefined symbols. Our ultimate comparison of simplicity must be between expressions in this primitive, undefined form. Otherwise it is all too easy to invent an appropriate definition that will—quite trivially and superficially—reduce a highly complex expression to a much simpler form. So Goodman could make the point that, if one starts with the 'grue' and 'bleen' terminology as basic, 'green' and 'blue' must be regarded as relatively more complex expressions, and therefore the paradox cannot be resolved by an appeal to the greater simplicity of the familiar colour-vocabulary when compared with the 'grue' and 'bleen' one. What apparently needs to be shown instead is that use of the latter vocabulary inherently disadvantages a hypothesis.

Goodman tries to show this via an account of what he calls 'entrenchment' and 'projectibility'. He begins by defining a hypothesis as being 'projected' at a particular time if it is adopted at that time *after* some of its instances have been examined and found to be true and *before* the rest of its instances have been examined. A hypothesis may be said to be 'projectible' if and only if it is validly projected. So a hypothesis that is falsified thereby becomes unprojectible. But not all hypotheses that avoid falsification are thereby rendered projectible. In order to introduce a further criterion of projectibility Goodman defines the concept of 'entrenchment'. Entrenchment is what accrues to a predicate in virtue of its occurrence, or of the occurrence of any predicate co-extensive with it, within a projected hypothesis. So some predicates become better entrenched than others. For example 'green' is much better entrenched than 'grue', because it has occurred much more often than 'grue' in projected hypotheses. Then relative entrenchment is a further criterion for separating the projectible from the unprojectible.

That is, if two conflicting hypotheses have the same number of evidential instances in their favour, and none against them, and there is just one difference in entrenchment between a predicate in the one and a predicate in the other, then the hypothesis with the better entrenched predicate is projectible and the other is not. So 'All emeralds are green' would be projectible and 'All emeralds are grue' would not.

Goodman insists that entrenchment is not the same as familiarity. 'Any wholesale elimination of unfamiliar predicates', he says, 'would result in an intolerable stultification of language. New and useful predicates like "conducts electricity" and "is radioactive" are always being introduced and must not be excluded simply because of their novelty.' And he points out that his criteria of projectibility legislate against novel or unfamiliar predicates 'only to the extent of eliminating projections of them that conflict with projections of much better predicates'. But is not that bad enough? If scientists followed Goodman's prescription they could easily come to eliminate one of two conflicting hypotheses because of its poorly entrenched predicate, even though, when more evidence became available, it turned out to be better supported. A more prudent policy might often be not to eliminate in advance the hypothesis with the novel or unfamiliar predicate, but to retain it for further consideration at a later date when more evidence becomes available. Indeed, this was how the pathogenic role of vitamin deficiencies came eventually to be understood, even where, as in the case of beri-beri, the presence of toxic micro-organisms was for long the favoured aetiology. In sum, Goodman's proposal for solving the paradox makes far too drastic an inroad on our terminological open-mindedness, and forces science into an excessively conservative posture. Nor does it take account of the gradualness with which fundamentally new ideas tend to spread within the scientific community.

It is not possible to avoid this difficulty by allowing predicates to inherit entrenchment from what Goodman calls 'parent' predicates. Goodman calls a predicate P a parent of a given predicate Q if P applies only to certain mutually disjoint classes and one of these classes is the extension of Q. For example, he says, the predicate 'army division' is a parent of the predicate 'soldier in the 26th division'. Similarly, no doubt, 'class of mutually similar sub-atomic particles' would be a parent of the predicate 'proton'. But there is no reason to suppose that in the relevant period of conceptual innovation the predicate 'class of mutually similar sub-atomic particles' was any better entrenched than the predicate 'proton'. So the latter would not inherit any entrenchments from the former.

Accordingly we must seek to resolve the paradox in some other way than by excluding terminology of the trouble-making kind. Obviously we have to invoke background knowledge in some way, in order to eliminate the paradoxical hypotheses. But it looks as though the background knowledge that we rely on must be factual rather than terminological. And there are perhaps two main ways of trying to put this knowledge to work in order to achieve the desired result. One uses Bayes's law, the other the Method of Relevant Variables.

If we employ a Pascalian measure for degree of confirmation we must presumably infer that the prior probability of 'All emeralds are grue' is much less than that of 'All emeralds are green', since in the past hypotheses about objects' changing their colour if not already examined have all proved false. Then by Bayes's law (p. 23) the hypothesis 'All emeralds are green' must also be much more probable on the evidence than 'All emeralds are grue' is, since in both cases the evidence is the same and so is the probability of the evidence given the hypothesis. At first sight this type of solution is admittedly open to the objection that it begs the question at issue. It assumes that there is inductive evidence in favour of the hypothesis that grue-type hypotheses are always subsequently falsified. And such evidence, Goodman might say, is just as much in favour of the hypothesis that grue-type hypotheses are always falsivered, where 'falsivered' applies to all hypotheses propounded before t just in case they have been falsified and to others just in case they are verified. So there is apparently a case for saying that background knowledge allows just as much prior probability to be assigned to 'All emeralds are grue' as to 'All emeralds are green'. However if our past experience is such as to assign only a low prior probability to the hypothesis about falsivering, Goodman's potential objection would lapse.

The Method of Relevant Variables can also exploit background knowledge in order to achieve a solution of the paradox.

It must treat grue-type hypotheses as being subject to an appropriate series of canonical tests, and presumably the first of these tests must manipulate the before-*t*/after-*t* variable, whatever time '*t*' denotes. After all, our past experience must be that 'grue-type' hypotheses are generally falsified by the manipulation of this variable: otherwise we should not find it so paradoxical to have an apparently well-confirmed prediction that emeralds are going to change their colour forthwith. Consequently, if all confirmatory evidence has to come from the results of canonical tests, there will never be such evidence, for any value of '*t*', unless the hypothesis under examination does indeed describe, for a specified value of '*t*', a genuine turning-point in Nature. Moreover, the argument that was used to answer a possible objection to a Bayesian resolution of the problem has an analogue in the Method of Relevant Variables. If we consider the hypothesis about tests and relevant variables that is assumed by the present treatment of the problem, we can see that, in any contest between it and a 'falsivere'-type hypothesis, it has as good a prospect of winning as common sense would think it to deserve. It too would just need to be tested over the crucial before-*t*/after-*t* variable.

In short, from a Baconian point of view Goodman's paradox, like Hempel's, may be seen as arising from the use of too coarse and global a concept of confirmation. Both paradoxes arise because this concept is neither graduated nor variative and is therefore insufficiently sensitive to background knowledge about locally relevant factors. Once we replace this concept by one that corresponds more closely to the actual practice of natural science the paradoxes can no longer be constructed.[27]

§ 26. THE LOTTERY PARADOX

Kyburg's lottery paradox discloses an apparent conflict between deductive cogency and any Pascalian criterion for the acceptance

---

[27] Many other discussions of Goodman's paradox are to be found, such as S. Blackburn, *Reason and Prediction* (Cambridge: Cambridge University Press, 1973), 61–96; H. Fain, 'The Very Thought of Grue', *Philosophical Review*, 76 (1967), 61–73; and M. Hesse, 'Ramifications of "Grue" ', *British Journal for the Philosophy of Science* 20 (1969), 13–25 (which includes a useful bibliography).

of a hypothesis. Levi proposes to resolve the paradox by insisting that acceptance must always be relative to some ultimate partition of the hypotheses under consideration. But the paradox also disappears if we base acceptance on a Baconian criterion.

Twentieth-century philosophers have used quite a variety of terms in their references to inductive reasoning as the topic of their analyses. They have spoken about a relationship of 'confirmation', 'justification', 'validation', or 'support', for example—with or without assistance from the adjective 'evidential'. Such terms have many differences in everyday nuance or implication that are irrelevant for present philosophical purposes. For example, as already remarked (§ 2), confirming items normally occur later than confirmed ones: a hotel reservation has to be made before it can be confirmed. On the other hand, supporting items are not normally either later or earlier than supported ones: the relationship is spatial rather than temporal. But this difference in ordinary language is of no importance in modern philosophical discussions of inductive reasoning, which treat temporal priority and spatial subjacence as equivalent metaphors for justification. The analysandum is the same, whether or not the proposed analyses are different. What is ultimately under discussion in each case is the nature of a certain epistemic relationship that can exist between one proposition and another—a relationship that, since the early seventeenth century, most philosophers have regarded as a matter of degree.

Nevertheless there are several purposes for which this relationist stance is inadequate, and what may conveniently be called 'the need for inductive detachment' arises. We want to be able not only to assert that E gives such-or-such a level of inductive support to H but also, in appropriate cases, because E is true, to detach as a conclusion the truth of H. Certainly engineers, physicians, navigators, law-courts, and other decision-taking agents often need in practice to detach conclusions from premisses which state both what the evidence is and how well that evidence supports such-or-such a conclusion. So do the writers of scientific text-books, though Carnap was inclined to deny that there was ever any need for it.[28] Indeed most scientists feel the

---

[28] R. Carnap, 'Inductive Logic and Rational Decisions', in R. Carnap and R.C. Jeffrey (eds.), *Studies in Inductive Logic and Probability* (Berkeley: University of California

need at some stage to translate the relational inductive gradations of their more cautious colleagues into the common-sense
categorical dichotomies of knowledge versus ignorance, or proof
versus disproof (see p. 154). This happens particularly when
some previous discovery, in the role of 'background knowledge', constitutes an indispensable premiss for the evaluation of
a new hypothesis, as when any measuring instrument is used in
a laboratory experiment. But it also happens when the effects of
a particular medical drug have to be predicted before it is pre-
scribed, or a causal law has to be derived before it can be
exploited, or a theory has to be established before it can be cited
as *the* explanation of anything, or juries have to bring in an
unconditional verdict of 'Guilty' before the accused can be
sentenced.

So it is natural to ask: what level of support for a proposition,
in the light of available evidence, justifies belief in its truth or
acceptance of it as being true? Obviously this would be justified
by a Pascalian probability of 1 or by maximal legisimilitude in
accordance with the Method of Relevant Variables. But in the
typical inductive situation we never have a probability of 1 and
we are never entitled to be sure that our list of relevant variables
is complete. So in practice we are often content with a lower
threshold, which we treat as the level at which, for the purpose in
hand (with whatever utilities it involves), further doubt or
hesitation would be unreasonable and an appropriate conclusion may be detached. But what should this threshold be? Any
attempt to fix it in terms of a stipulated level of Pascalian
probability seems at first sight to be exposed to the derivation of
a paradox which is often called 'the paradox of the Lottery' and
was first enunciated under that name by Kyburg.[29]

The core of the paradox may be formulated as follows.
Suppose three conditions:

Press, 1971), 29–30. See also Y. Bar-Hillel's comment in H.E. Kyburg and E. Nagel
(eds.), *Induction: Some Current Issues* (Middletown: Wesleyan University Press, 1963), 46.

[29] H. Kyburg, jun., 'Probability, rationality and a rule of detachment', in Y. Bar-
Hillel (ed.), *Proceedings of the 1964 Congress for Logic, Methodology and the Philosophy of Science*
(Amsterdam: North-Holland, 1965), 301–10. The first statement of the paradox is to be
found in H.E. Kyburg, jun., *Probability and the Logic of Rational Belief* (Middletown:
Wesleyan University Press, 1961), 197. A similar paradox is discussed by C.G.
Hempel, 'Deductive-Nomological vs. Statistical Explanation', in H. Feigl and G.
Maxwell (eds.), *Minnesota Studies in the Philosophy of Science* (1962), iii. 144–7.

(1) If E states all the available evidence, and the Pascalian probability of H on E is within some suitably small interval from 1, it is rational to believe H (i.e. justifiable to accept H).

(2) If it is rational to believe H_1, rational to believe H_2, . . . and rational to believe H_n, then it is rational to believe any logical consequence of H_1, H_2 . . . and H_n.

(3) It is not rational to believe an inconsistent proposition.

These three conditions all have a certain intuitive appeal. But they are demonstrably not co-tenable. Consider a lottery with a million (or more) tickets, that is assumed to be administered fairly. There is a very high probability on this evidence that ticket no. 1 will not win, and that ticket no. 2 will not win, . . . and that ticket no. n will not win. So, according to (1), it is rational to believe each of these propositions. Then, according to (2), in the light of the information that there are just n tickets it is rational to believe that no ticket will win. But also, according to (1), it is rational to believe that some ticket will win, since the lottery is assumed to be administered fairly. So, according to (2), it is rational to believe the conjunctive proposition that no ticket will win and some ticket will win. But that conjunctive proposition is inconsistent and, according to (3), it is not rational to believe an inconsistent proposition. Accordingly, we have demonstrated from (1), (2), and (3) both that it is, and that it is not, rational to believe the proposition that no ticket will win and some ticket will win. At least one of the three conditions must therefore be rejected.

Condition (3) is hard to reject. The intuitive connection between inconsistency and irrationality is in any case a strong one. And there is nothing much to be gained by objecting that it might be rational for a non-logician to believe a complex, non-obviously inconsistent proposition that was asserted by a competent authority. For it is possible to replace (3) by

(3′) It is not rational to believe an obviously inconsistent proposition.

and the paradox will still arise.

So those who, to meet the need for inductive detachment, wish to set up a Pascalian criterion, like (1), for the rationality of inductively based belief are naturally inclined to interfere with

(2). The idea that underlies (2) is often referred to as 'deductive cogency' or 'deductive closure'. It is the idea that rationality requires a commitment to the logical consequences of one's beliefs. But is this commitment to be understood as applying to one's beliefs collectively or distributively? The collective application, as in (2), helps to generate the paradox. But, if (2) is replaced by a distributive version, as in

(2′) If it is rational to believe H, then it is rational to believe any logical consequence of H,

the paradox cannot be constructed. And it is along these lines that Kyburg himself proposed to solve the problem. After all, if it is rational to believe that one *may* sometimes err, then even if one believes all and only the several propositions H_1, H_2, . . . and H_n it seems quite rational not to believe at the same time either that the conjunctive propositions $H_1 \& H_2 \&$ . . . $\& H_n$ is true or that it is false.

But here some rather subtle differences between rationality of belief and justifiability of acceptance are in play.[30] We need to check our intuitions rather carefully. It may well be rational to believe—in the everyday sense of that expression—that one may sometimes err. But if it is justifiable to accept H_1, justifiable to accept H_2, . . . and justifiable to accept H_n, it is certainly justifiable to accept both the conjunction $H_1 \& H_2 \&$ . . . $\& H_n$ and also any logical consequence of that conjunction. Indeed, unless we could assume the truth of (2) in *this* sense, we should be intolerably hampered in compounding the premisses for our inferences. We should never be entitled, as the phrase goes, 'to put two and two together'.

Levi,[31] however, has an argument against (2) even when this is its intended meaning. He claims that acceptance is always to be thought of as being relative to some ultimate partition of the hypotheses that are candidates for acceptance, where the evidence (including background evidence) entails that at least,

---

[30] For further discussion of the difference between belief and acceptance see L. Jonathan Cohen, *The Dialogue of Reason* (Oxford: Clarendon Press, 1986), 92–7.

[31] I. Levi, *Gambling with Truth: An Essay on Induction and the Aims of Science* (New York: Knopf, 1967), 38–42. See also I. Levi, 'Deductive Cogency in Inductive Inference', *Journal of Philosophy*, 57 (1965), 68–77, repr. in I. Levi, *Decisions and Revisions: Philosophical Essays on Knowledge and Value* (Cambridge: Cambridge University Press, 1984), 42–50.

and at most, one such hypothesis is true. (Compare Scheffler's approach to the paradox of the ravens in § 24.) For example, acceptance of the hypothesis that ticket no. 1 will not win the lottery is relative to a partition into the two possibilities 'Ticket no. 1 will win' and 'Ticket no. 1 will not win'. And, analogously, acceptance of the hypothesis that ticket no. 2 will not win is relative to a different ultimate partition, according to which the hypothesis that ticket no. 1 will not win is not even a candidate for consideration. So, if it is therefore required that the constraints of deductive cogency apply only in a way that is relative to the *same* ultimate partition, we must put this requirement in place of (2). We thus have no warrant, according to Levi, for inferring that *all* the tickets in the imaginary lottery will fail to win. And without such a warrant the paradox cannot get off the ground. Of course, in order to resolve the paradox in this way Levi has not only to reformulate the constraints of deductive cogency but also to modify (1). On his view a high probability for H, on E, does not provide sufficient grounds for accepting H outright, even if E is all the available evidence. It may provide grounds only for accepting H as against other hypotheses in the ultimate partition to which H belongs. Nor is a high probability *necessary* for H, if there are to be grounds for so accepting that hypothesis. If each rival hypothesis has a lower probability than H, H might still deserve victory over them in the struggle for acceptance, on Levi's view, even if the probability of H itself were in fact quite low.

Levi's thesis that a high probability is not a necessary condition for the acceptance of H, as against its rivals, has some plausibility in the context of inductive reasoning. If H and its rivals are generalizations that make conflicting predictions over an indeterminately large domain, we might expect that even the winning hypothesis has a low probability on the evidence because of the very low prior probability that is to be attached to any generalization of this kind. So, if any such hypothesis is to be accepted at all in science when its rivals have been eliminated—and many are in fact so accepted—it is no use insisting that a high probability is necessary, as in (1). But in order to resolve the lottery paradox this point does not need to be pressed. All Levi needs for the resolution of *that* paradox is his insistence on making acceptance relative to an ultimate partition. Or, at any rate, that is the situation if the criterion for inductive detachment is to be stated in Pascalian terms.

But there are some further points to clarify here. On Levi's view there can be no authority for a clear-cut, unconditional, non-relative acceptance or rejection that is parallel to belief or disbelief. Yet the paradox originates because of the felt need for a criterion to control detachments that are indeed of just that kind. Levi's resolution of the paradox has the disadvantage of presupposing that no such criterion is ever possible.

In practice the situation varies according to the nature of the issue and the evidence. Where there is apparently nothing to choose between several different ultimate partitions, there is no reason to regard the hypothesis that is more acceptable than any other within one particular partition as somehow superior to any hypothesis that is more acceptable than the others within any other partition. So, where more than one ultimate partition seems equally respectable, no single hypothesis can be the over-all winner and therefore declared to be the one that it is justifiable to accept *tout court*. For example, the hypothesis that in the above-mentioned lottery ticket no. 1 will not win is no more acceptable, in an absolute sense, than the hypothesis that ticket no. 2 will not win or than any other such hypothesis. But the situation is often quite different, especially in the natural sciences. Often just one set of rival hypotheses may be considered to contain all the serious candidates for acceptance, because of what we know already about the subject. And the best of these hypotheses, if the evidence is strong enough, may then be regarded as acceptable in an absolute rather than just a comparative sense. It is better than any rival within the only ulti-mate partition that is itself acceptable on the available evidence. Thus Galileo, in his famous *Dialogue Concerning the Two Chief World Systems*, discussed only whether the Ptolemaic or the Copernican theory was preferable, and did not entertain also some quite different partition of the fundamental possibilities. Nevertheless, the lottery paradox cannot be reproduced in this kind of situation, so it does not constitute an objection to Levi's resolution of that paradox. Levi can still maintain his claim that acceptance is always relative to an ultimate partition, even if in many cases only one ultimate partition needs to be considered.

Indeed, the lottery situation is unrepresentative of acceptance issues in more than one way. Not only does it allow the equal legitimacy of a large number of different ultimate partitions, with the consequences that have just been under examination. It is also insulated from any practical question about whether all the relevant facts are included in the available evidence. Since the lottery is explicitly assumed to be administered fairly we can treat it as a perfect game of chance and calculate the probabilities of the various outcomes according to an indifference analysis (§ 6). But where we are not dealing with aleatory probabilities questions about the extent or spread of relevant evidence may be highly pertinent. If the issue is, for example, whether it will rain tomorrow or not, then what Keynes called the weight (§ 14) of the available evidence is just as important as the probability on that evidence. It is justifiable to accept that it will rain only if the weight and the probability are both sufficiently high. So in this respect any Pascalian criterion for detachment needs some appropriate supplementation if it is to cover an important feature of many non-aleatory situations (as Levi recognizes: see p. 174).

Finally, it is worth noting that the lottery paradox arises only if the criterion for inductive detachment is stated in Pascalian terms. Suppose that we grade the evidence's support by the Method of Relevant Variables or in accordance with some derived scale of Baconian probability (pp. 167–8), and that, instead of adopting (1), we select some suitably high Baconian grade as the appropriate basis for acceptance. Then all we can at best say in these terms about ticket no. 1, or about any of the other tickets, is that the evidence is sufficient for us to accept that its chances of not winning are 999,999 in 1,000,000. That is to say, each ultimate hypothesis under consideration, and open to acceptance, is a proposition about the aleatory probability of winning, or of not winning, not a hypothesis about winning, or about not winning. And in this context (2) is quite innocuous: the hypotheses that we are justified in accepting have no para-doxical consequences, even when considered collectively. Moreover, this solution fits well with the fact that in normal circumstances it would seem queer for someone to buy a ticket to a lottery which he feels justified in accepting that he will not win. Since many people do buy lottery tickets, many people presum-ably do not feel justified in accepting that they will not win and would find the relevant implications of (1) counter-intuitive. Correspondingly the Method of Relevant Variables resolves the prima-facie conflict between the need for inductive detachment and the idea of deductive cogency—the conflict that underlies the lottery paradox—by retaining (2) but reformulating (1) in Baconian terms. It could well be argued, however, that, like Levi's analysis, the Method of Relevant Variables still makes inductively based acceptance relative to an ultimate partition of hypotheses, since any eliminativist analysis of induction presupposes such partitions (see §§ 2, 18, and 20).

So, just as (see §§ 23-5) the classical problem of induction, the paradox of the ravens, and the 'grue' paradox all admit of resolution both in terms of a Pascalian gradation for ampliative induction and in terms of a Baconian one, so too the lottery paradox can be dissolved both in Pascalian terms and in Baconian ones.[32] Indeed, even on the general issue of Pascalianism versus Baconianism, it may be best to refrain from supposing that this is an issue where in the end one side has to be supposed correct and the other incorrect. What we have are alternative kinds of proposal for the systematic reconstruction of inductive reasoning, each of which has both advantages and disadvantages (see also §§ 16-22). In such philosophical dilemmas it is normally worth while to carry forward both options.

---

[32] The underlying problem about detachment in inductive reasoning is discussed by H.E. Kyburg jun., Y. Bar-Hillel, P. Suppes, K. Popper, W.C. Salmon, J. Hintikka and R. Carnap, in I. Lakatos (ed.), *The Problem of Inductive Logic* (Amsterdam: North-Holland, 1968), 98-165.

INDEX